Ahsan Academy of Research
(Springs, South Africa)

Abdul Haleem Siddiqui and His Mission

Abdul Kader Choughley

Tawasul International
Centre for Publishing, Research and Dialogue
Rome, Italy

First Edition 2022
ISBN: 978-93-91601-67-6
Abdul Kader Choughley

Ahsan Academy of Research
(Springs, South Africa)
info@ahsanacademy.co.za
www.ahsanacademy.co.za

SHELVCRAFTTM Shelving | Racking |
Display | Shop Fiting Ph: 012 666 8933
Email: sales@shelvcraft.com Website:
www.shelvcraft.com

Tawasul International
Centre for Publishing, Research and Dialogue, Rome, Italy

DEDICATION

This book is dedicated to the loving memory of
Hajee Salim and Zubeida Essa Kurtha

My Lord! Bestow on them Your mercy even as they cherished
me in childhood.

(17: 24)

CONTENTS

Contents

Contents

Abdul Haleem Siddiqui and His Mission

Acknowledgements

Many individuals had shown a keen interest to the production of the book and made resources available, dating as far back as the 1930s. I cannot forget the unwavering support by the late Mawlānā Mahomed Ali Khan of Overport, a student of Dr Mawlānā Fazlur Rahman Ansari. He supplied me with rare documents and unpublished writings of Mawlānā Siddiqui, which gave me new perspectives into the domain of tabligh. Indeed, these archival materials have augmented the scope and format of the book.

Adam Kolia, former Associate Editor of Makki Publications, has made every effort to provide me with the relevant documents and magazines and has enriched my assessment of Mawlānā Siddiqui's multifaceted contributions. Likewise, he has a been a great help by supplying me with unpublished articles related to Dr Fazlur Rahman Ansari's Aligarh years: 1933-47.

My dear friend and mentor, Dr. Yusuf Bamjee (d.2020), was kind enough to provide technical guidance to ensure that the high-quality standard is maintained for the present volume. I am under great obligation to my wife, Muniera, for her enthusiasm and the technical production of the book. Like my previous works, her supportive role is again acknowledged. Hafidh Mahmood Khatib has been extremely helpful in providing me with specific resources to the study.

The guiding spirit behind the present work is Anver Essa. His inspiration and collaborative effort have brought to fruition a series of works dedicated to Mawlānā Siddiqui's and Mawlānā Ansari's life and thought.

And the reward is with Allah.

Abdul Kader Choughley
(Springs, South Africa) 30 November 2021

Preface

It has almost been eighteen years since the commemorative volume on Mawlānā Muhammad Abdul Aleem Siddiqui, (hereafter referred to as Mawlānā Siddiqui) appeared in 2003. The title of the volume *The Greatest Propagator of Islam*[1] suggests that his tabligh stature and mission have been unsurpassed in the first half of the twentieth century. Likewise, his contributions to Islamic thought and his multifaceted personality are considered an enduring legacy to the Muslims across the world.

Mawlānā Siddiqui's position as a *muballigh*[2] needs greater scrutiny in view of the many challenges faced by Muslims in the present century. The term 'tabligh' has undergone significant changes, which have been largely shaped by geopolitical developments.[3] In examining his conception of tabligh, two factors need to be carefully considered: first, the motivation for a departure from the traditional understanding of the term. Second, the nexus between tabligh and *tarbiyah* (moral training)[4] in relation to Western civilisation and other ideological systems. In other words, how did Mawlānā Siddiqui's presentation of tabligh show an interconnectedness to the Muslim communities affected by these foreign influences during his local and international travels. Viewed from a different angle, Mawlānā Siddiqui's understanding of tabligh offers interesting insights into the Islamic reawakening discourse, which is interchangeably used to describe the process of *islāh* (reform).[5]

The period under study, early twentieth century, was a crucial phase for the Muslim communities to define their collective Islamic

---

[1] Muhammad Younus Qadri, *The Greatest Propagator in Islam* (Karachi, 2003).

[2] The term *muballigh* has a broader connotation than the title of the special souvenir suggests. The present study covers a wide range of aspects associated with Mawlānā Siddiqui's tabligh outreach vision.

[3] An excellent study on the geopolitical developments in South Asia is Francis Robinson's *Islam, South Asia and the West* (New Delhi, 2007).

[4] The ambivalent responses to the tabligh-*tarbiyah* concept by Muslim groups have been examined in Dietrich Reetz, *Islam in the Public Sphere: Religious Groups in India* 1900-1947 (New Delhi, 2006).

[5] For a detailed commentary on *islāh*, see the contribution by Ali Merad in the *Encyclopedia of Islam* (Leiden, 1997).

identity in the background of modernism, Western culture and Communism. The ʿulama's response was wide and varied and represented the differing expressions of authentic Islam.[6] In many instances, these volatile situations prompted Mawlānā Siddiqui to make a clarion call for unity of the fragmented *ummah* - a theme that is explored in the volume. Likewise, his formulation of spiritual rearmament[7] for humanity was a radical step towards forging the interfaith dialogue. This issue is contextualised in a historical setting. Moreover, the *tasawwuf* accomplishments of Mawlānā Siddiqui and his mission are closely examined in his presentation of the inner dimensions of Islam.[8]

In recent years there have been critical works dealing with the life and thought of the versatile scholar to enrich our understanding about the dynamics of tabligh. This work, *Abdul Aleem Siddiqui and his Mission* (2013)[9] as the title suggests, focuses on his contribution to tabligh beyond the Indian subcontinent. The present study draws upon the recent works in English which present deeper insights into his life and legacy. Two works in particular offer a coherent presentation of his contributions within specific sociopolitical milieus. A scholarly piece of work, *Maulana Abdul Aleem Siddiqui: His Life, Thoughts and Message* (2019)[10] by Ibrahim Alladin covers a broader terrain of Mawlānā Siddiqui's eventful life. Alladin critically examines the erudite scholar's works, many of which were speeches delivered in several countries, as representative of his brilliant intellectual learning. The work is copiously illustrated with archival

---

[6] Mention may be made of the theological bickering which characterised the divergent versions of Islamic thought. See Ishtiaq Qureshi, *Ulema in Politics* (Karachi, 1974).

[7] Although rearmament has a military connotation, it is used in the text to describe the process of mobilisation or a readiness to be aligned spiritually. It is significant that Mawlānā Siddiqui reconfigured its meaning in the backdrop of the Second World War.

[8] For a general discussion on this aspect, see Annemarie Schimmel, *Mystical Dimensions of Islam* (Carolina, 1975), 344-402.

[9] Abdul Kader Choughley, *Abdul Aleem Siddiqui and his Mission* appeared in 2013. It is considered a seminal work on the tabligh perspectives in the light of Mawlānā Siddiqui's multidimensional personality. The present study is a revised version bearing the same title.

[10] Ibrahim Alladin, *Maulana Abdul Aleem Siddiqui: His Life, Thoughts and Message* (Curepipe, 2019).

material, adding new dimensions to the versatility of Mawlānā Siddiqui. A noteworthy study, *Allama Abdul Aleem Meeruti and his Contribution to Islamic Preaching* (2020)[11] by Muhammad Ashraful Kausar Misbahi covers in detail the life and times of Mawlānā Siddiqui. Apart from the timeline approach adopted by Misbahi, the unexplored areas of Mawlānā Siddiqui's tabligh have been meticulously covered. Another laudable feature of his research is the painstaking effort to procure the original sources from individuals and institutions. His visit to South Africa in 2019 reaffirms his commitment to present a scholarly study about this influential figure of Islamic resurgence.

It is a truism that the intellectual contributions of Dr Fazlur Rahman Ansari (d. 1974) are interconnected to the tabligh vision of Mawlānā Siddiqui. The latter's influence on his broader presentation of Islam in a contemporary setting is brought out in his several writings.[12] My latest work, *Fazlur Rahman Ansari: Aligarh Years (1933- 47)*[13] is a conspectus of the joint tabligh mission by these scholars. Keeping in mind that Mawlānā Siddiqui hailed from India, it was expected that a comprehensive study of his life and legacy would enrich our understanding about *The Roving Ambassador of Peace.*[14] A random survey of works available in Urdu suggests that the *Special Issues*[15] and translations of his speeches and writings[16] are marked features of the recent publications. Likewise, the embellished accounts of his multifaceted personality mar the readers' appreciation of his immense contributions to the Islamic resurgence that was taking place in the Muslim world.

A brief survey of the available literature on Mawlānā Siddiqui points out to the glaring lacuna of vital information about his versatile personality. There are several reasons for this void. First, Mawlānā

---

[11] The doctoral thesis written in Urdu was submitted in 2020 by Muhammad Ashraful Kausar Misbahi to the Department of Islamic Studies, Jamia Millia Islamia (New Delhi, India).

[12] For example, *Communist Challenge to Islam* (1950) was largely inspired by Mawlānā Siddiqui.

[13] Abdul Kader Choughley, *Fazlur Rahman Ansari: Aligarh Years, 1933-47* (Springs, 2021).

[14] Yasien Mohamed, *The Roving Ambassador of Peace* (Cape Town, 2006).

[15] See *Anwār i-Rizā, Hadhrat Shah Abdul Aleem Siddiqui* (Karachi, 2011).

[16] Muhammad Naeemullah Khan Qadri, *Tabarrukiit i-'Alami Muballigh i-Islami Sairul Islam Hadhrat 'Alliimah Abdul Aleem Meeruti Siddiqui* (Karachi, 2014).

Siddiqui's busy schedule did not allow him to write prolifically, which could have enhanced a systematic study of his contributions to Islamic thought. This is evident in the brief biographical account[17] given by his student and successor, Fazlur Rahman Ansari (hereafter Mawlānā Ansari). Second, his extensive travels did not give him much opportunity to record his personal accounts as these are covered by a few periodicals. Last, there were three phases in his productive life: Meerut, Karachi and Madinah were the principal cities where a substantial period of his life-enriching career was spent. The timeline of his activities included interactive meetings, lectures and spiritual training. Unlike his contemporary sufi scholars, the constraints of a rigorous schedule did not permit the establishment of a major network of ʿulama and scholars who could have advanced his tabligh mission.

The present work is a modest attempt to highlight Mawlānā Siddiqui's contributions as these are based on his published writings. *The Greatest Propagator of Islam,* a collection of articles in English and Urdu, deals with several aspects of his tabligh efforts. The noteworthy merits of this book are the documents, offering a synopsis of his missionary work in the far-flung corners of the world. South Africa has enjoyed an enviable record of promoting the works of Mawlānā Siddiqui and Mawlānā Ansari. Yasien Mohamed has made a sterling effort to edit the lectures delivered by Mawlānā Siddiqui during his historic lecture tours in 1934 and 1952 respectively. The thematic presentation of the lectures in *The Roving Ambassador of Peace*[18] captures the salient features of his mission. Another work, *Dimensions of Islam* by Mawlānā Abdul Hadi al-Qadiri[19] is a two-volume compilation of Mawlānā Siddiqui's booklets. Additional notes have been incorporated to make the text reader-friendly. Mohammed Makki who was actively associated with Mawlānā Siddiqui since 1934 had through his *Makki Publications*[20]

---

[17] See Qadri, *The Greatest Propagator of Islam*, 62-4.

[18] Abdul Hadi al-Qadiri, *Dimensions of Islam.* 2 volumes (Durban, 2005).

[19] Yasien Mohamed (ed.), *The Roving Ambassador of Peace* (Cape Town, 2006).

[20] Several issues of *The Muslim Digest* (1952) and *Ramadan Annual* contain articles about Mawlānā Siddiqui and his contributions to the Islamic reawakening (*nahdah*).

played a major role in promoting the latter's works and reporting on his tabligh travels. To this end, the present book relies on articles published in *The Muslim Digest* and *Ramadan Annual.*

Our study charts the various approaches to tabligh as envisioned by Mawlānā Siddiqui within the framework of the historical, social and political milieus of the countries he visited during this tabligh travels.

Chapter 1

Mawlānā Siddiqui: Man and Mission

The renewed global and national networking of Islamic organisations and revivalist movements has its origins in the late nineteenth and early twentieth century. From Jamaluddin Afghani's Pan-Islam to Mawlānā Siddiqui's dynamic concept of tabligh, the Islamic reawakening in its varied forms has shaped the Islamic discourse of *islāh*[1] (reform), which is based on the *salf al-sālih*[2] (earliest representatives of Islam) presentation.

The paucity of literature on Mawlānā Siddiqui's biography has limited the scope for the critical evaluation of his contributions to Islamic thought. Apart from the overstrained accounts which accentuate a distinct sectarian bias, other biographical sketches are generally reproduced and repackaged from a single source to promote the preconceived profile of this eminent scholar. Fortunately, the biographical account and other articles on Mawlānā Siddiqui by his successor, Mawlānā Ansari[3] are considered reliable sources as they provide an overview of his contributions, which are corroborated by documents and materials contained in magazines and newspaper articles related to the period under study.

Likewise, Mawlānā Siddiqui's monographs and published lectures are useful guides to reconstructing, albeit briefly, his life and times. His unassuming personality and aversion for publicity were inextricably linked to the Islamic ethos he rigorously followed. His *taqwā* (Allah-consciousness) was his beacon light which illumined his radiant personality. In sufi terms, *fanā* (absorption in divine love)[4] permeated the spiritual disciplines which he internalised in his daily

---

[1] Abdul Kader Choughley, *Fazlur Rahman Ansari: Life and Thought* (Springs, 2012), 26-34.

[2] Fazlur Rahman Ansari, "Shah Abdul Aleem Siddiqui: The Roving Ambassador of Islam" in *The Muslim Digest:* Jan/Feb 1996, 65.

[3] The title is used interchangeably for Dr Ansari in the study.

[4] The types of *fanā* in relation to *tasawwuf* are succinctly discussed in Amatullah Armstrong, *Sufi Terminology: The Mystical Language of Islam* (Kuala Lumpur, 1995), 46-7.

life. In his view, spirituality[5] formed the core message of the Islamic teachings. Therefore, an uncompromising faith and committed practice to the Islamic principles were the criteria for a believer's success in both worlds.

Mawlānā Siddiqui argued that laxity, for example, had the baneful effect on the proper understanding of the Islamic teachings. His standpoint is instructive as the following example shows:

Let me give you an important warning: Beware! You have a spiritual treasure during Ramadan. Take care! Just as thieves of material riches are always planning to rob people, similarly, the baser self and the devil are the thieves who are on the lookout for stealing the spiritual assets. Today is the day of Eid. You are in the midst of well-earned rejoicing. The doors of Allah's unbounded Mercy are wide open. The breeze of divine forgiveness is blowing. But beware of Satan's mischief. The wine shops and gambling houses are also open. The immoral attractions of the cinema are also here. The half-naked physical attractions are out on the roads with their immoral enhancements. Be on your guard! Save the delicate glass of faith and piety from the deceptive attacks of evil. Protect the labour you have made during the days and nights of Ramadan.[6]

Biographical Sketch

A synoptic overview of Mawlānā Siddiqui's manifold contributions is provided by Mawlānā Ansari (d. 1974), an erudite scholar and leading figure in the Islamic resurgence movement of the twentieth century. As Mawlānā Siddiqui's successor and private secretary, Mawlānā Ansari imbibed his missionary fervour through the establishment of the Aleemiyah Islamic Institute (Karachi, Pakistan), serving as the link between the traditional and progressive Islamic thought. His major writings show an unmistakable influence of Mawlānā Siddiqui's tabligh vision.[7]

---

[5] In the study, the term spirituality is loosely associated to *ruhāniyat*.

[6] Extracts from the Eid message delivered in 1950 in Port of Spain (Trinidad). The theme of moral regeneration resonates in his speeches which he delivered in major cities around the world during his tabligh tour.

[7] See Choughley, *Fazlur Rahman Ansari: Aligarh Years.*

The following biographical sketch is extracted from several articles written by Mawlānā Ansari and covers the multifaceted contributions of Mawlānā Siddiqui. It also demonstrates the unrelenting efforts of a *dā'i* striving to establish unity (*ittihād*) among the divided *ummah*; to restore the credibility of Islam as a civilisational force, and more importantly, reinforce the universal values of morality and tolerance shared by other faith-based communities. The personal narrative reveals the inner aspects of a *muballigh* committed to the Islamic ideal: *service to humanity*.

Early Years

Mawlānā Siddiqui was born on 3 April 1892 in Meerut (India). He was a direct descendant of the first Caliph of Islam, Abubakr Siddiq. Endowed with unusual intelligence and exceptional memory, Mawlānā Siddiqui commenced his education at the early age of three years and devoted himself to the acquisition of Islamic learning. Thereafter, he completed his studies in *Dars i-Nizami*[8] at the Madrasah Arabiah Qawmiyah, Meerut, at the age of sixteen. But the desire to understand the modern problems of mankind and to reach out the message of Islam to the world at large, urged him to acquire modern education as well.[9]

As regards his Islamic studies, he did not discontinue them even while pursuing modern education. In fact, he continued with his studies till many years after he had entered the field as an Islamic scholar and amassed further knowledge in Qur'ānic exegesis (*tafsir*), hadith, *tasawwuf* and *Fiqh* in Makkah and Madinah through discussion and interaction with the leading Islamic scholars of the day. As an erudite scholar he augmented his studies at the well-known Islamic libraries in the Arab world. He also benefited from the sufi

---

[8] The *Dars-i-Nizami* which is associated with `ulama of Lucknow was aimed at fostering an intellectual tradition in the period of political instability. The curriculum defined Islamic learning at the Islamic higher institutions. See Said Rafiq, Islami *Nizām i-Ta'lim* (Karachi, 1956).

[9] The 'ulama's response to modern education was influenced by colonialism. Politcal factors inhibited a positive outlook towards learning English and scientific disciplines. See Aziz Ahmed, *Islamic Modernism in India and Pakistan: 1857-1964* (London, 1967), 22-3.

masters such as Shaykh Ahmad al- Shams of Morocco, Shaykh al-Sanusi of Libya, Mawlānā Abdul Bāqi of Farangi Mahal and Mawlānā Ahmad Rāda Khan of Bareily[10].

Choice of Career

With the formal completion of education, various professions were open to him for earning his livelihood.[11] He was employed by the reputed firm of Haji Mohammad Husain Seedhi as a manager in Mumbai towards the close of 1918. Very soon he proved himself to be more than a match for the position and rose to be a partner. But he had been there hardly for a year when his restless soul took him to Islam's Holy Land (*muqaddas*) on his first pilgrimage (*hajj*). From there he returned with the decision to devote himself primarily to the moral and religious upliftment of humanity.

Spiritual Discipline

The atmosphere to which Mawlānā Siddiqui was exposed was saturated with spirituality and enviable scholarship. His mother was a deeply pious lady, while his father, Mawlānā Abdul Hakim Siddiqui, was not only a versatile scholar and a high-class poet but also a sufi of eminence.[12]

Being the youngest child and endowed with extraordinary talents, his father held him in great affection and kept him close to himself and transmitted to him the blessings of his personality until he was

---

[10]For a biographical account of these scholars, the following books may be consulted: Nicola Ziadeh, *Sanusiyah: A Study of the Revivalist Movement in Islam* (Leiden, 1983); Francis Robinson, *The 'Ulama of Farangi Mahall and Islamic Culture in South Asia* (Delhi, 2001), Usha Sanyal, *In the Path of the Holy Prophet* (Oxford, 2008). Cf. *Anwār i-Rizā*, 96.

[11] Mawlānā Siddiqui had completed his B.A. in Meerut Islamia College. Likewise, he completed another course in Punjab University, which deepened his understanding of Arabic literature and Persian. His law degree in Allahabad University is also mentioned. See *Anwār i-Rizā*, 171-2.

[12] A specimen of his poems devoted to the personality of the Holy Prophet (pbuh) is emblematic of his high - ranking position in *tasawwuf*. See Qadri, *Azim Muballigh-i-Islam*, 55.

nearly twelve. His initial training in *tasawwuf* was under his elder brother, Mawlānā Ahmad Mukhtar Siddiqui[13] from whom he received the *ijazah* (authority) in several great sufi orders (*silsilahs*).[14]

Spirituality thus became the marked feature which distinguished Mawlānā Siddiqui's life from the lives of many a religious leader, even as the combination of Western education with Islamic learning was his sign of distinction. Indeed, spiritual purification and illumination tempered with the moral, social and political salvation of humanity remained his mission throughout his life.

Oratorical Excellence

It has been said that orators are born and not made and it was literally true in the case of Mawlānā Siddiqui because he delivered his first public speech at the Jam'i mosque of Meerut at the age of nine. It must be noted that during his youth he had already made his mark as a successful public preacher (*khatib*) which earned him international fame decades later. An instance in point were his public lectures in Tokyo at several prestigious universities. As Professor

N.H. Berlas wrote from Tokyo:

> ... [for] a fuller appreciation one must hear Mawlānā Siddiqui from the platform. One is sure to be charmed like the audience here by his magnetic personality and oratorical powers, his loud and impressive but musical voice and splendid delivery.[15]

As an engaging conversationalist and as a charming orator, he was equally at home in Urdu, Arabic, English and Persian[16] and used the first

---

[13] The contributions of Mawlānā Ahmad Mukhtar Siddiqui to tabligh in several Muslim countries including Burma (Myammar), in particular, have not been fully examined. Likewise, his political activities have received a brief mention.

[14] The spiritual lineage is provided in Umair Siddiqui, *The Roving Ambassador of Islam* (Karachi, 2011), 95-6.

[15] Abdul Aleem Siddiqui, *Cultivation of Science by the Muslims* (Karachi, n.d.).

[16] Mawlānā Siddiqui was also conversant in Japanese and Swahili, which facilitated

three languages during his numerous tours in different parts of the world.

The capacity to express himself according to the intellectual temperament of his listeners was Mawlānā Siddiqui's great asset and he employed it with equal mastery in his lectures before learned societies[17] as well as during his missionary tours among the indigenous people of the African hinterland.

Spiritual Work

With these qualities of head and heart together with his accomplishments, Mawlānā Siddiqui resolved in 1919 to devote himself purely to spiritual work as a *muballigh* of Islam. It was not a new decision, however, because he had nurtured it in his heart for years. In fact, he wrote a poem while still a boy which proved in later years to be prophetic. An English rendering of two of its couplets is given hereunder:

> *My heart yearns to show its bleeding scars. Wrought by the spiritual perversions of man*
> *And to teach everyone on earth the Laws. This is my yearning and this is my aim. This is my intention and this my claim. With this, I yearn to scan the globe*
> *And deliver to humanity the message of hope.[18]*

The twin concept of humanity and hope were the ideals he cherished and through which he strove to highlight Islam's universal message. The decision once made was irrevocable in spite of the hardships which it entailed and the travels once commenced did not cease until virtually his final journey from this world. Even his last remains were not buried in his hometown but in the far-off city of

---

his mission to these countries.

[17] *The Forgotten Path of Knowledge* is an instance in point.

[18] Mohamed, *The Roving Ambassador of Peace, xxiv Cf. The Muslim Digest:* 1996. These articles are generally reproduced in several magazines.

Madinah. As a spiritual pilgrim, Mawlānā Siddiqui visited Makkah and Madinah several times, while as the Flag-bearer of the spiritual rearmament of mankind, he travelled to different regions of the world continually for forty years, returning to his family only for short breaks. This was remarkable in the field of tabligh.

Countries Visited

The countries he visited during those travels - many of them repeatedly were: Myanmar, Malaysia, Indonesia, Thailand, Vietnam, China, Japan, Philippines, Sri Lanka, Mauritius, Reunion, Madagascar, South Africa, Mozambique, Kenya, Tanzania, Uganda, Belgian-Congo, the Hijaz, Egypt, Syria, Palestine, Jordan, Iraq, France, Britain, West Indies, Guyana, Suriname, the United States and Canada.[19]

To travel for forty years is in itself a mighty feat of endurance. These strenuous journeys were undertaken by a spiritual pilgrim who gave to his spiritual labours sixteen to eighteen hours a day.[20] When we probe into his activities, and when we look at the many societies and institutions with diverse functions which he founded or inspired, the hundreds of converts who received the light of Islam through him, the hundreds of thousands of Muslims belonging to different races who were elevated through his preachings, we get an inkling into the greatness of this man.

His International Work

The following paragraph is a poignant description of Mawlānā Siddiqui's *jihād* which was synonymous with his tabligh endeavours:

Mawlānā Siddiqui's message of Allah- realisation (*taqwā*), of moral regeneration and of spiritual revival penetrated millions of hearts.

---

[19] Several of these countries have been renamed in order to discard their colonial past. For example, Belgian Congo was a Belgian colony from 1908 to 1960. The former colony adopted its present name, the Democratic Republic of Congo.

[20] In his early tabligh tours, Mawlānā Siddiqui was exposed to enormous challenges as the modes of transport were limited. The hurdles included rationing in the aftermath of World War One. Under these bleak circumstances, he was not deterred to spread the message of Islam in the remote areas of the world.

His visits everywhere gave new impetus to the religious fervour of the people. His work transformed sandy deserts of spiritual inertia into green orchards of moral dynamism. His spiritual magnetism purified the social conscience of the people and in the wake of his visits sprang up orphanages for the helpless youth, infirmaries for the destitute, hospitals for the suffering humanity, educational institutions for the propagation of knowledge, assemblies for the dissemination of spiritual discipline, mosques for the worship of Allah, missionary societies for the propagation of the Divine message, interfaith organisations for the consolidation of religious forces against the onslaught of materialism and atheism and Muslim unity boards for the creation of harmony among Muslims.[21]

The spiritual content of his mission gave renewed meaning to the Islamic reawakening discourse. In fact, the gamut of activities to which he was associated, underscored his commitment to the Islamic cause for which he devoted his life. It was, therefore, not surprising that he was instrumental in the establishment of institutions ranging from missionary societies to orphanages. This realisation was a profound commitment to conscientise the *ummah* on its revolutionary mission to serve humanity.

Service to the Cause of Pakistan

When Muslims in India launched their struggle for self-determination and for the creation of Pakistan,[22] Mawlānā Siddiqui who had already contributed to the cause of Muslim politics during the Khilafat movement put all his weight in favour of the struggle. He went even so far as to snatch one year from his spiritual work and to travel to the world for aligning the hearts of the Muslim world with the righteous cause of the Indian Muslims.

Mawlānā Siddiqui, who was perhaps the most suitable man for this purpose because of his fluency in Arabic and his contacts with Arab leaders, realised the urgency of the situation and undertook to visit

---

[21] Ansari, "Abdul Aleem Siddiqui's Role in Modern History" in *The Muslim Digest*: September 1959, 12.

[22] On the ʿulama's contributions to the Pakistani cause, see Qureshi, *Ulema in Politics*, 339-70.

Egypt, Palestine, Lebanon, Syria, Trans-Jordan (now Jordan) and Iraq. In Egypt, he stayed with his friend Shaykh Hasan al-Banna (d.1949), founder of the Muslim Brotherhood (*Ikhwān al-Muslimin*).[23] From there he contacted the Egyptian intelligentsia, media and statesmen and convinced them of the just cause of the Indian Muslim struggle. There were other `ulama from different theological (*maslak*) backgrounds who also contributed to the Pakistani cause.

Quest for Harmony

Fragrant sweetness was the keynote of Mawlānā Siddiqui's life. True peace - peace with Allah and peace with man - was his watchword; harmony between nations and races and parties was his aim; and the spiritual rearmament of humanity was his mission. Strife was alien to his nature and so were narrow-mindedness, bigotry and sterile religiosity. Throughout his long career as an international religious leader, there was no occasion when even his critics could point out a flaw in his religious personality[24] or in his sincerity and moral earnestness.[25]

His position as a messenger of peace on behalf of Islam did not, however, mean compromise. He was a staunch believer in the absolute truth of Islam, in its great mission, in its ennobling principles and in its elevating practices. What he was deadly against was baseless strife founded on egotism and not on altruism.

Goodwill and Harmony

Mawlānā Siddiqui struggled not only to remove the differences

---

[23] For his biographical account see I.H. Husaini, *The Muslim Brethren: The Greatest of Modern Muslim Movements* (Beirut, 1956); Brynjar Lisa, *The Society of the Muslim Brothers in Egypt* (Reading, 1998).

[24] A detailed discussion appears in his *Quest for True Happiness*. See Siddiqui, *Dimensions of Islam* (Durban, 2005), 15-28.

[25] In the early years of his mission Mawlānā Siddiqui was subjected to a tirade of misrepresentations by his critics. See Siddiqui, *The Clarion Call*, 30-31. This was understandable in view of his global profile that transcended sectarian affiliations.

and antagonisms existing between Muslims rooted in political oppositions, social dissensions, and juristic differences (*ikhtilāf*)[26] but also to bring about understanding and goodwill between Muslims and non-Muslims.

His writings reflected his non-sectarian outlook; his preachings acquired the character of presenting Islam on the fundamental level, to which all his published English lectures bear witness, and to avoid all inter-school theological bickering. He made a positive effort to bring about goodwill and harmony. His participation in the establishment of an organisation, under the presidentship of Muhammad Ali Allouba Pasha of Egypt with Dr. Shawarib as its Secretary- General was significant. The organisation was named as *Taqrib bayn al-madhāhib Islami* (Society for the promotion of harmony between Muslim Islamic schools of thought).[27]

Society for the Promotion of Interfaith Cooperation

Mawlānā Siddiqui's yearning to see peace and goodwill established on earth was well known to everyone who came into contact with him. He carried in his heart the conviction that peace is unattainable by modern humanity unless every man and woman strove for spiritual rearmament.

With this end in view, Mawlānā Siddiqui initiated in 1949 a movement among the leaders of different religions in Singapore: Muslim, Christian, Jewish, Buddhist, Hindu, Sikh, etc. His sincerity of purpose and persuasive eloquence succeeded in opening a new chapter in religious history.[28] A society known as The Inter-Religious Organisation (IRO) and composed of eminent leaders of different religions was formed to realise these objectives.

---

[26] Mohamed, *The Roving Ambassador of Peace*, xxi.

[27] A similar effort was initiated by Shaykh Mahmud (d. 1963) of Egypt. See Kate Zebiri, *Mahmud Shaltut and Islamic Modernism* (Oxford, 1993), 24-6, 172. Cf. Ansari, "Muhammad Abdul Aleem Siddiqui ki Dini khidmāt ki Mukhtsar Ta'aruf" in *The Minaret*: April 1996, 30.

[28] Qadri, *The Greatest Propagator of Islam*, 63-5.

Personal Character

The very first thing that struck everyone who came into contact with him was the profound charm of his personality, which created a sense of awe and respect.

His unassuming character was reflected in his sincerity, independence and self-respect. This independence, however, never took the form of haughtiness or arrogance. His humility touched the hearts of thousands of people from all walks of life. He was ever polite, ever sweet, ever persuasively eloquent, and independent of all ulterior considerations and dependent on principles alone. This gave him dignity and personal self-respect.

Cheerfulness in adversity and reliance in Allah were the hallmarks of his exemplary character. He was at his best when confronted with obstacles, and he possessed a special aptitude for undertaking tasks for which he possessed apparently no material resources. Whatever gifts his very close friends presented to him with love and humility, he spent them most liberally in the way of Allah.

In his daily interaction, Mawlānā Siddiqui personified the true meaning of consciousness of duty. This trait of character was most conspicuous in his personality and the guiding force of his life. For instance, when he started his memorable world tour (1949-1950), it gave him a unique distinction in the history of Islam because he (and Mawlānā Ansari) was the first Muslim missionary to have performed it.[29] His physicians advised him complete rest in view of his delicate state of health. Not only was he physically weak at that time but had also already lost the sight of one eye while the other eye also was suffering from cataract, but those considerations could not deter him. "This body of mine is a trust from Allah," he told his remonstrating physicians, "and is meant to be exhausted in Allah's way. How, therefore, can I suspend my activity even for a day for considerations of bodily comfort. No, gentlemen, that is not possible."[30]

---

[29] There were several scholars who made pioneering efforts of tabligh in the West. However, the scope of their tabligh was limited. See, Muhammad Mojlum Khan, *Great Muslims of the West: Makers of Western Islam*. (Leicester, 2017).

[30] Mohamed, *The Roving Ambassador of Peace*, xvi.

Demise

There are two noteworthy factors which stand out in connection with Mawlānā Siddiqui's demise:

- He died while in harness, remaining active to the cause of his mission practically up to the last day, although before his death he had been seriously ill for nearly one year.
- He died and was buried in Madinah, which is an enviable blessing of Allah for every righteous Muslim. His death occurred at such a time of the year when Muslims from all over the world assemble at Madinah after the *hajj*. He had served the cause of Islam all over the world. He was Islam's world-class missionary. And Allah, in His infinite mercy, blessed him with a world congregation for his funeral prayers. Muslims from far and near came and paid their last respects to him.[31]

Major Contributions

Wherever Mawlānā Siddiqui went, both laymen and intellectuals among non-Muslims were inspired to enter the fold of Islam through his inspiring lectures. He wrote about twenty books in Arabic, Urdu and English. He took an interest in world politics generally and Muslim politics particularly. On his own initiative he advocated the cause of Pakistan in the Arab world and other Muslim countries. He moved for the elimination of the unjust imposition of the *hajj* tax, which the Saudi government reduced after protracted negotiation when they recognised his moral force.

Mawlānā Siddiqui's mastery of languages lent charm and beauty to his thoughts and ideas. His eloquence was evident during his lectures before such learned societies as the Royal Asiatic Society of Shanghai and the Oriental Culture Society of Japan, as well as during his lecture travels to the African continent. Whether on the

---

[31] Ansari, "His Eminence Muhammad Abdul Aleem Siddiqui Al- Qaderi: A Pioneer 'World Missionary" (Adapted) in *The Minaret*: May 1996, 8-18.

public platform   or in private conversation, Mawlānā Siddiqui's exposition of contemporary problems was invariably marked by such lucidity, profundity and spiritual dynamism which were unrivalled. He belonged to both the worlds - traditional and modern; he was equally well- acquainted about the past, the present and the future; and he was equally impressive among the conservatives and the modernists. He was traditional in the sense that he carried on his venerable shoulders the responsibility and the obligation of delivering to humanity the message which Allah granted to the Prophets and Messengers in the different parts of the world. At the same time, he was modern in the sense that he possessed the ability to expound that message in contemporary idiom. He believed that science and religion, far from being antagonistic, are complementary to each other and can be optimally pursued in the best interest of mankind.

In sum, Mawlānā Siddiqui's tabligh vision transcended the traditional understanding of this term; his missionary spirit focused on the unity of the Muslim *ummah* which regrettably was fragmented into sectarian groupings. Disunity had weakened the spirit of brotherhood *(ukhuwwah)*, the bedrock of Islam's universal message. For forty years he strove to perpetuate the idea that the unity of the *ummah*, embedded in the primary sources of Islam, was the benchmark of Muslim progress across the world.

For forty years Mawlānā Siddiqui's travels extended to major countries of the world. The modes of travels were hazardous in several countries especially in Africa which were under colonial rule. Flights between India and European countries including USA were in their initial stages; however, perseverance was his inner strength which he drew from the Qur'ān and the Prophetic model.

With no organised financial backing, with apparently insurmountable difficulties constantly facing him, with broken health and continuous illness and with many to criticise and few to cooperate, he had to tread this lonely path. Under these adverse conditions, he maintained an admirable composure which imparted a spiritual glow to his every action. With his battle-cry: *Back to the Qur'ān and the sunnah*, his watchword: *the unity of Islam* and his conviction that *"[the] more religious Muslims become, the better will they succeed in solving all their problems,"* he fought against the forces of disruption and disintegration, creating harmony between the forces of conservatism, sectarianism and modernism.[32]

In the wake of his endeavours came a new awakening, a fresh consciousness and a stronger will to work, and these factors resulted in the establishment of missionary societies, youth movements, organisations of the `ulama, educational institutions, mosques, orphanages, magazines and newspapers. And this new awakening captured the minds of all classes of Muslim society. Before the greatness of his work as also of his personality bowed princes and governors, judges and lawyers, students and professors, business magnates, bureaucrats and professionals from diverse backgrounds. His disciples in the 1950s exceeded nearly one hundred thousand souls while his admirers and friends numbered by the millions.

Survey of Writings by Mawlānā Siddiqui

Mawlānā Siddiqui's works must be understood in the context of historical developments in Egypt and the Indian subcontinent during the late nineteenth and early twentieth century. Both countries under British rule were exposed to a sustained form of Western civilisation.[33] Alongside this incursion of new intellectual thought was the rise of reformist Islam[34] challenging the ritualistic Islamic practices. Thus, the bold step to refer to the sources of Islamic authenticity was resisted by the polemical writings from those `ulama who vigorously identified themselves with ritualistic Islam. The tendency to confinate Islam in its pristine form with cultural accretions was very much evident in the Indian subcontinent. Other Muslim countries, too, were exposed to different forms of religious syncretism.

---

[32] See Choughley, *Fazlur Rahman Ansari: Life and Thought* (Springs, 2012).

[33] For a detailed discussion about Western civilisation's influence on the Muslim world, see Francis Robinson, *Islam, South Asia and the West* (New Delhi, 2007), 99-123.

[34] According to Mazheruddin Siddiqui, the Muslim modernists were largely interested in the reconstruction of the Muslim society. Their worldview covered the intellectual, social and political bases which brought them into confrontation with the traditional `ulama. See Siddiqui, *Modern Reformist Thought in the Muslim World* (Islamabad, 1982), 1-40.

Again the period under discussion brought in its wake a cadre of the Muslim modernists - `ulama and scholars- who critically reviewed the legacy of Islam through the lens of Western civilisation. It would, therefore, be not surprising that the `ulama establishment, scholars of traditional Islam, were pitted against the Muslim modernists who were unequivocal in their condemnation of *taqlid*[35] and advocated new strands of Islamic intellectual thought. In view of the religious autonomy enjoyed by the `ulama over the centuries, the battle lines of Islam and Western civilisation were drawn. Instead of appropriating the technological benefits of the West, the `ulama perceived these as an encroachment to Islam's faith and practice. As a corollary, the study of English was vehemently frowned upon as it was considered the bastion of Western art and culture. Ishtiaq Qureshi's assessment of the conflicting relationship between the `ulama and the colonial society is revealing:

The European powers saw danger in this doctrine and the word Pan-Islam became obnoxious to all imperialists, not only because they did not want to let go what they held, but also because they were determined to grab more. It was not easy to hide this sentiment which was sometimes expressed openly, and sometimes clothed in ambiguous and less offensive words. With the growth of European power, European languages came to be studied in varying degrees in the various Muslim countries and the subcontinent was no exception. An access to European journals, reports and books gave the Muslims an insight into Western policies and ambitions. The knowledge percolated to the masses and the `ulama, who had mostly, almost universally, abstained from learning any European language.[36]

The post-1857 syndrome illustrated the unbridgeable gaps between the `ulama and the new opportunities to acquire modern education. The representatives of modernism in Egypt and India like Muhammad Abduh, Sayyid Ahmad Khan and Syed Ameer Ali saw no

---

[35] The debate about the validity of *taqlid* (adherence to the authoritative explanation by the four Imams) continued unabated in the twentieth century. Mawlānā Siddiqui's exposition of *taqlid* is cogently expressed in his *The History and Codification of Islamic Law* (Karachi, n.d.).

[36] Ishtiaq Qureshi, *Ulema in Politics*, 231.

conflict between Islam and science. They harboured no illusions that the Islamic civilisation was the precursor to the European Renaissance and, therefore, possessed the innate potential to assimilate the scientific progress appropriated by the West. Of course, the Muslim modernists disregarded the negative impact of the rationalist trends which gave rise to Marxism and Communism and other hybrid movements, displacing religion in the collective life of man. Sadly, the Muslim countries were not immune to the pernicious influence of these isms.[37]

In its divide and rule policy, British colonialism, in particular, supported the deviant Islamic movements that served their political interests. Qadianism[38] rose from the ashes of obscurity in Punjab and worked in complicit with the British government to dislodge the concept of the finality of Prophethood (*khatm al-nabuwwat*). The 'ulama's position was swift and decisive. Their writings and debates with the Qadiani cohorts stemmed the tide of the Muslim community falling prey to the conspiratorial campaign against the Holy Prophet (pbuh). Iqbal, the Poet of the East, made a profound remark regarding the Finality of Prophethood:[39]

Islam as a religion, consists of a uniform belief and the law, but as a social entity its existence rests on the creed of the finality of Prophethood. Islam can subsist on its law but the sense of Islamic unity springs from the belief in the finality of Muhammad's prophethood.

In an insightful article, Maroof Shah comments that Iqbal's interpretation is irrefutable proof that Islam as a *din* (way of life) has been perfected and there is no room for improvement, evolution or development.[40]

---

[37] For a critical assessment of Marxism and Communism, see Ansari, *Islam versus Marxism* (Karachi, 1982) and *Islam and Communism* (Karachi, 1980). Cf. Khalifa Hakim, *Islam and Communism* (Lahore, 1994).

[38] Leading scholars undertook a critical study of Qadianism. See Elias Burney, *Qadiani Movement* (Durban, 1955); Abul Hasan Ali Nadwi, *Qadianism A Critical Study* (Lucknow, 1976).

[39] Muhammad Iqbal, *Harf i-Iqbal*, 136-7.

[40] Maroof Shah, "Legitimating the Modern Project" in *Hamdard Islamicus*: vol. xxxi, 13:20.

Tasawwuf in the Political Spectrum

Apart from the critique of these deviant sects, the modernists and the Salafi groups challenged sufism (*tasawwuf*) as the legitimate expression of Islamic spirituality. In the Indian context, *tasawwuf* had established itself as the transmitter of the universal values of Islam in a land dominated by Hinduism. The *mashā'ikh* were responsible for the mass conversion of Hindus to Islam through their distinct style of tabligh. Over the centuries, *tasawwuf* evolved within the Indo-Islamic cultural environment. As a result, the syncretic practices associated with popular Islam was evident. This did not imply that *tasawwuf* degenerated completely. On the other hand, the presence of the *mujaddids* (reformers) was responsible for realigning the course of *tasawwuf* to be shariah compliant.[41] Moreover, the amalgam of the sufi-'alim tradition provided a positive catalyst to establish the message of Islam in its pristine form.

Another development that took place was in the realms of political structures. Pan-Islamism which stood against the West's dominance of Muslim countries did in some measure allow for self-introspection of Muslim decline. Scholars like Mohamed Ali, Mawlānā Abul Kalam Azad played pioneering roles in the Islamic renaissance project. However, their focus was, by and large, on the liberation of India from the British rule.[42] Their contributions to the Islamic intellectual thought were interwoven with the nationalist aspirations composed of multi-faiths. The destiny of Islam, according to them, could be strengthened by pursuing policies that were best suited to the Indian cause. Their collective voice did not necessarily represent the unitary expression of Muslim aspirations. On the contrary, Mohamed Ali was committed to the corporate Muslim identity which outlined the blueprints of an independent Muslim country, Pakistan.[43] From the spectrum of Indian politics, Mawlānā Abul Kalam Azad and a number of `ulama,

---

[41] A comprehensive account of *tajdid* in the subcontinent is given by Muhammad Mujeeb, *The Indian Muslims* (Lahore, 1986) 113-67.

[42] This vision is clearly evident in Mohamed Ali, *My Life A Fragment* (Lahore, 1966); Khaliq Ahmad Nizami, *Mawlānā Abul Kalam Azad and the Thirty Pages of India Wins Freedom* (Delhi, 1989).

[43] Afzal Iqbal, *Life and Times of Mohamed Ali* (Lahore, 1979), 338-77.

by their unwavering standpoints, championed the cause of composite nationalism. In other words, Muslims could co-exist with the Hindu majority in the undivided India. It was the Partition of India in 1947 that determined the future of the Muslim collective identity. Mawlānā Siddiqui's efforts to advance the Pakistan cause among the Arab world were in many instances impressive.[44]

Tabligh: Multidimensional Approaches

There are several dimensions associated to Mawlānā Siddiqui's personality which are gleaned from his writings. Although they were limited owing to his preoccupation with tabligh and lecture tours, they, nevertheless, give an overview of the areas of his work.

Broadly speaking, Mawlānā Siddiqui presented a rational exposition of the Islamic faith and practice. For example, *The Universal Religion* and *Universal Teachings*[45] are relevant works as these discuss the phenomenon of religions and its relevance to mankind. The philosophical explanation combined with psychological observation is signposted in order to appreciate Islam as the universal religion.

Progressive orthodoxy, a term developed by his successor, Mawlānā Ansari was also indelibly etched in Mawlānā Siddiqui's writings about the Islamic faith and practice. A lucid presentation of the perennial sources of Islam are contained in *The Principles of Islam* and *The History of the Codification of Islamic Law.*[46] These monographs are an elaboration of the distinctive features of Islam. The codification of Islamic law as shown by the formation of the *madhabs* (schools of thought) - the formative years of Islam - reveals Mawlānā Siddiqui's mastery over the Islamic textual sources. The last-mentioned monograph has a greater relevance today in view of the anti-*taqlid* movements that have attempted to undermine the *turāth* (legacy) as the integral component of the established schools of thought.

---

[44] Qadri, *The Greatest Propagator of Islam*, 22.

[45] The monographs together with other booklets of Mawlānā Siddiqui have been compiled by Mawlānā Abdul Hadi al-Qadiri bearing the title *Dimensions of Islam.* Some of these titles were originally published by Makki Publications and Islamic Publications Bureau of Cape Town.

[46] Siddiqui, *The Principles of Islam*, (Karachi, 2002).

Mawlānā Siddiqui's spiritual credentials were reflected in the *tasawwuf* tradition. His stature as a Qadiri shaykh and his profound insight into the inner dimensions of Islam are derived from the influential works of the eminent *mashā'ikh* like Sayyid Abdul Qadir Jilani[47], Imam Ghazali, Rumi, etc. In a similar vein, *The Forgotten Path of Knowledge*[48] and the *Quest for True Happiness* are concise spiritual guidelines for the aspirants in the *tasawwuf* tradition. Mawlānā Siddiqui's scholarly presentation of *tasawwuf* is brought out in the *Spiritual Culture in Islam*. Like a spiritual physician, he diagnoses the maladies affecting the *ummah* and prescribes remedies that are life-enriching and meaningful. An important Urdu monograph, *Kitāb al-Tasawwuf*[49] belongs to the genre of classical sufi works. The eloquence, rhetorical powers and stylistic usage of language are compressed in this excellent work. In a specific sense, it is an accurate reproduction of the essence of *tasawwuf* explained by the *mashā'ikh* over the centuries.

The history of Islam had witnessed deviant sects making audacious claims to prophethood. The charisma associated to the founders of these sects was meant to distort the Islamic teachings by bolstering their false claims. Qadianism emerged during the period of political upheaval in India by coining new forms of prophethood. Mawlānā Siddiqui also contributed to the series of anti-Qadianism literature. His A'ina Qādianiyat (The Mirror) exposes the bizarre claims of Qadianism. Likewise, he edited a number of monographs to raise awareness in the Muslim world about this deviant movement.

Overall, the intellectual legacy of Mawlānā Siddiqui has been largely marginalised as no systematic study has been undertaken during the last seventy years. A number of his writings dealing with his intellectual contributions are no longer extant. Only *A Shavian and a Theologian*[50] offers a glimpse into his mastery of comparative religion, Qur'ānic studies and world history. This widely-acclaimed monograph had carved out a niche for Mawlānā Siddiqui as the

---

[47] Mawlānā Siddiqui's profound love for Shaykh Abdul Qadir Jilani is poignantly expressed in *Dhikr i-Habib* (Karachi, 2018).
[48] Siddiqui, *The Forgotten Path of Knowledge* (Karachi, 1980).
[49] Siddiqui, *Kitāb al-Tasawwuf* (Karachi, 1994).
[50] Siddiqui, *A Shavian and a Theologian* (Durban, 1955).

erudite scholar of international acclaim.

Love for the Holy Prophet (pbuh) permeated the personality of Mawlānā Siddiqui. –Back to the Qur'ān' and 'Back to the Holy Prophet (pbuh)' bore the unmissable traces of his deep-seated attachment to the Holy Prophet (pbuh).

Belonging to this genre, *Dhikr i-Habib*[51] serves as a reminder to the *ummah* that love for the Holy Prophet (pbuh) and his *uswah al-hasanah* (excellent model) are true markers of the perfect faith (*imān*).

Western civilisation possessed the paraphernalias of superiority due to its imperialist policies. It also bought in its wake a number of Orientalist writings committed to undermining the Islamic civilisation and culture. 'The Backward nations of the East', a derogatory term applied to Muslims, was calculated to demean Muslims psychologically. One of the strategies employed by the Orientalists was to highlight Islam's unscientific worldview. Unlike the Muslim apologetics, Mawlānā Siddiqui wrote *Cultivation of Science by the Muslims*[52] to demonstrate Islam's enduring scientific outlook. Its legacy is concisely explained and supported by relevant Qur'ānic *āyāt* (verses).[53]

Democratic institutions with claims to the protection of human rights and equality had failed to counter the emergence of Marxism and Communism in the twentieth century. These **isms**[54] in turn were also existential threats to the Muslim countries, some of which embraced them after gaining independence from the colonial rule. Egypt, in particular, promoted a rebranded version of Socialism to show that Islam was compatible with the wayward policies of this ideology. This growing menace prompted Mawlānā Siddiqui to write a critique of these movements. In his *How to Face Communism* Muslims

---

[51] The Urdu books have seen several reprints in the subcontinent.

[52] Siddiqui, *Cultivation of Science by the Muslims* (Karachi, n.d.).

[53] Siddiqui, *How to Face Communism* (Karachi, 1955).

[54] This term (ism) has a long history of the anti-Islam rhetoric. In the twenty first century, it has assumed a rebranded form of hostility towards Islam. Islamophobia, is an instance in point. It is a global campaign by portraying Islam as anti-civilisation, anti-West, anti-human rights, etc. Indeed, it has deepened the Clash of Civilisations debate.

were reminded of their obligations as *Khalifat Allah* (representative of Allah).

In the historical perspective, the world tabligh tours undertaken by Mawlānā Siddiqui did not offer him the opportunity to write comprehensive works on the myriad issues affecting the Muslim *ummah*. His series of lectures in countries were, however, recorded. Sadly, over a prolonged period of time many of his recorded lectures were lost. It was during his epoch-making lecture tours to South Africa in 1934 and 1952 respectively, that special arrangements were made to record and transcribe his lectures. *The Roving Ambassador of Peace*[55] is an edited version of the lectures delivered by Mawlānā Siddiqui in the Cape and other provinces.

In the following pages a thematic presentation of Mawlānā Siddiqui's varied contributions to the Islamic reawakening project is highlighted. Relevant passages from his writings and articles contained in the magazines and lectures (which have been transcribed) and arranged under specific topics provide an organic structure to his thoughts. This format is aimed at reinforcing the key themes that guided Mawlānā Siddiqui's tabligh mission. Also, the relevant historical information gives a clearer understanding of his writings.

A notable feature of the present volume is the inclusion of excerpts of articles, documents and historical photographs that have a direct bearing on his world tabligh tours. While a chronological narrative is not strictly followed, the resource material is a useful guide to assess his contributions to the countries he visited. Again, the political and historical settings as well as the social milieus under which he undertook these lecture tours, and on many occasions single-handedly, are examined to highlight his extraordinary achievements in response to the changing landscapes of tabligh.

---

[55] Yasien Mahomed, *The Roving Ambassador of Peace* (Cape Town, 2006).

Chapter 2

Dimensions of Tabligh

The dimensions of tabligh assume greater importance in relation to Mawlānā Siddiqui's role as both a scholar and sufi. His tabligh efforts in Muslim countries and in regions where Muslims constituted a minority or as emerging communities provide an overview of the scope and function of the tabligh he promoted. There is no doubt that his methodology was at variance with the existing forms of tabligh, particularly in the subcontinent. The motivation for adopting this approach was largely in response to the geopolitical developments in these countries. Again, the discourse of tabligh rooted in the *tasawwuf* context had far-reaching implications in terms of Islam's universal influence.

The chapter attempts to examine the distinctive features of Mawlānā Siddiqui's conception of tabligh, based largely on his major writings and lectures which he addressed to the diverse communities in many parts of the world. A brief discussion of other revivalist movements serves to illustrate the dynamics associated with Islam's role as a missionary religion. The timeline adopted also explores the trends of revivalism affecting Muslims in specific countries.

Tabligh: Meaning and Context

The word tabligh is derived from the root **b-l-gh**, meaning to reach one's destination, to achieve one's objective or to come of age. Tabligh as a verbal form denotes "to make something, to reach, to communicate or to report."[1] In its grammatical form, the term requires an object, for example, *risālah* (message) which is frequently used in the Qur'ān. Thus, the term tabligh appears in several *āyāt* (verses) in relation to *risālah* and is invariably linked to revelation (*wahy*) or message. In the modern usage, tabligh and *da'wah* are interchangeable terms and have specific semantic connotations.

In the Qur'ānic parlance, the verbal form of tabligh has been used in conjunction with *risālah* to communicate a prophecy or revelation or –to fulfil a mission.[2] The Qur'ān also defines the form of tabligh to the Muslim *ummah* in explicit terms:

> *You are the best of peoples, evolved for mankind, enjoining what is right and forbidding what is wrong and believing in Allah.*

(3:110)

From this *āyāh*, the doctrine of *amr bil ma'ruf* and *wa'al nahy al-munkar* (enjoining good and forbidding evil) is established and forms an essential element of tabligh. Since the nineteenth century, it has become synonymous with tabligh and *da'wah* and has developed as a discourse with respect to its objectives and methodology in the backdrop of the evolving Muslim societies. In fact, the multiple interpretations of tabligh have been based on historical circumstances and ideological formations[3] as the following section will reveal.

---

[1] Raghib Isfahani, *Al-Mufradāt i-Gharā'b al-Qur'ān* (Cairo, 1961), 60.

[2] A detailed treatment of tabligh and its variant meanings are discussed in Muhammad Khalid Masud (ed.) *Travelers in Faith* (Leiden, 2000), xx.

[3] Masud, *Travelers in Faith*, xxi-xxix.

Historical Development of Tabligh

Our study also focuses on the development of tabligh during the nineteenth and early twentieth century for this purpose. A common description of the term, translated as 'mission' in the nineteenth century, was employed in response to the debate over the missionary activities with particular reference to the Indian subcontinent. According to Max Muller, a wider redefinition of Islam as a missionary religion, which raises the work of converting unbelievers is a sacred duty. The missionaries, committed to the spirit of truth embodied in their religion, make every effort to manifest this ideal in thought, word and deed.[4]

T.W. Arnold echoes a similar sentiment: "[It] is such a zeal for the truth of their religion that has inspired the Muhammadans[5] (Muslims) to carry with them the message of Islam to the people of every land into which they penetrate, and that justly claims for their religion a place among those we term missionary."[6] It must be borne in mind that these statements have a historical connotation and do not suggest a sympathetic line of approach to the Islamic civilisation and culture. Therefore, these works have to be read cautiously.

The issue of tabligh became crucial in the background of British colonialism, which promoted the cause of Christian missionary work. In fact, the Western colonial governments were inseparable from the Christian missionary thrust in the Muslim world.[7] Essentially, the establishment of mission schools entrenched the Christian presence with an avowed missionary agenda. Thus, the mobilisation of Muslim masses by the ʿulama was aimed at stemming the rising tide of missionary work which received political and economic support from the colonial government.[8] In many respects,

---

[4] T.W. Arnold, *The Preaching of Islam* (Lahore, 1960), 81.

[5] This description is a misnomer and refers to the stereotyping in the nineteenth century of Muslims as Muhammadans by the Orientalists in order to challenge the divine status of the Qur'ān.

[6] Arnold, *The Preaching of Islam*, 1.

[7] It was the mercenary ambition and missionary fervour that strengthened the Orientalist presence in the colonised Muslim countries.

[8] Robert Hefner and Muhammad Qasim Zaman (eds.), *Schooling Islam: The Culture and Politics of Modern Muslim Education* (Princeton, 2007), 52.

tabligh served as a bulwark of religious and political defence against Christianity and colonialism.

The nineteenth century also saw notable cases of the `ulama acting as Islamic champions against the claims of other faiths. The famed Agra debates of 1854 in which Mawlānā Rahmatullah Kayranwi (d. 1891) got the better of the German missionary, Dr Pfander to advance the Muslim argument against the Christian doctrines were in many respects aimed at establishing the supremacy of Islam. The work[9] produced by Kayranwi is an indispensable critique of Christianity.

A new approach was, however, discernible in the early twentieth century, and context was thus important to the development of new ideas. The `ulama saw how the encroachment of Western civilisation had marginalised Muslims in their beliefs and culture. They also witnessed the emergence of a Muslim generation gradually alienated from the Muslim society. The tabligh approaches did not establish, in the long term, the supremacy of Islam as envisaged by the `ulama.[10] As they came to realise the full impact of the British rule in the world, they, too, sought to counteract these foreign tendencies by reassessing their role in the changing society.

The `Ulama and Tabligh

The establishment of the madrasahs by the `ulama with a reformist vision was evident in their interpretation of tabligh. The corpus of Islamic scholarship was incorporated into the curriculum to maintain the unbroken link with the Waliyullah tradition.[11] Parallel to the dissemination of Islamic knowledge through the production of texts was the vigorous promotion of tabligh by its graduates. It

---

[9] *Izhār al-Haq* (The Truth Revealed) was written in reply to the polemical tract entitled *Mizan-ul-Haq* by Rev. Pfander. See Kayranwi, *Izhār al- Haq* (London, 1989). Cf. Goolam Vahed, *Ahmed Deedat: The Man and his Mission* (Durban, 2013), 32-6.

[10] The challenges faced by the `ulama are summarised in Francis Robinson, *Islam, South Asia and the West* (New Delhi, 2007), 59-98.

[11] The Waliyullah tradition influenced the various schools of thought (*maslaks*) in South Asia. See Mahmood Ghazi, *Islamic Renaissance in South Asia 1707-1867* (Islamabad, 2002), 189-252.

assumed greater importance for two reasons. First, the authentic presentation of Islamic belief (`aqidah) and teaching (ta'lim)[12] was considered essential to curb the syncretic practices deemed Islamic over the centuries. In this way, their reformist activities were intensified largely in the villages where the distinction between Islamic and un-Islamic practices was blurred. Second, the mission schools posed a potential threat to tabligh as their Muslim students invariably challenged the `ulama over doctrinal issues. In fact, the rising generation of the modernist Muslims[13] shared ideological commonalities with the Christian missionaries: to dislodge the established traditional interpretation of Islam's foundational texts. The culture of polemics was rooted in scepticism and nurtured by the Christian individuals and organisations who were hostile towards Islam. By and large, the `ulama had to devise new strategies to expand the implementation of tabligh. They had to contend with the new armory of ideas (anti-Islamic) by the Christian missionaries possessing questionable academic interest in Islamic studies. They represented the face of Orientalism which was yet another challenge to Islam. Two countries were directly affected by this new menace and over a prolonged period: India and Egypt. British colonialism had subtly created a generation of Muslim intellectuals who were swayed by Western civilisation. Although the response of the `ulama varied in both countries regarding the Western encroachment, the forms of tabligh were redirected to meet the challenges of the day.

In Egypt the close encounters with the Christian missionaries gave Muslims the motivation to adopt new tabligh approaches. This encounter prompted the reformist scholar, Rashid Rida to establish the *da'wa wa'l-irshad* (*da'wah* and guidance) project for similar purposes. Likewise, the *da'wah* activities initiated by Hasan al-

---

[12] Regardless of their sectarian backgrounds, the newly established Islamic institutions made tireless efforts in their reformist (*islāhi*) vision to root out these un-Islamic practices, See Ghazi, *Islamic Renaissance*, 256-7. Cf. Sherali Tareen, *Defending Muhammad in Modernity* (Ranikhet, 2020).

[13] The modernists of varying backgrounds have reinterpreted Islam apologetically. See Mazheruddin Siddiqui, *Modernist Reformist Thought in the Muslim World* (Islamabad, 1982).

Banna, founder of the Ikhwan movement was aimed at reforming the Egyptian Muslim society.[14] Also his presentation of *din* as a comprehensive term that encompassed all facets of human activity brought the Ikhwan into the arena of politics. Imam al-Banna promoted *da'wah*[15] which embodied the ideals of the *salaf*. This form of *da'wah* urged Muslims to reassess their past glory on the basis of their adherence to the Islamic teachings. Hence, the future success for Muslims was dependent on following this ideal.

The nineteenth century was in marked contrast to the early twentieth century. The struggle for independence in the Muslim world gained momentum in the form of *jihād* movements like Al-Sanusiyah. It must be noted that the Grand Sanusi was primarily a sufi and most of his intellectual legacy revolved around this spiritual discipline. Again, the defining feature of his writings reflects the revival of sufi thought.[16] Also, geopolitics determined the course of events that directly affected particular Muslim countries emerging from the shadows of colonial rule. This phenomenon was more evident in the Arab world which had to redefine its Islamic identity. Its affiliation to Islam was in several instances tenuous as Marxism and Socialism had made inroads into several Arab countries.[17] For *da'wah* to succeed, ideals had to give way to pragmatism. There was, no doubt, that the fortunes of *da'wah* swayed between Islamic commitment and the challenges of the ideological systems.

Tabligh in the Subcontinent

In the subcontinent, the process of democracy and modernity

---

[14] Albert Hourani, *Arabic Thought in the Liberal Age* 1798-1939 (London, 1962). The chapters on Afghani, Abduh and Rida provide a detailed background and analysis of their lives and views.

[15] The Ikhwān al-Muslimin extended the scope of *da'wah* to all aspects of life. Thus, *din* was comprehensively developed in their discourse. Saeed Hawwa, *The Muslim Brotherhood* (Salama,1985).

[16] See Ghulam Shams-ur-Rehman, "Two Conflicting Paradigms of Puritanical Islam" in *Hamdard Islamicus*: vol. xxxiv, 48.

[17] A summative assessment of Islam and Communism appears in Fazlur Rahman Ansari, "Islam and Muslims in the Soviet Union" in *Voice of Islam: 1955*, April-July, 295- 312.

produced secularism – a potential threat to the traditional Islamic values. In response to these emerging ideologies, it was felt that tabligh among the Muslims was a prerequisite in order to create the ideal Muslim society.

Founded by Mawlānā Muhammad Ilyās[18] (d.1944), his tabligh project sought to make Muslims true, self- conscious and strictly abiding by the dictates of faith.[19] Two points formed the core of his movement in its initial stages: strengthening the faith (*imān*) and raising awareness about the importance of the Islamic ritual obligations.[20] According to Mawlānā Ilyās, the method he proposed was simply a means to the higher goal of bringing other facets of Islam in accordance with the dictates of the shari`ah.[21] The tenor of his tabligh project was the responsibility it placed on every individual to uphold the basic tenets of Islam. It was through the –six principles' that the Tabligh Jama'at (TJ) was organised to promote its message among Muslims. Also, formal travel from place to place was the distinctive mark of the movement.[22]

Mawlānā Ilyās emphasised a reformed *tasawwuf*[23] that suited the scope and function of the tabligh project. This was in keeping with the worldview of the `ulama who criticised the deviant practices in the name of Islam and, instead, presented Islam based on the foundational texts and elucidated by the *salaf*.

The *tasawwuf* element was shared by both the Ikhwan and the TJ. However, the *da'wah* propagated by the Ikhwan extended beyond the boundaries of conventional tabligh. Their involvement in politics was in direct contrast to the TJ's apolitical position.[24] Both of them

---

[18] On the growth of and development of the Tabligh Jama'at, see M. Anwarul Haq, *The Faith Movement of Mawlana Muhammad Ilyās* (London, 1972).

[19] Yoginder Sikand, *The Origin and Development of the Tablighi-Jama'at* 1920-2000 (New Delhi, 2002), 66.

[20] Ibid.

[21] Haq, *The Faith Movement*, 167.

[22] The tabligh literature sets out guidelines regarding the purpose and function of tabligh. See Masud, *Travelers in Faith*, 80-45.

[23] The reformed *tasawwuf* implied a rejection of practices borrowed from the un-Islamic sources. Haq, *The Faith Movement*, 75-6.

[24] In a broader sense, these movements differed in their approach to politics, which served as the leverage to effect changes in the Muslim society. See Masud, *Travelers*

derived their source of inspiration from the *salaf* with varying degrees of interpretation. The tumultuous period that marked the Ikhwan's *da'wah* activities pointed out to its ideological commitment which it sought to advance. On the other hand, the TJ adopted a quietest, pietest approach with the revitalisation of faith (*tahrik-i-imān*) as its goal.

Tabligh: Mawlānā Siddiqui's Presentation

An overview of tabligh and *da'wah* illustrates the differing perception of these trends. Mawlānā Siddiqui's decades-long career offers interesting insights into his understanding of the defining features of tabligh. His approach was derived from his forty years of rigorous travels and earned him the title of *The Roving Ambassador of Islam*. His travels within India and beyond have not been comprehensively covered. However, the information available in the form of his lectures, monographs and posters does in some measure present a fair account of his efforts. His busy schedule was intertwined with the expanding notions of tabligh. While committed to its basic formulation, Mawlānā Siddiqui saw greater opportunities to reach out to the Muslim communities in the far-flung areas of the world by imparting Islamic values. In this regard, he enjoyed the singular advantage over other *muballighs* for several reasons. His competence in modern education and several languages together with his profound Islamic learning and absorption in *tasawwuf* was his outstanding trait. His goal was unambiguous: to project the message of Islam through the establishment of Islamic institutions. Among his notable achievements was the creation of interfaith forums to foster peace and harmony among mankind. His broad concept of tabligh was impactful:

> According to the Islamic teaching, every Muslim must act as a born missionary. For, Muslims have been described in the Holy Qur'ān as the "best of nations" on the ground that "they enjoin what is right and forbid what is wrong." Therefore, if

---

in Faith, 97-8.

Muslims of the present day fulfil this obligation, they will deserve this title. If the Muslims neglect to do so, they can only be classified in the reverse category both in this world and their accountability before Allah. History bears witness to the fact that so long as Muslims continued to fulfil this great task of the active and dynamic realisation of Islam, they continued to enjoy an enviable position in the comity of nations.[25] Its neglect brought them down and we may be sure that if they return to it once again, they will regain their lost position.

The need for such a revival, the call of Islamic missionary activity is indeed more pressing today than ever before.

The dissemination of Islamic knowledge is, therefore, the crying need of the day and calls for a determined, organised and well- coordinated effort, which should be planned in accordance with modern conditions.

I wish to warn Muslims against the type of formal and lifeless propaganda which certain people have learnt to carry out in the name of Islam. Superficialities cannot carry us far as they are always short lived. What we need is a high-class and honest Islamic intellectual campaign, on the one hand, and the radiation of the light of Islam by personal example on the other. My thirty years' labour in this field has convinced me that it is ultimately man which attracts man. It is the personal and practical example set by the preacher in his total personality which counts above everything else. This is a fact which many of us seem to have forgotten today and we have thus belied our own history. I remind my Muslim friends that it was the personality of the Holy Prophet (pbuh) which, besides the correct intellectual presentation of Islam, was responsible for the most wonderful revolution of human history. Again, the whole history of the spread of Islam revolved around the personalities of those who were, in their own persons, shining illustrations of Islam and possessed not only the knowledge of

---

[25] In other words, Mawlana Siddiqui argued that tabligh was an essential feature of promoting Islam as the universal religion. The term 'comity of nations' has also undergone dramatic changes in view of the geopolitical developments.

Islam but also a share of the spiritual magnetism of the Holy Prophet (pbuh). Read and re-read the history of the propagation of Islam in India or Indonesia or China or Africa or any other part of the Muslim world and you will come across the same story everywhere.[26]

Mawlānā Siddiqui personified the tabligh ideal in his presentation of Islam. His unwavering commitment to promote Islam in the changing socio-political landscapes was a testament to his vision of embracing change without compromising the Islamic teachings. Like the spiritual luminaries who spread Islam in the far-flung countries of the world through their charismatic personalities, Mawlānā Siddiqui, too, belonged to this unbroken chain of the saviours of Islamic spirit. His tabligh was a marked departure from the conventional understanding and practice as was prevalent in the early twentieth century. He developed a methodology that was flexible and well-suited to the needs of the different Muslim communities, some of whom were refugees, political asylum seekers or those who sought economic opportunities in countries with a neglible presence of Islam. These diaspora communities needed guidance in the Islamic teachings and a mentor of his calibre who could steer their collective Islamic identity under adverse circumstances. In this perspective, the well-structured contributions of Mawlānā Siddiqui to tabligh may be understood.

Mawlānā Ansari's Elaboration of Tabligh

The concept of tabligh envisaged by Mawlānā Siddiqui was elaborated by Mawlānā Ansari in his *The Qur'ānic Foundations and Structure of Muslim Society,* a major work on Qur'ānic studies. According to Ansari, the Qur'ān has equated tabligh to the status of an institution. Its objectives are preservation, development and perpetuation of the Islamic community. The dimensions of this duty are:

---

[26] Siddiqui, "The Islamic Ideal" in *The Minaret:* June 2004, 14-5. This lecture was delivered in the 1940s.

- Education of new generations of Muslims in Islam. Improvement of Islamic knowledge.
- Dissemination of the knowledge of Islam to Muslims and all non-Muslims.

Tabligh stands out "as a duty towards other individuals and respect of their spiritual and moral progress. It has also served to keep the Islamic community alive and functioning generally into the body politic of Islam." Mawlānā Ansari warns against the rigid approach to tabligh. The field of tabligh should be enlightened, dynamic and multidimensional and not a ritualistic or professional performance.[27]

The common vision underlying their perceptions of tabligh strengthened their respective goals in countries they visited. They also wielded considerable influence on the academic circles and Islamic movements supporting the revival project. Indeed, they had played an important role in the Arab and Islamic world.

It would be worthwhile to comment on Mawlānā Siddiqui's popularity within India. It is generally assumed that his tabligh outreach activities were outside the subcontinent for which he gained immense fame. Although no detailed study has been undertaken to shed light on his interaction with the local organisations due to the sketchy details available, the following information gleaned from several documents are indicative of his success in the field of tabligh. The 1930s saw his extensive travels which in some instances covered countries as far as Canada. The personal accounts or travelogues recorded by Mawlānā Ansari focus, albeit briefly, on the challenges and successes achieved by Mawlānā Siddiqui. The oral sources do point out to his extraordinary mission; however, the filtering of embellished accounts and unverifiable reports tend to mar the veracity of Mawlānā Siddiqui's accomplishments.

It is difficult to visualise the travel hazards Mawlānā Siddiqui had to face in his tabligh activities beyond the Indian subcontinent. Keeping in mind that his was a solitary mission in the early years of

---

[27] Ansari, *The Qur'ānic Foundations and Structure of Muslim Society*, vol. 2, xxv–xxvi.

the twentieth century, the insurmountable hardships that were associated with travel by sea was a grim reality. Not all of his tabligh activities were smooth sailing. From Mumbai, for example, to the vast swathes of the remote regions in Africa, the prospects of travel were a hazardous venture. In fact, the sea route was a tortuous journey prolonged by intermittent delays to reach the countries earmarked for tabligh. Amid these daunting challenges, Mawlānā Siddiqui remained steadfast in his resolve to communicate the message of Islam to the indigenous people of Africa. His approach was simple and direct to making the teachings of Islam accessible to these reverts.

Another plausible explanation to his tabligh success was his outstanding ability to acquire proficiency in several languages. This is particularly relevant to Swahili, which was widely spoken in East Africa. His regular visits to Kenya as a port of call reaffirmed his competence in the language and his effortless interaction with the local population. In several instances, the nodal points of his tabligh activities were Kenya, Mauritius and South Africa. In later years, the improved sea travel enabled Mawlānā Siddiqui to expand his tabligh footprints in many parts of Africa. The famous dialogue with the eminent playwright, George Bernard Shaw on the Union Castle Liner in Mombasa (Kenya) in a way represents the upgraded facilities which he utilised for the purpose of tabligh.

Barely twenty years old, Mawlānā Siddiqui made his tabligh foray into Colombo, Sri Lanka in 1914. He was invited to attend the Muslim Education Conference, which had passed resolutions to review the traditional Islamic education offered in *maktabs* and craft national policies for its reform. A graduate from Allahabad University and majoring in Humanities, Mawlānā Siddiqui was the ideal choice to address the distinguished audience. His subsequent visits spanning a twenty-year period saw the establishment of mosques, Islamic centres and institutions of higher learning. The construction of mosques was symbolic: to unify the Muslim communities and build a collective Islamic voice in the predominantly Buddhist population. The Memon Hanafi Mosque is an instance in point.[28]

---

[28] *Anwār i-Rizā*, 171-3.

Another interesting development of Mawlānā Siddiqui's tabligh network was his meeting with the renowned entrepreneur and philanthropist, Abdool Razack Mohamed in 1928. His father owned several businesses in Colombo and Abdool Razack was a frequent visitor to oversee the family's established business interests. His meeting with Mawlānā Siddiqui paved the way for the latter's tabligh visits to Mauritius. The key features of his busy schedule included the interfaith dialogues with the Christian missionaries, resulting in a number of priests accepting Islam. The name of Reverend F. Kingsbury features prominently in the list of conversions. An influential figure, he played an important role in spreading Islam among the non-Muslims.[29] Likewise, he inspired a generation of Sri Lankan Muslim intellectuals and scholars to carry forward the message of Islam. As they were exposed to new trends of religious thought their contributions were significant. Many Muslims had been exposed to the Western influence due to the pervasive presence of missionary schools and their ambivalence, often streaks of scepticism, was glaringly evident. The seminal Islamic magazine titled *The Star of Islam* was inspired by Mawlānā Siddiqui. Among the contributors to this cultural weekly were the articulate pieces of writings by Justice M.T. Akbar, a senior judge of the Supreme Court in Sri Lanka. He played a prominent part in the educational and judicial life of the country. Akbar made outstanding contributions towards the development of Muslim Personal Law, very much reminiscent of Mawlānā Siddiqui's efforts in Mauritius. He was an ardent admirer of the learned scholar's writings; his own published works are a cogent presentation of the Islamic moral philosophy and teachings. His article 'Allah of the Qur'ān' is an exploration of *tawhid* as opposed to polytheism and the ideological systems like Communism.[30] Akbar also contributed a series of articles to the *Ramadan Annual*[31] and was closely associated with Mohammed Makki of South Africa. His writings bore the distinct traces of his mentor's scholarly acumen. All in all, Mawlānā Siddiqui was the guiding spirit of

---

[29] Fazlur Rahman Ansari, *A New Muslim World in the Making* (Karachi, 2018), 88.

[30] *The Star of Islam*, vol. 1: 14, 1.

[31] See *Ramadan Annual*: December 1998/January 1999, 33-9. The article "What I Believe" bears close resemblance to Mawlana Siddiqui's *Choice of One's Religion*. Ibid, 155-60.

the Islamic resurgence taking place in Sri Lanka. Therefore, his contributions underscore the contours of his tabligh mission.

While not following strictly the timeline of Mawlānā Siddiqui's tabligh outreach activities in the Indian subcontinent, we focus on an important lecture delivered by Mawlānā Siddiqui before a learned audience in Mumbai (1935). The Jami'at al-'Ulama arranged several conferences in this metropolis, drawing a number of distinguished scholars and leading sociopolitical activists. Framed from the Islamic intellectual discourse perspective, *The Universal Teaching* hosted under the auspices of fifty-one organisations in the Townhall, Mumbai, underpinned Mawlānā Siddiqui's intellectual stature. The salient features of the lecture are a pointed reference to Islam as a universal religion. According to Mawlānā Siddiqui, Islam promotes the 'golden mean' which directs Muslims to achieve material progress within the ambit of spiritual culture. In other words, the pursuit of science and technology should equip Muslims for their "journey towards the centre of all life and light and embodiment of all perfection -Allah."[32]

In a similar vein, Mawlānā Siddiqui draws the readers' attention to the unbroken link between *wahy* (revelation) and the sunnah as representing the comprehensive character of the Holy Prophet (pbuh). The Qur'ānic declaration in this regard is unambiguous:

Whatever the Prophet gives you, that accept; and whatever he forbids you, that avoid. (59:7)

Without delving into the growth and development of Islamic studies, there are clear indications that Mawlānā Siddiqui was familiar with the trends of contemporary Islamic thought. Likewise, he was acquainted with the writings of his contemporary, Muhammad Asad (d. 1992).[33] Asad earned international fame for his celebrated work, *Islam at the Crossroads*[34] which was published in 1934. Mawlānā Siddiqui's analysis of the sunnah has resonance in the words

---

[32] Ibid., 245.

[33] On the life and legacy of Muhammad Asad, see Ikram Chagatai, *Muhammad Asad: Europe's Gift to Islam* (Lahore, 2006).

[34] Muhammad Asad, *Islam at the Crossroads* (Lahore, 1969).

of Asad.

Thus, the personality of the Greatest Man becomes deeply embodied in the very routine of our daily life, and his spiritual influence is made real, ever-recurring factor in our existence. We learn to regard him not only as the bearer of a moral revelation but also as a guide towards a perfect life.[35]

Reference has been made to the Jami`at al-Hind (Kanpur). As an executive member of the organisation, Mawlānā Siddiqui was invited to deliver a series of lectures on the theme: *The Muslims: Their Past, Present and Future.*[36]

His leadership and scholarly credentials were reaffirmed and so was his stature as a *muballigh* of repute.[37] This period (1933) also saw his *hajj* travels, which revealed a sensitive soul immersed in the love of the Holy Prophet (pbuh). Also, the *hajj* experience allowed him to record his impressions about the Saudi kingdom's economy, poor maintenance of roads and security concerns.[38]

The extracts below by three Indian organisations refer to Mawlānā Siddiqui's epic journey, covering a year (1933) of tabligh to several countries in Africa and the Far East.

Islamic Discourses

The gratifying news of your exceptional, well-reasoned discourses on Islamic subjects delivered in the City of Madras and elsewhere through India, Malaya Peninsula, Ceylon, etc. has spread like wild fire in all the towns and villages of this Presidency, and we deem ourselves very fortunate indeed for having such an eagerly coveted opportunity of listening to the enlightening and edifying speech of your Holiness discussing the teachings of Islam in their pristine purity. We earnestly request your Holiness to pray to Almighty Allah to give us the inclination and strength to follow the precepts of Islam in the light of Your Holiness's true and genuine interpretation.[39]

---

[35] Ibid., 147.

[36] *Sind Observer* (Karachi). August 01, 1933.

[37] *Wahdat Delhi.* March 02, 1933.

[38] *The Hindustan Times* (Delhi). August 08, 1933.

[39] *Members of the Reception Committee: Pandaravadai,* 18 June 1934.

Inspiring Lectures

Your fame as a master theologian and master preacher of Islam, the religion of humanity in its pristine purity is so great and wide throughout the length and breadth of India, Ceylon, Burma, Malaya, Dutch East Indies, South Africa, Mauritius, etc. That wherever you deliver your most eloquent, learned and inspiring lectures, thousands of people of all colours and creed flock together without any prejudice to benefit themselves in their search for truth. We thank the Almighty for having bestowed upon us the golden opportunity of availing ourselves of your highly beneficial advice.

Oh! Knight of Islam!

You are sacrificing your life and your all for the cause of Islam and the cause of Islam only. Constantly afflicted with cold, cataracts, bronchitis, etc. you have braved the worst ill-health for the sake of proclaiming to the world the Truth. Single handed and with no backing from any organised missionary society you are most successfully fighting your weary way against the stormy waves of materialism by which the world is fast being sunk today. Indeed, many thousands of human souls have been rescued and brought to light.[40]

Islam Personified

Allah has granted you all the wisdom and virtues of the Islamic religion, and your thorough mastery of the several languages of the world is a manifest indication of His blessings upon your gracious self to spread His mission in lands unacquainted with the principles of our religion. Easy is to talk and difficult is the task to act. But the voluntary institutions which your Eminence has founded and established in the different parts of the globe are monuments of your altruistic accomplishments[41] in the cause of

---

[40] *Gowthia Association*: Nagore, 30-3-44.
[41] Altruism refers to the selfless concern for the well-being of others. It is the

Islam. In a word, it is no exaggeration to assert that your precious words end in deeds and convictions.

Lastly, we most humbly request your Eminence to accept our heartfelt gratitude for having so kindly given us an opportunity of presenting this humble farewell address on the eve of your departure to Japan and we sincerely pray the Almighty to bless you with long life, prosperity and strength to carry out His laudable mission, for which you have dedicated your life.[42]

Mawlānā Siddiqui addressed the Muslim communities with a single-minded purpose: to spread the teachings of Islam. He did not discriminate between low-profile organisations and leading institutions. In his estimation, tabligh took precedence over other worldly considerations. The emotive contents in the above extracts also reveal the international fame of Mawlānā Siddiqui whose arduous travels illustrated his unwavering dedication to the tabligh cause. It was his altruistic accomplishments that projected his goals of reaffirming the values of peace and tolerance among mankind. These organisations appreciated his single-minded dedication to promote the cause of Islam. His vision was remarkable in many ways. First, his tabligh mission was not a collective effort or undertaken in the name of an organisation (*tanzim*) possessing sufficient resources to advance its cause. Second, he was fully conscious of the challenges associated with such a journey - a hazardous undertaking in view of the modes of travel. However, this did not deter him from reaching out to the Muslim communities who were eager to listen to his lectures and take practical measures to practise Islam in its totality. The transformative spirit of Mawlānā Siddiqui's personality was evident in the countries he visited and which left an enduring legacy - visible markers of his contributions to the Islamic reawakening project.

---

unselfish regard or devotion to the welfare of others. The word *ithār* in *tasawwuf* has a broader definition in terms of the spirit of self-sacrifice.

[42] *Kamalia Muslim League*, Negapatam (India).

Chapter 3

Tabligh in East Asia

Tabligh in Shanghai

Lest it be assumed that Mawlānā Siddiqui's primary focus was on the Indian Muslims who had settled in many parts of the world, his travels to China and Japan, however, a different picture. Mawlānā Siddiqui raised an awareness through his lectures on the plight and challenges faced by Muslims in countries he visited. In Shanghai (China) he addressed the Turko-Tartar community at several meetings in June 1936.[1] The Turko-Tartar Muslims had exercised their autonomy over the centuries and preserved their Islamic identity by sharing common cultural and linguistic traits with other Turkic people who were spread across Central Asia and the hinterlands of present-day Turkey. Like other Muslim nations in Soviet Russia, they, too, suffered a similar fate under the Communist regime.[2] Its totalitarian policies were aimed at eradicating any expressions of their Islamic identity in this predominantly Muslim region. The Muslim organisations were forced in the 1920s to conscientise other Muslim countries about their traumatic experiences under the Communist rule. It is against this background that Mawlānā Siddiqui's contributions must be examined.

The Religious National Geo-fraternity of Turko-Tartar Muslims which was based in Shanghai was greatly impressed by Mawlānā Siddiqui's efforts to address their concerns and restore their faith and confidence in the Islamic teachings. He also reminded them that the panacea for the sufferings of mankind required steadfastness and perseverance. In a *Welcome Address* to Mawlānā Siddiqui, the society gave a graphic description of the threat to the Turko-Tartar Muslims'

---

[1] Qadri, *The Greatest Propagator of Islam*, 77.

[2] For a historical account on the persecutions of the Tartar Muslims, See J.G. *Tiwari, Muslims under the Czars and the Soviets* (Lucknow, 1984), 93-124.

collective Islamic identity under the Bolshevik regime:

> The regard you have for us as your brothers in Islam is of great consolation to us especially at this juncture when we are passing our days in a homeless state of our life. Your Eminence is aware of the miseries we had to face owing to the cruelties of the Bolsheviks in our homeland. Our homes are ruined, our relatives are murdered and for the last fifteen to twenty years we are exile in this country. We have listened to your discourses on some occasions in Shangai and have come to know of your selfless sacrifice and come to know of your selfless activities.[3]

The iron-fist rule of Communism in Soviet Russia had two distinct features: the veneer of technological progress and the intimidating presence of dictatorship. Large-sized photos and statues were a grim reminder that the citizens were under scrutiny by the intelligence and security apparatus.[4] Any attempts of resistance were brutally quelled and the punitive measures were equally gruesome.

Communism: A Critique

According to Mawlānā Siddiqui, the prevalent ideological systems posed a powerful challenge to tabligh. In this respect, his critique of Communism (interchangeably used for Marxism) brought into sharp relief its distinguishing features. A telling example shows how it had shackled millions of souls in total subservience to entrench its ruthless policies. He observed:

It is said that the evils of capitalism have compelled the starving millions to rise in revolt; that the exploitation of the power by the rich have forced them into conflict and that the only way in which to establish justice is nothing but war. There is no doubt that the exploitation and oppression of mankind should be stopped and the destiny and prosperity of the common man should be secured. We

---

[3] *Welcome Address*, 7th January 1936.
[4] Fazlur Rahman Ansari, *Communist Challenge to Islam* (Karachi, 2018), 116-7.

have to be on guard against those who are out to use this struggle for social justice for gaining certain ulterior ends of their own. The Marxists or the Communists, for instance, are employing the poverty line in certain countries as an instrument of their aggression. They appeal to the people in the name of human equality and ask them to wage class warfares, but the theory as well as the actions of the Marxists and the Communists is a positive proof that the success of Marxism puts the people into evils even worse than those which it aims to fight.

The success of Marxism means the way to atheism and the mechanical acceptance of certain creeds which are after all man-made. Marxism further means wide suppression of the faith in God. Who has not heard the words of Karl Marx that belief in God is a fraud and that religion is the opium for the people. Marxism cannot tolerate the faith, the brotherhood and the unity of mankind which is based on the faith in the one Supreme Being, the true God. Anyone who has studied the books of Marx will completely agree with me.[5]

In other words, Communism purports to be concerned about the welfare of its people in the name of social justice. However, it uses propaganda ploys to undermine religion to show its 'toxic' effects on the people. Mawlānā Siddiqui expended his energies to counter the menace of Communism during his tabligh travels. Books written under his guidance especially by Mawlānā Ansari[6] were intended to raise a global awareness about the tragic consequences created by these ideological systems. The fate of Turko-Tartars was a microcosm of the large chunks of Muslim nations suffering miserably under the Communist regime.

Mawlānā Siddiqui was a rare prodigy; his writings on Communism bear definite traces of deep study about this ideological system, which had suppressed the innate desires and aspirations of man to forge a spiritual bond with his Creator. Through devious means the

---

[5] Siddiqui, *How to face Communism* (Karachi, n.d.), 15-6.
[6] The following books written by Mawlana Ansari were meant to refute Communist doctrines: *Islam versus the Communism* (Karachi, 1982); *Islam versus Marxism* (Karachi, 1982).

propaganda tool of expediency was employed to create its messianic message: liberation from the shackles of capitalistic exploitation. Under the guidance of Mawlānā Siddiqui, the collaborative effort with Mawlānā Ansari was started to counteract the menace of Communism. In fact, *The Communist Challenge to Islam* was the culmination of a series of books devoted to the critical study of this ideological system. Mawlānā Ansari elaborated:

> The [present work] forms the third literary work in English undertaken at the instance of the Islamic Research Academy (Karachi, Pakistan). The Academy was inaugurated in 1943 at the Aligarh Muslim University (AMU) under the patronage of the celebrated Islamic missionary (*muballigh*) and international leader, His Eminence Muhammad Abdul Aleem Siddiqui, and under the guidance of the revered Islamic philosopher, Professor Syed Zafarul Hasan. The Partition of India caused it to be shifted to Karachi in 1947.[7]

The correspondence between Mawlānā Ansari and Mawlānā Siddiqui[8] offers refreshing insights into the former's mastery over the topic. Indeed, his academic studies at AMU (1933-47) developed his international image. In more ways than one, Mawlānā Ansari was the *tarjumān* (spokesperson) of Mawlānā Siddiqui in the intellectual sphere. His cogent reappraisal of Communism is based on logical arguments, well-documented research and irrefutable evidence about the Islamic position of *khilāfah*. Overall, the thrust of the Communist philosophy is expediency. Additionally, half- truths, iron-fist rule and anti-faith - these are the toxic elements that drive its agenda to the path of social disintegration.

Mawlānā Siddiqui had a thorough grasp of Communism's intrusive influence on several Muslim countries. Mention may be made of *Islam and Communism* which was published by Makki Publications in 1945. Like several other works pertaining to Islam and the West theme, Mohammed Makki was responsible for producing Islamic literature

---

[7] Ansari, *Communist Challenge to Islam*, 38-9.

[8] See Umair Mahmood Siddiqui, *Makātib i- Ansari* (Karachi, 2018).

under the supervision of Mawlānā Siddiqui. The following extract from the correspondence to Makki is illustrative of his visionary spirit:

> My dear Makki
> The great service which you are rendering to Islam by the publication of missionary periodicals and magazines is indeed a great achievement and is an emulation for others. Your selfless enthusiasm for Islam makes me extremely happy and I congratulate you with all my heart. May the Almighty give you further strength and enable you to render greater services to Islam.[9]

The intellectual contributions of Mawlānā Siddiqui are succinctly expressed in his meetings with the literary societies in Shanghai. The China Muslim Literary Society in Shanghai recorded its impressions of Mawlānā Siddiqui's scientific approach to issues confronting the Muslim intelligentsia:

> Whilst you were addressing the large gathering in the Royal Asiatic Society Hall, the audience was deeply impressed with the logical and scientific discourse you made on the most important subject of science and religion. Your reasoning and arguments were quite sufficient to convince even an atheist into believing in the existence of One God, the only reality in the universe. In fact, all your lectures have enlightened to a great extent the Muslims as well as the non-Muslims in this city.[10]

It may noted that these organisations were made up of Islamic intellectuals, professionals and Islamic scholars who were very much familiar with the emerging trends of Western philosophy, science and technology and comparative religions. In this strain, the Muslim political asylum seekers were exposed to the new challenges in their host country and had to present Islam as a rational religion. The choice of Mawlānā Siddiqui to articulate the scientific temper of the

---

[9] *Fifth Pillar*, November 1945, 24.
[10] Qadri, *The Greatest Propagator of Islam*, 72.

sacred text is illustrative of his fame as a leading exponent of the Islamic teachings. His tabligh vision was embedded in the broader framework of Islam as a civilisational force.

Islamic Perspective on Science

The scientific discourse finds resonance in Mawlānā Siddiqui's other writings as well. His logical presentation of the universe from the Islamic perspective is persuasive:

> The beautiful panorama of the heavens and the earth which we see around us carries in its bosom the testimony that it is the creation of a great artist. The existence of order and design in the universe, which modern science teaches us, leads us to the belief in the existence of a supreme power and sublime intelligence who is responsible for this complex but orderly design - of a Supreme Being who brought it into existence and supplied it with all that it needed for its life and growth - in the language of the Holy Qur'ān, of the *Rabb al-'Alamin.*
>
> The universe, as we know it in science, is an organic whole, all of whose parts are beautifully and harmoniously interrelated. It is, further, a domain of law in which every particle exists and moves in subjection to a prescribed and immutable course of law. Neither the huge planets that swim in space, nor the tiny particles of sand that lie scattered on the sea- shore, can deviate even slightly from the course. Their life is a life of complete submission to the laws of nature, in the language of science, and to the laws of God, in the language of religion. Their life is the life of Islam, which means submission to divine commands. In other words, they are Muslims.[11]

The 'immutable laws of nature' are pithily expressed in this verse:

> *... Not a leaf does fall but with His knowledge. There is not a grain*

---

[11] Siddiqui, *The Principles of Islam* (Karachi, 2002), 1-2.

in the darkness (or depths) of the earth, nor anything fresh or dry (green or withered), but is inscribed in a Record which is clear (to those who can read). (6:59)

Two points emerge from Mawlānā Siddiqui's interaction with the leading organisations in Shangai. First, the looming presence of Communism was an existential threat to the nascent Muslim communities who had sought political asylum from the ruthless Soviet regime. The crisis of confidence if remained unchecked would have a debilitating effect on the Muslims searching for Islam-friendly environments. Shangai, at the time, was a haven of peace where Islam could be freely practised. Second, the ascendancy of science and technology influenced the mindset of the Muslim intellectuals in this region. In fact, these Muslim organisations represented a new generation seeking answers about the Islamic teachings, message of the Qur'ān from a scientific perspective. They were equally conversant with Western learning and, therefore, required an Islamic scholar who could address these issues on a rational basis. Keeping in mind the dearth of *muballighs* who could deliver on the Islam and Science theme, the contributions of Mawlānā Siddiqui are remarkable.

Establishment of Islamic Institutions

The progressive trends adopted by Mawlānā Siddiqui to communicate the message of tabligh were in keeping with his broader objectives of reaching out to the larger Muslim constituency who had settled in many parts of the world. As a British colony (protectorate), Hong Kong had an interesting history in terms of its religious harmony that existed among the different faith groups. Mawlānā Siddiqui was instrumental in the establishment of an orphanage and the foundation stone laid by him was considered a 'praiseworthy project' by *The Morning Post*.[12] Mawlānā Siddiqui maintained that institutions like the orphanages were havens for

---

[12] "Muslim Orphanage" in *The Morning Post:* October 3, 1926.

destitute children who required religious and emotional support. The Qur'ānic directives for supporting such causes are clearly explained in the following *āyah* (verse):

> *If you disclose (acts of) charity, even so it is well. But if you conceal them, and make them reach those (really) in need, that is best for you. It will remove from you some of your (stains of) evil. And Allah is well acquainted with what you do.*[13]

The article in the newspaper raised an important point: "These orphanages would be extended to non-Muslim children in the spirit of Islam's fundamental principle of universal brotherhood." Mawlānā Siddiqui strongly urged the Muslim organisations to build a national consciousness through such humanitarian projects. For him, the interfaith dialogue was not a soulless gesture buried in reams of resolutions. On the contrary, the spirit of universal brotherhood as envisaged by Islam was a tangible expression of forging ways to alleviate the plight of humanity. In this instance, the orphanage was a practical example.

A similar initiative was undertaken by his elder brother, Mawlānā Ahmad Mukhtar Siddiqui in Durban (South Africa). He founded the *Dar-al-Yatāma wal Masākin*[14] to address the plight of the orphans and destitutes. Mawlānā Siddiqui's endeavours bore tangible results. Islamic institutions were established under his guidance for the purpose of strengthening the dynamic Islamic presence in countries which had a marginal Muslim population. He maintained that the Islamic legacy had to be perpetuated in order to articulate the concept of *tabligh wa'l irshād* (preaching and guidance). Mauritius also established orphanages, several of which were inaugurated by Mawlānā Siddiqui.

Islam in Japan: Brief Overview

Islamic relations with Japan are quite recent as compared to other

---

[13] Qur'an: 2: 271.

[14] Dar-al-Yatama Pamphlet: *Journey Through Time*, n.d.

countries around the world. There are no documentary records to suggest Islam's coming into Japan through *da'wah* work except for some isolated cases of individual efforts by Japanese converts and Muslims of other countries before 1866. The early Muslims who came to Japan were from the Indian subcontinent towards the end of the nineteenth century. They were largely engaged in trade and also were instrumental in the establishment of *maktabs* (elementary Islamic schools). They founded the first permanent mosque in 1935 which served a pivotal role as the centre of tabligh. However, their activities were limited on account of the paucity of Islamic literature in Japan. Likewise, they had limited resources to expand the network of *da'wah* among the Japanese who were spiritually inclined and sought an authentic expression of Islam in line with their intellectual temperament.

The second generation of Muslim emigrants comprised Tartars (Kazan Turks), who came to Japan to escape the Communist atrocities in the early twentieth century. Together with the Indian Muslims they formed the nucleus of the Muslim community. Mawlānā Siddiqui's contact with the Fledgling Muslim community of Japan commenced as early as 1936. According to documentary sources, 10 Tartar Muslim families migrated to Japan following the surge of anti-Islamic activities by the Russian regime. The Tartars established a temporary structure for the purpose of the five daily prayers (*salāh*). In 1936 the foundation stone for the Nagoya Mosque was laid by Mawlānā Siddiqui. The mosque was constructed in 1937 and largely funded by the Turkish and Indian migrants.[15] Another mosque, Tokyo Mosque, was erected by the Tartar Muslims, who were led in their Islamic activities by Haji Qurban Ali, a noted 'alim and social activist.

The timeline of Mawlānā Siddiqui's visit to Japan is illustrative of his growing popularity in East Asia. His close affinity with the Turko-Tartar Muslims in Shangai also explains his warm reception in Japan:

We wish you long life and prosperity and a successful voyage

---

[15] *The Nagoya Muslim Mosque: A Souvenir Booklet* (Nagoya, 1937).

to Japan so that the world may benefit by your right and up-to-date exposition of the only true divine religion- Islam.

The first Japanese was "mar Yamauka[16] who played a pioneering role to the dissemination of Islam in the country. With the establishment of the first mosque in Kobe, the Muslim community of Japanese and foreign nationals was established. Apart from delivering public addresses in Kobe Mosque and at other Muslim institutions, Mawlānā Siddiqui's landmark contribution was his lecture at the Oriental Culture College in Tokyo. The topic *Cultivation of Science by the Muslims* was relevant to the Japanese audience on account of their rationalist interpretation of religion. Professor Noorul Hasan Berlas: Head of Tokyo School of Foreign Language made a noteworthy assessment of Mawlānā Siddiqui's intellectual stature:

It is a pleasure to meet a personality of such versatile abilities as Mawlānā Abdul Aleem Siddiqui. I made his acquaintance through *Genuine Islam* of Singapore and when he came here two years ago, I tried to make the best of his presence here. As it was summer, I arranged for some of his speeches at Karuizawa, the summer resort of the Far East, the present one being delivered at the Summer College held under the auspices of the Oriental Culture Society. It shows us his profound learning and what is more effective, a thorough command over Western terminologies through which he can effectively appeal to the modern mind coupled with his persuasive eloquence which has a force of attracting our attention. I wish there were more English knowing Muslims of his ability among us. He came here with the noble object of delivering his message of Islam and of establishing the friendly relations between the Muslim world and Japan.[17]

---

[16] *Islamic Culture Forum*: 28 February 1975.

[17] Siddiqui, *Cultivation of Science by the Muslims* (Foreword). It was also through the efforts of Professor Berlas that the tabligh contributions of Mawlana Siddiqui were covered in the prestigious *Ma'ārif* journal (Azamgarh, 1938). Sayyid Sulayman Nadwi's appreciation of the latter's tabligh zeal is indicative of the growing presence of Islam in Japan.

The concluding remarks made by Mawlānā Siddiqui in the lecture do not betray strands of apologia that were a marked trait of the modernist Muslim thinking during the early twentieth century. As Islam was rooted in divine revelation, its impetus for scientific quest led man to the knowledge of the Creator. This observation was a timely reminder for Muslims to rediscover their links to Islam's past glory. Mawlānā Siddiqui explains:

> In truth Islam intends the Muslim community to be a community of intellectuals, and the cultivation of science and all other forms of learning is one of the primary aims of Islam. Had it not been for the Muslims, Europe would never have seen its way to the Renaissance and the modern scientific era would never have dawned. Those nations who have received their knowledge of science from Europe are in fact indirectly the disciples of the Islamic community of the past. Humanity owes to Islam a debt which it can never repay and gratitude which it can never forget.[18]

Our focus is on the lecture series delivered by Mawlānā Siddiqui at several institutions in Tokyo. Of particular relevance are the topics before an academic audience. The range and depth of these lectures have an intellectual tenor; they reveal a brilliant exposition of the Qur'ānic meaning and message without showing any semblance of apologia. The learned scholar succintly conveys the Islamic viewpoint on issues that are generally tinged with a modernist slant, very much in line with the worldview of the Muslim modernists. We may refer to the apologetic presentation of polygamy by the widely acclaimed Muslim scholar, Syed Ameer Ali (d. 1928) whose celebrated work, *The Spirit of Islam* is a must-read in Islamic studies. While citing extensively from this work to demonstrate the enduring Islamic legacy, Mawlānā Siddiqui adopts a balanced approach to bring to the

---

[18] Ibid, 44. European Renaissance owed a debt of gratitude to the Islamic civilisation which in its heydays made enormous contributions to 'Western science'. For a detailed discussion on this theme, see Abdul Azim Islāhi, –Mercantilism and the Muslim States' in *Hamdard Islamicus*: vol. xxxii, 23-39.

fore the authentic Islamic teachings in the light of the Qur'ān and the sunnah.

A close examination of the lecture, *Status of Women in Islam* makes interesting reading. The speech was delivered on 27 July 1936 at the 'Orion in Ginza' in Tokyo at the invitation of the Tokyo International Club. An accomplished historian, Mawlānā Siddiqui draws upon the Western sources to provide a graphic description of the period of *Jāhiliyyah* with particular reference to the position of women. The litany of woes suffered by women in pre-Islamic Arabia is contrasted with the Prophethood of Muhammad (SAW), who is described as the *Saviour of Womanhood*. Mawlānā Siddiqui elaborates:

> Such was the condition of the female sex in the world when Muhammad, the Saviour of Womanhood, stood up in Arabia and, through the divine revelation of the Lord of the universe, who created both the male and the female and who loves them equally, preached to the world that females are just like males, having equal rights, equal honour and equal status in life. They were on no account to be treated as the property of the males. They have the right of ownership, of property in the same way as the males have, though no doubt under the principle of the division of labour the female sex has specialised duties to perform in life, just as the male has its own special duties.[19]

Mawlānā Siddiqui presents a conspectus of women's rights which preceded the Charter of Human Rights. His incisive analysis of the psychology of the veil is based on the unambiguous Qur'ānic verses which recognise the separate function of males and females. Likewise, he examines the nature of gender relations in the light of scientific studies. Moreover, the dignity of women is cogently expressed to reaffirm her status in Islam. To this end, Ibrahim Alladin has made some pertinent remarks about Mawlānā Siddiqui's perceptive analysis:

---

[19] Siddiqui, *Women and their Status in Islam* (Karachi, n.d.), 5.

Mawlānā Abdul Aleem gave a historical overview of gender. Throughout history, he argued men and women have been perceived differently, and their roles have been confused and blurred. The gender debate, particularly women in Islam, catches a lot of attention. He indicated that many of the comments and opinions are often as a result of misinterpretation and misunderstanding. He pointed out quite rightly that Islam does not discriminate women, quite the opposite: women are elevated to a higher status. Men and women are core characters, with key roles in fulfilling their family obligations.[20]

Mawlānā Siddiqui made a significant impact on the Muslim intellectuals in Japan. His tabligh career represented the amalgam of the Islamic *'ulum* and modern science. In this respect, he embodied the Islamic ideal of holistic knowledge. The thrust of his several lectures illustrated the scientific spirit promoted by the Qur'ān through the presentation of the natural phenomena. Mawlānā Siddiqui observed:

The basic principle of Islam, or in other words, the goal of a Muslim is the gnosis (recognition) of the Creator of the universe. The philosophical speculation and the principles of harmony and design working in nature plainly point out to the fact that there is a Creator of the universe and that this whole universe is His creation and a manifestation of His attributes. Guided by this belief, a Muslim ponders over every phenomenon which he comes across and strives to appreciate its reality, so that he may be able arrive at a knowledge of the Absolute Reality which may lead him to the knowledge of the Creator Himself.[21]

The sweep of Mawlānā Siddiqui's mastery over modern science is remarkable. He cites the works of non-Muslim scholars who have acknowledged the scientific outlook of the Qur'ān. The key themes explored include the sacred text's rational approach and revolutionary tenor to things scientific. Interestingly, his familiarity with the contemporary writings of Muslim scholars like Syed Ameer

---

[20] Ibrahim Alladin, *Maulana Abdul Aleem Siddiqui: His Life, Thoughts and Message*, 100.

[21] Siddiqui, *Dimensions of Islam*, 32.

Ali attests to his discerning approach to academia. In a particular sense, Mawlānā Siddiqui reveals his deep study and grasp of the progressive trends that were unfolding in the Muslim world. His reference to the Osmania University (Hyderabad, India) is revealing:

> The Osmania University which imparts all education in traditional and modern learning through the medium of Urdu and stands in proud contrast against other universities in India, where the medium of instruction is English, might be regarded as a modern prototype (model) of the Nizamia University of Baghdad, established in the fifth century of the *hijra*. The Translation Bureau, which bears upon its shoulders the responsibility of translating all modern knowledge as also all important books of classical learning into the Urdu language, may well be compared with similar institutions which Flourished under Ma'mun (Abbasid ruler) and other Muslim rulers.[22]

In sum, Mawlānā Siddiqui adopted a practical approach to tabligh in view of the geopolitical developments during this crucial period in modern history. The formation of Muslim identity required visionary leadership that could inspire activism without compromising the Islamic values. He stood out as an eminent 'alim-sufi who advanced the cause of tabligh as the base for Islamic reform. Like his contemporary scholars, he stood firm in his *Back to the Qur'ān, Back to Muhammad* call which yielded positive results in the countries he visited during his world tabligh travels.

Chapter 4

Da'wah in the Arab World

A versatile personality, Mawlānā Siddiqui's tabligh activities transcended the geographical boundaries. As a diplomat, the motivation for his political activities was promoting the cause of the Pakistan movement to the Arab world.[1] His meetings with the leading Islamic scholars, 'ulama and politicians were aimed at raising an awareness about the emergent Pakistan, established in the name of Islam in 1947. It was through his unremitting efforts that the Arab press advanced the Pakistani cause, which was confronted with negative publicity as a result of the strong lobby representing an influential segment of Muslims who vehemently opposed its creation.[2] The All-India Muslim League[3] mandated Mawlānā Siddiqui, in recognition of his excellent command of Arabic and established contacts in the Arab world, to carry out this responsibility.

The Khilafat Movement: An Overview

The Khilafat movement[4] which preceded the establishment of Pakistan was led by the charismatic brothers, Mohamed Ali[5] and Shawkat Ali. As the name suggested, the movement was established

---

[1] Qadri, *Azim Muballigh i-Islam*, 79.

[2] For a detailed discussion about the strained relations between the leading Muslim individuals and political parties regarding the Pakistani movement, see Qureshi, *Ulema in Politics*, 240-274.

[3] The All-India Muslim League established in 1906 was a powerful political party articulating Muslim separatism. See Francis Robinson, *Separatism among Indian Muslims* (New Delhi, 1993), 345-53.

[4] The Khilafat Movement under the charistmatic leadership of Mohamed Ali (d. 1931) played an active role in championing the Caliphate in Turkey. Its religious aspirations and participation in the agitational politics have been critically analysed in the following works: Robinson, *Separation among Indian Muslims*, 257-344; Iqbal, *Life and Times of Mohamed Ali*, 63-283.

[5] Qureshi, *Ulema in Politics*, 249-50.

to counteract the European incursion into the Ottoman Empire in the background of political upheaval and in the aftermath of World War One (1914-9). The following assessment of Mohamed Ali's active involvement with the Khilafat reveals the pivotal role of the movement:

> For the better part of the year 1920, Mohamed Ali pleaded passionately the cause of the khilafat (caliphate) in Europe. From every platform he had proclaimed that his was a religious mission; to him khilafat was a matter of faith and the khalifah, the centre of the structure of Islam which would fall apart like a house of cards if the pivot were once removed. Islam and khilafat were synonymous; and the identity to him was so complete and pervasive that he could not reconcile his own existence as a Muslim. In a world deprived of both the person and the institution of khilafat, how could a body survive without a heart? With singular clarity and conviction, he had hammered on this simple theme in the knowledge and belief that his views were shared by the mass of Muslims at home.[6]

The political fortunes of the Muslim leadership in India prompted an ambivalence towards the khilafat. As a result, the course of action pursued by Mohamed Ali did not yield the desired results as its dissolution occurred simultaneously with the balkanisation of the Ottoman Empire. Nevertheless, the movement during its active period created a transnational reawakening among the Indian Muslims who saw Turkey as the symbolic seat of the khilafat (caliphate).

Mawlānā Siddiqui and the *Hajj* Tax

Mawlānā Siddiqui shared an affinity for Mohamed Ali's political ideals and was unsparing in his condemnation of Sharif Husayn[7] for his complicity with Britain to undermining the Ottoman caliphate.

---

[6] Iqbal, *Life and Times of Mohamed Ali*, 249

[7] Qureshi, *Ulema in Politics*, 290.

Likewise, he led a delegation on behalf of the All-India Muslim League in 1946 to address the concerns of the Muslim *ummah* regarding the *hajj* tax - an unjust imposition that added financial burdens to the *hujjāj* (pilgrims). The mandate had the support of several countries of the Muslim world, and the Saudi government eventually acknowledged it by reducing the amount of the *hajj* tax. The following article published in the *As-Sajal daily* in Baghdad (Iraq) illustrates Mawlānā Siddiqui's prominence in the Arab world.

Imposition of Taxes on the *Hujjāj* (*Hajj* Pilgrims)

Muslims who visit Makkah Al-Mukarramah repeatedly complain about the taxes that they are required to pay. Some Islamic organisations continue petitioning the government of the Saudi kingdom to abolish these taxes so that it would be easier for more people to perform this injunction (of the shari`ah). Added to this grievance are the exorbitant expenses that the pilgrim has to bear for his transfers (within the Kingdom).

Yesterday we met with `Allamah Abdul Aleem Siddiqui who was mandated by the Muslims of India and South Africa to deliberate with the kingdom of His Majesty Ibn Sa`ud. He presented us with documents containing the negotiations between the delegation led by him and His Majesty. These highlighted the desire of pilgrims from those countries that the taxes be abolished because Allah never revealed any proof regarding them. Furthermore, neither the rightly guided *khulafā* (caliphs) nor those who came after them stipulated such taxes. Enforcing these taxes is, therefore, an evil innovation. After expressing his willingness to abolish these taxes, His Majesty requested the delegation to solve this issue by suggesting economic alternatives. It (the delegation) urged the Saudi government to find other sources of revenue, whether it is petrol, gold mines or resources throughout the kingdom.[8]

After a series of protracted negotiations, the *hajj* tax was substantially reduced by the Saudi kingdom. In a similar vein, the khilafat committee had voiced their concerns to Ibn Sa`ud for

---

[8] *As-Sajal* (Baghdad), Sha'ban, 25, 1366 *hijri*.

instituting the monarchy. He had made himself further unpopular by the "excesses of his followers in destroying parts of historical monuments of religious importance."[9]

Tabligh Travels to Egypt

The fluidity of political events in the Arab world followed by the establishment of Pakistan renewed Mawlānā Siddiqui's commitment to reaffirm the Islamic values and the importance of spirituality (*ruhāniyat*) among the Muslim communities. Hence, his visit in 1949 to another Arab country, Egypt, the citadel of Islamic learning. His first visit to the country in 1947 had already facilitated his interaction with the eminent `ulama and leading personalities associated with the Islamic reawakening (*nahdah*)[10] across the world.

The following account of Mawlānā Siddiqui's second visit to Egypt is a summative assessment of his contributions to the moral regeneration mission through his network of Islamic activities in the country. Notwithstanding his brief stay in Egypt, Mawlānā Siddiqui's impact was considerable. Mawlānā Ansari, his private secretary, accompanied him. The close relationship between the two luminaries embodied the *tasawwuf* concept of *munāsibah* (spiritual fellowship) by defining the trajectory of progressive orthodoxy[11] in which knowledge (*'ilm*) enjoyed a distinctive position. According to Mawlānā Ansari, the concept of *'ilm* was the reference point to a clearer understanding of this ideal.

The first Qur'ānic message came for *'ilm*. Muslims are encouraged to "unearth all the treasures of knowledge that are buried in the different civilisations of the world: to preserve, to classify and to rectify all the different types of knowledge to advance the cause of knowledge."[12]

Mawlānā Siddiqui was accompanied by Mawlānā Ansari, who resigned

---

[9] Qureshi, *Ulema in Politics*, 291.

[10] A critical assessment of the *nahdah* movement appears in Ibrahim Abu Rabi, *Intellectual Origins of Islamic Resurgence in the Modern Arab World* (New York, 1996).

[11] The progressive orthodoxy as conceived by Mawlana Siddiqui was later developed by Mawlana Ansari at the Aleemiyah Institute in Karachi.

[12] Mohamed, *Islam to the Modern Mind*, 188.

from his government post in Pakistan, on 14 January 1950. When they arrived in Cairo (Egypt) they were received by the leading Muslim industrialist, Muhammad Bey Salim.

Interaction with Islamic Personalities

As soon as Mawlānā Sidiqqui's arrival was announced in the Egyptian press, his host's residence was thronged with people from all walks of life. His interviews were conducted at the offices of Young Men's Muslim Association, a premier Islamic movement of the Arab world which contributed immensely to the Islamic reawakening initiative. It may be recalled that Mawlānā Siddiqui had already established a close relationship with Shaykh Hasan al-Bannā, founder of the Ikhwān movement[13] in 1947. Their shared commitment of Islam as a *din* (way of life) and *da'wah*[14] were recurrent themes in their respective writings and public lectures. Mawlānā Siddiqui expressed his admiration of al-Banna in eloquent terms:

> In 1950, however, the great man (Hasan al-Bannā) was no more. The assassin's bullet through the darkness of political manoeuvring had snatched away this illustrious son of Islam. Cairo presented a gloomy picture. The voice of reason had been stifled; their headquarters were sealed; their leaders languished in prison.[15]

Conspiracy theories and a web of political propaganda were woven to undermine the Ikhwān's (Muslim Brotherhood) stature as the collective voice of the Muslims in the Arab world. In his memoirs (*Mudhakkirāt*)[16] Hasan al-Bannā provided his personal

---

[13] A number of biographical accounts highlight the multifaceted personality of Hasan al-Bannā. Refer to Abu Rabi, *Intellectual Origins of Islamic Resurgence in the Modern Arab World.*

[14] The *Majmu'at Rasā'il* expresses the clarity of Imam al-Bannā's vision of *nahdah* (resurgence). Both he and Mawlana Siddiqui referred to the Qur'an as the manifesto of the *mu'min* (believer) towards the realisation of Islam as the universal religion. See Bannā, *Majmu'at Rasā'il* - six monographs of Hasan al-Bannā (Kuwait City, n.d).

[15] Siddiqui, *The Ambassador of Peace*, 2.

[16] Hasan al-Bannā, *Memoirs* (Karachi, 1981).

reminiscences about the establishment of the Ikhwān. There are conspicuous traces of his and Mawlānā Siddiqui's visionary leadership to promoting the cause of Islam in the modern idiom. The Islamic teachings embedded in sociopolitical changes were prioritised by them to stem the tide of irreligiousness among the youth and the cohort of intellectuals nurtured in the portals of Western institutions. In a particular sense, their common concern of promoting the unity (*wahdat*) of the *ummah* is articulated in their respective writings. In *Majmu'at Rasā'il,* al-Bannā deplores the disunity among Muslims as a result of the rigidity of views, intolerance pertaining to the culture of disagreement (*ikhtilāf*) and condemning the legacy of the Islamic legal thought, notably the rich repository of *Fiqh*[17]. Mawlānā Siddiqui echoes a similar view:

> In mentioning this classification of Islamic sciences, my purpose is just to give an idea to my simple-minded brothers and sisters who are being thrown into confusion concerning the Islamic legal schools by certain unconscientious people, who wish to establish their own hegemony and leadership, and hence they propagate all sorts of confusion. Some of them have their ulterior sectarian ends to gain. Most of them are ignorant of Islamic sciences and the safest way they can adopt their leadership is that of the denial of the validity or the necessity of those sciences.[18]

During the twenty days in Cairo, Mawlānā Siddiqui's presence had a magnetic appeal. Every day from morning till late in the evening he was extremely busy receiving visitors, discussing Islamic problems with the leaders as well as lay Muslims, addressing meetings and visiting institutions. The first among all notables to meet Mawlānā Siddiqui was Sayyid Amin al-Husayni,[19] the Grand Mufti of Palestine.

---

[17] Hasan al-Bannā, *Majmu'at Ras'āil*, 100-104.

[18] Siddiqui, *The History of the Codification of Islamic Law* (Karachi, 1980), 24.

[19] Several studies highlight the role of Al-Husayni to the Palestinian struggle. An unbiased assessment and historical objectivity of his pioneering role have been downplayed by recent works. Philip Mattar, *The Mufti of Jerusalem: Al-Hajj Amin al-Husayni* (Columbia, 1988) is representative of the polemical works concerning this illustrious Islamic figure.

The two leaders discussed at length the plight of Palestinians, the alarming encroachment of Zionism and the way forward to alleviate the Palestinian problem.

A contemporary of Mawlānā Siddiqui, the poet of the East, Muhammad Iqbal (d. 1938) wrote a soul-stirring poem to raise an awareness about the sinister plot of the Zionist movement to usurp the Palestinian lands. Like the political stalwart of Khilafat fame, Mohamed Ali who was buried in Jerusalem, Iqbal, too, expressed his agitation over the conspiratorial role played by the British government and the League of Nations to create a Jewish homeland in Palestine. Iqbal's terse verses capture the political fortunes of the Arab world:

> Iqbal does not doubt Europe's nobility of every oppressed nation she is buying, but my heart burns for Syria, Palestine
> And this hard riddle of fate none can lay bare. Freed from Turkey's 'savage grasp' they pine Poor wretches! Now in civilisation snare.

Iqbal makes caustic remarks about the Arab uprising against the Ottoman Caliphate through intrigue and complicity with the imperialist policies of Europe. They, in turn, have lost their autonomy by being dismembered into petty kingdoms and devoid of the true spirit of unity, a rallying call of the Caliphate that strengthened the cause of Islam.[20]

The Palestinian problem, a misleading term coined in Western academia to downplay the centrality of this sacred land in the eyes of the Muslims, was a major cause of concern for the Ottoman caliph, Abdul Hamid II. He outrightly rejected the Zionist manouvres and financial inducements to alleviate the plight of the Caliphate which was in the throes of deep debt due to political reasons. Theodore Herzl, leader of the Zionist movement, offered to settle the burgeoning debt in exchange of permitting the Zionist settlement in Palestine. Sultan Abdul Hamid's response was reflective of his unconditional

---

[20] Nadwi, *Glory of Iqbal* (Lucknow, 1973), 159.

veneration of Jerusalem. He even took upon himself the responsibility of administering directly the Ottoman *sanjak* (district) of Palestine. His communique on this critical matter is illustrative:

> Advise Dr Herzl not to take any further steps in his project. I cannot give away a handful of the soil of this land as it is not mine; it belongs to the Islamic nation who have fought for the sake of this land and watered it with their blood. The Jews may keep their millions; if the Islamic Caliphate is one day destroyed then they should take Palestine without a price. While I am alive, I would rather push a sword into my body than see the land of Palestine is taken away from the Islamic state. This will never happen. I will not start cutting our bodies while we are alive.[21]

Cairo: Seat of Islamic Learning

Cairo, the citadel of Islam, had attracted scholars and activists from the Arab world. Amir Muhammad bin Abdul Karim and his brother Sayyidi Muhammad,[22] Moroccan leaders in exile were close associates of Mawlānā Siddiqui. Liberation from foreign rule was the key theme in their series of discussions. Like the great Sanusi leader and *jihād* activist,[23] through whom he received his spiritual authorisation (*ijāzah*), Mawlānā Siddiqui condemned the Italian presence in Libya and offered concrete solutions with respect to the country's freedom. It was also in the realm of *tasawwuf* that Mawlānā Siddiqui articulated the shari`ah-*tariqah* amalgam. His meeting with Shaykh Muhammad Hafidh al-Tijani (d. 1978), the supreme guide of the Tijaniyah order[24] (*silsilah*) typified their respective global vision

---

[21] Cited in Ebrahim Moosa, *Masjid Al-Aqsa: A Journey through Time* (2020), 149.

[22] These Moroccan scholars were sufi activists who played a leading role to the liberation of the country against French imperialism.

[23] The Sanusiyah movement represented the *tasawwuf-jihād* ideal. It created 'upright conduct' to restore the Islamic authenticity paradigm an among the Muslim communities in North Africa. See Nichola Ziadeh, *Sanusiyah: A Study of the Revivalist Movement in Islam* (Leiden, 1983). Cf. Shoayb Ahmed, *Muslim Scholars of the Twentieth Century* (2006), 72.

[24] The early twentieth century saw the rise of pre-eminent sufi movements in the Maghrib and Egypt. The Tijaniyah under Shaykh Muhammad Hafidh al-Tijani

of *tasawwuf*. The shaykh was a specialist in hadith and authored many works in tafsir, history and *tasawwuf*. Al- Azhar University, the seat of Islamic intellectual legacy[25] was the focal point of Islamic religious and cultural life for Egypt and the entire Islamic world. During the first millennium it produced scholars of universal acclaim. Over the centuries, the institution saw the rise and decline of powerful political rulers who in many ways maintained a symbiotic relationship[26] with it in order to retain credibility of their professed allegiance to Islam. It was after the eighteenth century that Al-Azhar became the battleground for reform which indirectly challenged the autonomy of the institution.

Muhammad Abduh's reforms[27] in the nineteenth century was a turning point in the nationalisation of this institution.

It is in the context that Mawlānā Siddiqui's interaction with the ʿulama fraternity must be understood. Shaykh Abdullah Draz (d. 1958),[28] a renowned Qurʾānic scholar of Al- Azhar, and the chief mufti of the institution, Shaykh Abdul Majid Salim, were counted as his admirers. The reception accorded to him by these leading figures was a testimony to his erudition and international fame. Apart from his meeting with political leaders, academics and educationists, Mawlānā Siddiqui's focus of Islamic reform related to unity (*ittihād*). The core mission he promoted was the unity of Islamic schools of thought and unity of mankind through the interfaith dialogue. These overlapping aspects had a sociopolitical relevance, and he strove

---

consolidated its presence among the 'ulama circles in Egypt. For background information about this sufi movement, see Jamil Abu Nasir, *The Tijaniyya, A Sui Order in the Modern World* (Oxford, 1965). See also Fakhruddin Owaisi, *Shaykh Muhammad al-Haiz al Misri*. www.tijani.org/shaykh-muhammad-al-hafiz-al-misri

[25] *Encyclopedia of the Modern Islamic World*, Vol. 1, 168.

[26] The relationship between the ruling dynasties and Al- Azhar during the eighteenth century is explored in Yunus Gilani, *The Socio-Political Rule of the 'Ulama in Egypt: 1798-1870* (New Delhi, 2007).

[27] The reformist movement initiated by Abduh had widespread ramifications in the Muslim world in terms of its interpretation of the *salaf al-sālih* concept. See Charles Adams, *Islam and Modernism* (Kuala Lumpur, 2010). Cf. Hisham Sharabi, *Arab Intellectuals and the West: The Formative Years, 1875-1914* (New York, 1970).

[28] According to Adil Salahi, Shaykh Abdullah Draz's scholarly treatment of Qurʾanic literature was reflected in his profound understanding of *'ulum al-Qurʾān* (sciences of the Qurʾan). See Abdullah Draz, *The Qurʾān: An Eternal Challenge* (Leicester, 2001).

unfailingly to achieve them during his lifetime.

The Islamic Unity Project

In Cairo, several forums were established to promote the *Taqrib al-Madhāhib* association through which the Sunni and Shi`ah schools of thought would be equally recognised. Allouba Pasha, President of the Association consulted Mawlānā Siddiqui for fostering a climate of harmony among these schools of Islamic jurisprudence. His own work, *The History of the Codification of Islamic Law,* examined the validity of the key juristic (*Fiqh*) issues in a changing world. In a similar vein, Shaykh Mahmud Shaltut (d. 1963)[29] continued with the *Taqrib* project. As the rector of Al-Azhar, he channelled some of his reforming zeal in another direction: the cause of promoting harmony between the various schools of law, in particular between Sunnis and Shi`ahs. Although Shaykh Shaltut had an academic interest in comparative jurisprudence, nonetheless, his *fatwās* (legal rulings) in several instances were controversial and provoked a series of debates among the `ulama. In the sphere of politics, Mawlānā Siddiqui's pro-active participation to the Pakistani cause was acknowledged. His series of meetings with Abdur Rahman Azzam[30] (d. 1976), secretary-general of the Arab League related to the brotherhood (*ukhuwwah*) efforts that transcended the racial and geographical barriers. At a reception to welcome him as the 'Apostle of Muslim unity', Mawlānā Siddiqui delivered a powerful message, reminding the members of the Association that their function was not to abolish different schools of thought, but to work unitedly for solving common problems affecting the *ummah*.[31] He deplored the tendency to waste energies in meaningless debates and, therefore, urged Muslims to cultivate the habit of looking to the future for the common Islamic glory. He reiterated the urgency of forming a representative committee of the

---

[29] A similar effort was launched by Shaykh Muhamad Shaltut which caused much controversy within the Al-Azhar hierarchy. See Kate, Zebiri, *Mahmud Shaltut of Islamic Modernism,* 24-6, 172.

[30] The secretary general of the Arab League, Abdur Rahman Azzam was also acquainted with Muslim affairs, particularly in South Asia. On his literary contributions, see *The Eternal Message of Muhammad* (London, 1979).

[31] Siddiqui, *The Roving Ambassador of Peace,* 4-5.

`ulama of different groups, which should undertake to solve the modern problems in the light of Islamic teachings.[32]

The positive approach endorsed by Mawlānā Siddiqui to relieve the *ummah* of its past burdens of sectarian strife was glaringly evident in the Indian subcontinent. He, too, had witnessed the baneful effects of sectarian formations[33] that had sapped the vibrant character of the Islamic civilisation, which was thriving for centuries in that part of the Muslim world. On the other hand, as the premier seat of Islamic learning, Al- Azhar remained unsurpassed in its global influence through the vast network of scholars and institutions promoting its vision of unity. Mawlānā Siddiqui's own initiatives and his transnational links were recognised by the shaykhs of Al- Azhar. Among the eminent `ulama, Shaykh Abdullah Draz may be mentioned who paid glowing tributes to Mawlānā Siddiqui's missionary zeal and advancing the Islamic cause. *Al-Azhar* magazine published articles relating to Mawlānā Siddiqui's tabligh. Furthermore, the accolades showered by the `ulama of Al-Azhar on him were a fitting tribute to his intellectual contributions.

Islamic Youth Movements

Two important organisations deserve special mention in terms of their interaction with Mawlānā Siddiqui's stated missionary vision: Jami'ah Rabita Islamia and Jami'at al- Shabab Muhammad. The former organisation expanded *da'wah* on a broader level with its network of activities extending to the African continent. In a soul-stirring speech delivered in Arabic, Mawlānā Siddiqui expounded the concept of *ummah*[34] which repudiated Arab nationalism, a trend that assumed exaggerated importance among the Arab intellectuals who saw Islam as an impediment in their advocacy of Western civilisation. In

---

[32] Mawlana Mahmud al-Hasan (d. 1920), a leading figure in the struggle for India's freedom also stated that Muslim disunity contributed to the ummah's decline in the subcontinent. See Shah Alampuri, *Mahmud- ul- Hasan: A Political Biography* (Karachi, 1988), 144-5.

[33] Siddiqui, *How to Face Communism* (Karachi, n.d.)

[34] Siddiqui, *Ambassador of Peace*, 5.

a specific sense, the Jami'ah served as a counterweight to these modernist trends.

Mawlānā Siddiqui was critical of the religious indifference by several segments of Egyptian society for their uncritical embrace of socialism and Arab nationalism. In the wake of these disturbing trends, the Islamic teachings were discarded in favour of liberal interpretations which, by and large, were dictated by self-interest. Essentially, territorial interest emphasised a narrowly-defined Islam, functioning under the constraints of a socialist manifesto seemingly compatible with the Qur'ānic message of brotherhood. This observation by Mawlānā Siddiqui was echoed on another occasion in respect of the Muslims' abject surrender to these 'isms':

The heart of man cannot be conquered by the atom bomb but I believe through fellow feeling and sympathy. It is not until the moral foundation of human lives are restored that true peace shall remain at a standstill. If you go deep into the working of the human mentality today, I am sure you will realise that it is self-conceit or superiority complex which is the root cause of the strife and war which we find in the world today. The superiority complex leads man to pride, pride leads to haughtiness, haughtiness leads to intolerance and intolerance leads to quarrels and wars. The hearts of man cannot be conquered by atom bombs, they can only be conquered by regarding each individual as a brother or sister.[35]

In fact, Mawlānā Siddiqui joined the ranks of other scholars in South Asia[36] who critiqued the rise of Arab nationalism, which expressed strong anti-Islamic overtones. The Jami'at-al-Shabab as the name suggested consisted of youth enrolled at the tertiary institutions and dar al-'ulums.

They were committed to the Islamic ideals as demonstrated by the *uswah* model of the Holy Prophet (pbuh). They drew their inspiration from the tabligh mission of Mawlānā Siddiqui who was impressed by their 'sublime ideal'[37] of imparting the true contents of the Islamic faith. Parallel to Mawlānā Siddiqui's lecture tours was the

---

[35] Siddiqui, *How to Face Communism*, 17.

[36] See Nadwi, *Western Civilisation, Islam and Muslims* (Lucknow, 1974). The book makes a critical assessment of Arab nationalism in Egypt.

[37] Siddiqui, *Ambassador of Peace*, 7.

groundswell of Islamic activities initiated by the Ikhwān movement. Needless to add, their activities had far-reaching implications for the Egyptian society. *Da'wah* tempered with spirituality[38] was the common refrain of Hasan al-Bannā and Mawlānā Siddiqui in their reformulation of the Islamic message to contemporary life.

Islamic Missionary Society

It was no fortuitous circumstances that Mawlānā Siddiqui established a missionary society to realise his ideals to which he had devoted almost forty years. His *da'wah* outreach activities, albeit limited in scope and confined to Cairo, yielded positive results, particularly among the foreign students pursuing their education at tertiary institutions. The following account delineates his successful efforts towards this goal:

Mawlānā Siddiqui's one great mission during his stay in Egypt was to arouse the Muslim leaders and intelligentsia to a correct realisation of the missionary needs of Islam in various parts of the world. For twenty five days he was continuously speaking on this problem to all those numerous persons who came in contact with him. And he not only spoke about it, but took practical steps to actualise it. On the one hand, he addressed several meetings of *Ta'ārif bil-Islam,* an Islamic missionary society, he established and during this visit he reorganised and revitalised it. On the other hand, he instilled the missionary spirit into those students of Al-Azhar who came in contact with him. Inspired by his presence, the foreign students held three meetings, two of which were addressed by Mawlānā Ansari and the last by Mawlānā Siddiqui. The students received a plan and an ideal and resolved to carry the scheme into execution. Mawlānā Siddiqui also spoke to a representative gathering of foreign students at

---

[38] Hasan al-Banna's *Memoirs* offers useful insights into the evolution of spirituality (*ruhāniyat*) which served as a tool for his *da'wah.* See Hasan al-Banna, *Memoirs of Hasan al-Banna Shaheed.*

the Abdul Hamid Said Bek Hall on *The Ideal of an Islamic Student.*[39]

Zainab Ghazali: Embodiment of Islamic Activism

During the tumultuous period in Egypt there were varied responses to the role of women in the Islamic discourse. Just as Egypt was in the throes of socialism, the rise of feminist movements posed a serious challenge to the Muslim women's role in society. The Ikhwān since its establishment eschewed all forms of chauvinism by setting up structures specifically for the advancement of Muslim women in various fields. Under al-Banna's visionary leadership, the Islamic women's organisation, Jama'at al-Sayyidat al-Muslimat was founded by one of the Ikhwān 's activists, Zainab al-Ghazali (d. 2005) who played an active role in the reorganisation of the movement following al-Banna's assassination in 1949. She was a formidable figure against the feminist movements advocating a liberal interpretation of Islam. By her personal example and charismatic personality, she also stood as a bulwark against these un-Islamic tendencies. Her political involvement and suffering under the Nasserist regime are poignantly recorded in her memoir.[40] She also carved out a niche as a Qur'ānic scholar. Her two-volume *Nazarāt*, written in the shadows of her prolonged years in prison is based on her deep reflections of the Qur'ānic methodology and *da'wah*- focused themes.[41]

During Mawlānā Siddiqui's stay in Cairo, Zainab met with him several times and his influence in restating the status of women in Islam also supplemented her understanding about the Jama'at al-Sayyidat's[42] scope and function within the Ikhwān hierarchy. Zainab, the embodiment of Islamic erudition and activism, upheld the Islamic principles and was unapologetic in her critical evaluation of

---

[39] Siddiqui, *Ambassador of Peace*, 6-7.

[40] Zainab al-Ghazali's autobiography focuses on the ordeals she experienced in Egypt under Nasser's oppressive rule. See Zainab al- Ghazali, *Return of the Pharoah: Memoir in Nasser's Prison* (Leicester, 1994).

[41] See Choughley, *Tradition of Tafsir (Qur'ānic Exegesis) in the Indian Subcontinent* (Springs, 2021), 188-9.

[42] Siddiqui, *Ambassador of Peace*, 6-7.

the prevailing feminist movements. Mawlānā Siddiqui elucidated this ideal regarding the Islamic concept of equality between the sexes:

> The doors of spiritual elevation are open to women in the same way as they are open to men. They are commanded to educate themselves in the same way as the men, and if they attain a high position in learning even the men are expected to learn and benefit from their knowledge and wisdom. It is reported that after the Holy Prophet's (pbuh) death his disciples used to visit Ayesha, the wife of the Holy Prophet (pbuh), and seek knowledge from her. Islamic history is resplendent with a long list of the names of ladies who received the highest honour in society, the highest degree in learning and the highest qualifications in different branches of human activity. It was through the influence of other societies, which were not Muslim, that the idea of the inferiority of the female sex already existing in those societies, spread to the uneducated classes among the Muslims, who knew very little about the teachings of Islam. If they had known the teachings of Islam, they would have known that in Islam the female sex deserves the same position, the same respect and the same dignity as the members of the male sex who, in their turn, are not allowed to degrade and insult them and make them their tools.[43]

Mawlānā Siddiqui also reached out to the female students attending tertiary institutions. He vociferously maintained that seeking knowledge was the inalienable right of every Muslim. In his address to the personnel and students of the King Farouq Royal Society,[44] he reminded the audience of Islam's scientific legacy. The Qur'ānic revelation opened up a scientific era through which it charted the destiny of humanity. Mawlānā Siddiqui made the following observation:

In the Holy Qur'ān the mission of the Holy Prophet (pbuh) has been

---

[43] Siddiqui, *Women and their Status in Islam*, 18.
[44] *Ramadan Annual:* 1994, 183.

described in these words:

> *It is He who has sent amongst the unlettered a messenger from among themselves, to rehearse to them His Signs, to sanctify them, and to instruct them in the Scripture and Wisdom, although they had been, before, in manifest error.*[45]

It is evident from the above statement that it was the Holy Prophet's (pbuh) mission to awaken humanity to the importance of the cultivation of learning, and that the Holy Qur'ān was revealed by Allah to open the gates of knowledge for mankind and guide them towards scientific research. The Holy Qur'ān does not only propound laws relating to worship and religious ceremonies; its broader mission and main thesis are to teach us laws pertaining to every walk of life and to act as a perfect guide for humanity.[46]

Concluding Remarks

Mawlānā Siddiqui's stay in Cairo was described as "a veritable festival for the Muslims."[47] His position in the Arab world was enhanced by his academic and spiritual pre- eminence through his interaction with the distinguished 'ulama and political activists especially in Hijaz. To this end, Shaykh Ahmad al-Shams of Morocco typified the 'alim- shaykh ideal. The *ijāzah* conferred on Mawlānā Siddiqui was a channel through which the transmission of knowledge and *tasawwuf* was internalised. The *ijāzah* system[48] has its origins in the early years of Islamic history, which was a certificate used to indicate that one has been authorised by a higher authority to transmit a certain discipline (*adab*) or text of Islamic knowledge. The face-to-face interaction between the students and teacher was emphasised. *Tasawwuf,* too, followed the *ijāzah* system and maintained the element of *tasalsul* (continuity)[49] in the spiritual lineage of the *tariqahs* (spiritual

---

[45] Qur'an: 62: 2.

[46] Siddiqui, *Islam and the Scientific Quest,* 4.

[47] Siddiqui, *Ambassador of Islam,* 7.

[48] www.quran-institute.org/ijazah.program

[49] The spiritual lineage of Mawlana Siddiqui appears in Umar Siddiqui, *The Roving*

orders).

Sayyid Ahmad, the Grand Sanusi of Libya (d. 1933) represented the sufi-activist paradigm. Like Shaykh Abdul Qadir al-Jaza'iri,[50] the freedom fighter of Algeria against the French colonial rule, Sayyid Ahmad strove hard to maintain the strong Islamic presence in Libya. His efforts were shortlived, forcing him to withdraw himself from all military activities. His final days were spent in Hijaz where he taught various branches of Islamic sciences (*'ulum*) and initiated many people into *tasawwuf.*

The impact of these distinguished scholars on Mawlānā Siddiqui was evident in terms of his presentation of *tasawwuf.* In this perspective, he drew guidance from the Qur'ān, the sunnah and the *salaf* whose writings and influence redefined their role in a contemporary setting.

Ambassador of Islam (Karachi, 2011), 92-6.

[50] Abdul Qadir al-Jaza'iri advanced the cause of *tasawwuf* through *jihād*. See Mustafa Talas, *Amir Abdul Qadir*, (Algiers, n.d), 196.

Chapter 5

Peace and Dialogue in the West

In the previous chapters, the Islam versus the West dichotomy was explored. The factors contributing to the hostility were largely colonialism and Western encroachment into the Muslim world. The technological progress advanced by the West affected the Muslim countries which were colonised by British imperialism. In this respect, the Indian subcontinent owing to its unique position was exposed to the multiple influences of Western civilisation.[1] No less important was Egypt as it also became vulnerable to the modernist forces and gave birth to a generation of intellectuals whose impact was far reaching on the *nahdah* (resurgence) movement[2] that sprang up during the late nineteenth century. The impasse between Islam and the West intensified and resulted in the myriad of responses along these fault lines. Alienation and assimilation[3] were the core issues that reflected the Muslim attitude towards the West. In other words, the tension between the traditionalist and modernist Muslims hindered the possibilities of a meaningful dialogue with the West.

---

[1] The colonial narrative was inseparable from the Muslim identity in the subcontinent before 1947. See Francis Robinson, *Islam and South Asia and the West* (New Delhi, 2007), 99-145.

[2] Ibrahim Abu Rabi, *Intellectual Origins of Islamic Resurgence in the Modern World*. Mazheruddin Siddiqui has made a comparative study of the ʿulama and Islamic scholars who represented the orthodoxy and modernism dichotomy. See his *Modernist Reformist Thought in the Muslim World* (Islamabad, 1982). Cf. Aziz Ahmad, *Islamic Modernism in India and Pakistan 1857-1964* (Oxford, 1967).

[3] These responses were evident in those Muslim countries under colonial rule.

Message to the West

Mawlānā Siddiqui maintained that the message of Islam had to reach Europe and America as these continents were symbolic representations of economic prosperity and strong democratic institutions. However, the early twentieth century witnessed a downturn of moral degeneration following the entrenched presence of Marxism and Communism in several countries of Europe. In a similar vein, Capitalism did not alleviate the plight of millions of people. Instead, it created an enclave of elitist groups promoting materialism at the altar of religion.[4] Against the background of the changing fortunes in the West, Mawlānā Siddiqui's tabligh travels were the key to understanding Islam's pivotal role as a harbinger of faith and universal values.

A brief mention may be made of Mawlānā Siddiqui's earlier attempts to forge a better understanding between Islam and the West. Under his guidance, *Genuine Islam* was published in 1936 in Singapore, containing articles related to his tabligh vision. Two strands of articles - intellectual and historical - were based on Islam's links with the European thought,[5] the mutual encounter in the field of science and Islam's enduring legacy as a civilisational force in Europe.

A thorough familiarity with the intellectual temperament of the West facilitated Mawlānā Siddiqui's recognition as a missionary with impeccable Islamic credentials. His lecture tour to Canada was a memorable event in 1950. As Daood Hamdani correctly observed that the nascent Muslim community in Edmonton (Canada) set the precedent for a viable Islamic presence in the West. He says:

Al-Rashid Mosque built in 1938 in Edmonton, Canada, and founded by both men and women was one of the first North

---

[4] In fact, the secular policies of several Muslim countries in the early twentieth century had strong Marxist and Communist learning. See Nadwi, *Western Civilisation, Islam and Muslims* (Lucknow, 1974).

[5] Muzaffar Iqbal explores the Islam and science nexus within the historical framework. See Muzaffar Iqbal, *The Making of Islamic Science* (Kuala Lumpur, 2009), 153-88.

American institutions of its kind. It created an inclusive community where social issues were discussed and leaders were nurtured. Women played a key role in establishing this community which valued the voices equally with men.[6]

The mosque was built by the immigrants from Syria and Lebanon of Shi`ah and Sunni persuasions. It had the synergising elements of a local culture with essentials of the Islamic faith.[7] In 1938 Mawlānā Siddiqui laid the foundation of the first mosque in Canada and one of the very first in North America. During his tour in 1949-50 he addressed the fledging community in Arabic and English.[8] Likewise, his public addresses in New York and Washington dwelt on the *Islam and West* theme. In Mawlānā Siddiqui's estimation, the impasse between these two civilisations had a negative effect of promoting the values contained in the Islamic belief system. His candid approach to the issues affecting the American society was indicative of his profound knowledge about the growth and development of the Western culture. Likewise, his critique on its shortcomings did not exonerate Muslims living in the West from discharging their fundamental duties of *da'wah*. According to Mawlānā Siddiqui, tabligh was a collective responsibility for the emerging Muslim community and Islam could be preserved through building mosques and other Islamic institutions. In this way, the interaction between Muslims and non-Muslims could engender the spirit of tolerance.[9] He warned Muslims against insulating themselves from the mainstream activities as these were counterproductive to the cause of interfaith relations.

Mention may be made of prominent intellectuals who accepted Islam after several meetings with Mawlānā Siddiqui. In the earlier years of his mission other eminent personalities like Merwate Tifinch, French governor of Mauritius, and Mr. F. Gengson, the Christian

---

[6] For a detailed discussion on the Edmonton Mosque, see Daood Hamdani, *The Al-Rashid – Canada's First Mosque* (Ottawa, CCMW, 2011).

[7] Hamdani, *Canada's First Mosque- a Model for Canadian Mosques today.* http://www.commongroundnews.org/article.

[8] A.B. Naeem, "Islam in Canada" in *The Muslim Digest:* September 1952, 27.

[9] Siddiqui, *The Islamic Ideal*, 15.

minister in the Sri Lankan cabinet also accepted Islam after meeting Mawlānā Siddiqui.[10] The eminent scientist, Maria Levinskaya and her philosopher husband, Professor George Antono responded positively to his and Mawlānā Ansari's rational exposition of Islam. Levinskaya's monograph, *Scientific Religion or Reverent Science*[11] has clear traces of Islamic thought regarding the Qur'ānic elaboration of science and religion. She says:

> Science is concerned with the study of the laws of nature. In its applied form it serves to better the conditions of living. In its pure form it elucidates and opens the way to the understanding of nature's law. Religion deals with the relationship of man to God and the spiritual commandments and laws through which man can live in peace and harmony with himself and with his fellow-creatures. It should lead to an inner awakening and a more elevated approach to moral values. Both are dedicated to the search for Truth amidst the grandeur, beauty and mystery of the universe and to greater understanding of that primordial force which is the origin of all created things.[12]

Levinskaya's observation finds resonance in the insightful comments made by Mawlānā Siddiqui on the relationship between science and religion:

> While speaking before the Royal Asiatic Society of Shanghai I expounded the view that to regard science and religion as opposed to each other was based on a misconception of facts and it gave me great pleasure to note that my view was highly appreciated. In fact, those who hold the view of conflict between religion and science labour under a wrong notion of religion. Those notions and ideas to which they give the name of religion are not really religion but mythology and superstition. The fact is that religion is itself a science. It carries its

---

[10] See Personality Profile: "Mawlana Siddiqui" in *Al-Hadil Ameen*: 2010: 1, 13.
[11] Maria Levinskaya, *Scientific Religion on Reverent Science* (Karachi, WFIM, 1983).
[12] Ibid., 4.

investigation into the realms of spiritual and moral values while physical science concerns itself with material entities. The main difference lies in the *methods* employed in physical science and the science of religion. The criterion of reason, however, works in the domain of religion as much as in the field of physical science.[13]

On the subject of Islam and science, the famous dialogue between Mawlānā Siddiqui and the Irish playwright, George Bernard Shaw is instructive. His reference to the lecture delivered by Mawlānā Siddiqui in Nairobi (Kenya) on this theme elicited an interesting question about Islam's compatibility with scientific enquiry. Mawlānā Siddiqui's reply was in keeping with his scholarly pursuits.

All the teachings of Islam are rational; there are no mysteries and no dogmas. They only require to be explained in a proper light in order to transfuse (transmit) their correct sense. It is difficult to understand the literature of any art with which we are not conversant. Hence, in order to grasp and assimilate the problematical points related to any art, we must first acquire knowledge and cultivate intimate acquaintance with that art.[14]

Simply put, the Qur'ānic message and teachings are based on rational thought.

A remarkable aspect of the science and religion discourse is Mawlānā Siddiqui's focus on the spiritual values which are derived from the Qur'ān and the sunnah. To the intellectuals who view religion critically, his message is clear: science without *wahy* is a meaningless venture. It cannot bring mankind to appreciate the wonders of nature, the perfection of the universe and Allah's grand design. By contrast, Islam strikes a balance between reason and faith; it elevates the status of man by reminding him about the purpose of his creation. The end result is gaining the pleasure of Allah. This point is important to contextualise Mawlānā Siddiqui's elaboration of the science and religion theme. He was exposed to the multiple layers of rational thought for which a cogent response was essential. This line of

---

[13] Siddiqui, *Cultivation of Science by the Muslims*, 7.
[14] Siddiqui, *A Shavian and a Theologian*, 18.

thought or approach, however, did not pose a dilemma for him because his vision was tabligh-centred. His academic background, too, strengthened his resolve to present Islam to the modern mind. In this way his contributions left an enduring imprint on the intellectuals searching for spiritual solace.

World Tabligh Tour: 1949-50

Mawlānā Siddiqui accompanied by Mawlānā Ansari made a second visit to United States of America in 1949-50. By now tabligh had expanded its footprint in the major cities largely due to immigration and the steady growth of Islamic institutions. Mawlānā Siddiqui was no stranger to the multiple layers of Islamic thought following the influx of Muslims from different countries and the emergence of Afro-American Islam[15] with its strong racial overtones. No doubt it was a daunting task to address the Muslim communities with distinctive ideological mindsets. Mawlānā Siddiqui's intuitive grasp (*basirat*) of the religious attitudes and his unwavering promotion of unity (*ittihād*) among the Muslims underpinned his success. He eschewed sectarian representations of Islam; instead, he urged Muslims to rally around the –Back to the Qur'ān, Back to Muhammad'[16] call. This unity of purpose was based on the Qur'ānic teachings and the Prophetic practice.

Tabligh and Salafiyyah: An Assessment

During the momentous period of change which swept across the Muslim world, particularly Egypt, the Salafiyyah movement,[17] tracing its origins to the Muslim reformers like Afghani and Mufti Abduh articulated a return to pristine Islam (*al-awda ilal Islam*). The worldviews of Mawlānā Siddiqui and Salafiyyah were different and in

---

[15] On the formation of the Nation of Islam, see Edward Curtis, *Black Muslim Religion in the Nation of Islam*, (Chapel Hill, 2006).

[16] To this end, Mawlana Ansari gave practical guidelines to this call in his major work, *The Qur'ānic Foundations and Structure of Muslim Society*.

[17] On the social milieu of the Salafiyyah, see Hourani, *Arabic Thought in the Liberal Age: 1998-1939*.

many respects expressed conflicting positions. Tabligh and *tasawwuf* were essential features of Mawlānā Siddiqui's interaction with the Muslim communities he visited. Through the prism of his multifarious activities there was an unconditional commitment to advance the cause of Islam. In contrast, the Salafiyyah's *da'wah* activitiess followed a confrontational course in its rejection of practices deemed un-Islamic by them. *Tasawwuf*, for example, was vehemently opposed as they found no textual evidence in the Qur'ān and the sunnah.

In fact, the rich repository of *tasawwuf* was jettisoned by them in their rigid interpretation of the authentic version of Islam.

Although the phenomenon of Salafiyyah was not pronounced among the Muslim communities straddling the major centres in the USA, the formation of societies along ideological lines required effective strategies. Mawlānā Siddiqui addressed a cross-section of Muslims of different backgrounds in Washington. His monograph, *Quest for True Happiness* outlined the Islamic concept of guidance within the ambit of spirituality. The key issues of his lecture were specifically meant for the American audience. A prominent feature of Mawlānā Siddiqui's writings is the spiritual nurturing of the Muslim community to earn Allah's pleasure. He says:

In that Divine book of guidance, the Holy Qur'ān, Allah corrected all those mistaken notions and ideas under which humanity was promoted, and expounded that philosophy of life and that system of living which is based on the eternal laws appointed by Him. The underlying principle of this philosophy is that just as there are laws that govern the physical existence and growth of man, there are also spiritual and moral laws that govern the spiritual and moral life. And just as the violation of the physical laws brings about physical disease and deterioration, similarly the violation of the spiritual and moral laws creates spiritual and moral ailments and disintegration. Consequently, true happiness and real success can be obtained only by means of a harmonious development of the physical, moral and spiritual aspects of life in accordance with those laws which our Creator has appointed for us and revealed through His chosen Messengers.[18]

---

[18] Siddiqui, *Quest for True Happiness*, 9.

The recurrent theme of moral and spiritual harmony is aimed at raising the religious consciousness of the Muslim communities. By way of example: if disunity and sectarian prejudice are visible in the Muslim society, then the prospects of harmony are illusory. As a result, the spiritual growth will be stunted while the responsibility of *khilafāh* will be diminished in importance. This concern was reiterated by Mawlānā Siddiqui in his tabligh travels. Following the footsteps of the Holy Prophet (pbuh), he made every effort to remind the Muslim communities about the detrimental effects of disunity. Obviously, there were cultural practices that were religiously upheld by different Muslim communities and for many individuals these were regarded as Islamic. Mawlānā Siddiqui, guided by his intuitive grasp (*basirat*) and wisdom (*hikmah*), pressed home the importance of observing the pillars of Islam. He fervently believed that a knowledgeable Muslim community would make positive contributions to society at large.

The impact of Mawlānā Siddiqui's lectures transcended the sectarian barriers. In many respects, the success of his endeavours was noticeable in the countries where capitalism and secularism were firmly entrenched. Both USA and Europe were not immune to these pervasive influences. Although professing Christianity as the state religion these countries were not averse to secularism because "it reached deep into the foundation of the faith." Overall, secularism was "the natural theological outcome of Christianity."[19]

In a pamphlet published by the Muslim Society of America, Mawlānā Siddiqui, accompanied by Mawlānā Ansari, was welcomed by the American Muslims. His fame as an accomplished scholar and spiritual guide is highlighted:

His Eminence (Mawlānā Siddiqui) has no connection with any new-fangled sects or movements and does not stand for sectarianism. He represents the *Ahl-Sunnah al-Jamaat* as a progressive and enlightened exponent, and as such he enjoys the confidence of the ʿulama of the world and is held in high esteem by such eminent personages of the ʿulama of Al-Azhar university who paid tribute to

---

[19] An incisive discussion of these terms is found in Abdulkader Tayob, *Religion and Modern Islamic Discourse* (London, 2009), 3.

him only recently (1950) by holding a welcome reception in his honour during his stay in Cairo.

His Eminence is essentially a man of peace and toleration. His audiences always include large numbers of non-Muslims whose respect and admiration he enjoys. While standing and working essentially as an exponent and philosopher of Islam, he acts as a messenger of goodwill unto all. His Eminence is one of those few prominent Islamic religious leaders who combine Islamic learning with modern Western education. This enables him not only to work effectively among the masses but also among the intelligentsia, and not only among Muslims but also among non-Muslims. His Eminence who has for thirty five years toured the earth as a religious ambassador of peace, bringing comfort, peace and goodwill to humanity by his non-sectarian lectures, his teachings and glorious writings have also inspired the souls of practically every human being who read or heard of him. As the *Messenger of Peace* he was warmly received in major cities of the country."[20]

The recurrent theme of 'The Message of Peace' was intertwined with Mawlānā Siddiqui's tabligh initiatives. He was a scholar who had devoted almost forty years of his life lecturing throughout the world, bringing peace and comfort to humanity. More importantly, he was able to demonstrate that the timeless message and teachings of Islam are the anchors of mankind's salvation in a world driven by greed, corruption and self-interest. Peace, as explained by Mawlānā Siddiqui, is not an abstract concept or an illusory quest proposed by the philosophers and intellectuals but a manifestation of Allah's divine planning and wisdom that can only create real happiness. Thus, his speeches and writings are a cogent expression of the Islamic ideal, which are clearly brought out in the Qur'ān and the sunnah.

Islam and Western Civilisation

Mawlānā Siddiqui's acknowledgement by the West as an ambassador of peace was in recognition of his cosmopolitan outlook and his

---

[20] Pamphlet issued by the Muslim Society of America, 1950.

commitment to promoting the universal message of Islam. His encyclopaedic knowledge of the contemporary movements and comparative religion gave him the consummate skill to critique Communism and Marxism which were gaining ground not only in the West but in Muslim countries as well. In this respect, the writings of Mawlānā Ansari served as a rebuttal to these 'isms'. In his *Islam and Western Civilisation*, Mawlānā Ansari stated that the three stages through which Western Civilisation has passed since the Renaissance are those of secularism, materialism and Communism:

> Secularism, materialism and Communism are interrelated. In the materialistic interpretation of life, the first stage which the Western civilisation attained was the stage of secularism wherein the state was separated from the church and the different branches of knowledge were divorced from the belief in Allah. This stage ultimately opened the doors wide for materialism which says that reality is material and material alone. This philosophical materialism, after it had penetrated sufficiently into the different departments of western life, transformed itself into "scientific materialism" in the hands of Karl Marx who, in the 19th century, gave to the world for the first time in human history the most thorough and the most aggressive materialistic philosophy.[21]

Mawlānā Ansari's reference to –scientific materialism' is a euphemism for Communism's aggressive policies of eradicating religion (in this case, Islam) and spreading the culture of materialism where belief in the Afterlife has no relevance. A similar sentiment was echoed by the poet of the East, Iqbal about the debilitating effects of these ideological systems afflicting Western society:

> The modern age prides itself on its progress in knowledge and its matchless scientific development. No doubt, the pride is justified. Today space and time are being annihilated, and man

---

[21] Ansari, *Islam and Western Civilisation* (Karachi, 1983), 3.

is achieving amazing successes in unveiling the secrets of nature and harnessing its forces to his own service. But in spite of all these developments, the tyranny of imperialism struts aboard, covering its face in the masks of democracy, nationalism, Communism, and fascism. Under these masks, in every corner of the earth, the spirit of freedom and the dignity of man are being trampled in a way, of which not even the darkest period of human history presents a parallel. The so-called statesmen to whom government and leadership of men were entrusted have proved demons of bloodshed, tyranny and oppression. The rulers whose duty it was to protect and cherish those ideals which go to form a higher humanity, to prevent man's oppression of man and to elevate the moral and intellectual level of mankind, have, in their hunger for dominion and imperial possessions, shed the blood of millions and reduced millions to servitude simply in order to pander to the greed of their own particular groups. After subjugating and establishing their dominion over weaker peoples, they have robbed them of their possessions, of their morals, of their religions, their cultural traditions and their literatures. Then they sowed divisions among them that they should shed one another's blood and go to sleep under the opiate of serfdom, so that the leech of imperialism might go on sucking their blood without interruption.[22]

The above extracts clearly demonstrate the affinity of views between Mawlānā Siddiqui and Iqbal - an undeniable proof of their intellectual acumen and shared concerns about the destiny of the *ummah*. At the same time, Iqbal's poems are an expression of his critical evaluation of the Western civilisation. Iqbal has employed philosophical language to describe the plight of mankind under these imperialist forces. The word imperialism conjures up images of slavery, tyranny and irreligiousness. It has spawned in different ways a number of ideological systems that dominate the world. In addition, it has brought untold misery to mankind. As events have unfolded in the

---

[22] Iqbal, "A Clarion Call to Humanity" in the *Voice of Islam*: Feb/ March 1938, 129.

last decades, the critiques by Mawlānā Siddiqui and Iqbal reveal a frightening story of mankind's perilous future.

Moral Regeneration of Western Society

At the reception hosted in honour of Mawlānā Siddiqui by several Muslim embassies, prominent scholars were invited as well. George Kheirallah, a distinguished Islamic scholar whose publications on the classical period of Islamic learning are widely acclaimed, was greatly impressed by his erudition and unassuming personality. There is no doubt that his intellectual expertise accumulated over his four decades of involvement with tabligh across several continents enabled him to address audiences of varied backgrounds.[23]

During his extensive travels to Europe and America between the period 1930-50, Mawlānā Siddiqui observed the rapid decline in morality caused by the Western civilisation. A permissive society undermined traditional norms and values; challenged cohesion in family life and promoted promiscuity. The barriers of modesty were lifted; instead, immorality dominated the collective life, thought and practices of the West. In contrast, Mawlānā Siddiqui asserted that the Islamic law of morality enshrined in the divine framework (*wahy*) was the unerring guide for a stable society. Tragically, the Western society disregarded the divine injunctions in favour of pieces of legislation that created an imbalance between the functions and duties of men and women.[24] In its quest for equality it created an anomaly that distorted gender relations, which were a clear violation of the natural laws advocated by the Islamic teachings. In the Qur'ānic language, *Fitrat* is the natural disposition of man that operates within the divine system. According to Mawlānā Siddiqui, the West had lost its moral compass and the pathetic conditions prevailing in its societies have created a mood of disillusionment and pessimism.

Addressing the Muslim youth, Mawlānā Siddiqui urged them not

---

[23] *Ramadan Annual,* 1996.

[24] Maryam Jameelah, a vocal critic of the Western civilisation has also examined the moral decline in Western society. The following work is representative of the Western trends which Mawlana Siddiqui also highlights in his writings: Maryam Jameelah, *Western Civilisation Condemned by Itself.* 2 vols. (Lahore, 1970).

to be entrapped by the superficialities of the Western culture. It was only Islam which could redeem the society from the 'web of destruction.'[25] He expressed his candour about the intrusive presence of the Western culture in the Muslim homes. Likewise, he was critical of Muslim parents' apathy towards their children's un-Islamic conduct: In many instances it transgressed all norms of decency (*hayā*). To these parents he issued a stern warning - a declarative announcement of divine punishment:

> [Parents] will definitely taste the severest torment of the wrath of the powerful Almighty Allah in the tight chamber of the grave and deep dungeons of hell.[26]

Mawlānā Siddiqui was deeply concerned about the deteriorating behavioural problems of the youth in several Muslim societies. For him, it was the onus of parents to address these issues by creating the Islamic ambience at home. They had to be role models for their children and instill excellent manners so that they could be the future ambassadors of Islam. This was only possible if *tarbiyat* (character development) complemented *ta'lim* (Islamic instruction).

Islam in Britain

The British colonial order had a direct impact on its relations with the colonised nations. Among its major designs was to consolidate 'civilising' missions through the network of institutions. Its influence extended to the study of Islamic culture and civilisation by actively supporting the Orientalist project.[27] At the same time, the steady stream of immigrants largely from South Asia prompted a reassessment of policy making with its former colonies. In Britain, the Muslim immigration also included the presence of intellectuals

---

[25] Siddiqui, *The Blossom of Youth*, Translated into English by Abdul Hādi al-Qādiri (Durban, 2004), 89.

[26] Ibid., 90.

[27] The relationship between British colonialism and Orientalism is critically examined in Zafar Ishaq Ansari and John Esposito (eds.) *Muslims and the West: Encounter and Dialogue* (Islamabad, 2002), 89- 102.

who made concerted efforts to create a viable Muslim society. There was no doubt that the Muslim communities in   many towns were formed along racial and ethnic lines and retained religious and cultural characteristics which were resistant to the assimilation trends taking place.[28] In cities like London, the hybrid communities comprising Muslim immigrants and hailing from different countries evolved. Their religious aspirations were mirrored in their output of Islamic activities and commitment to the Islamic faith and practice. Mawlānā Siddiqui on several occasions during his visits to Britain reinforced the need for Muslim unity which held out promises of *da'wah* success among the non-Muslims. His last visit in 1950 to Britain was significant for two reasons. First, his interaction with the intellectuals and Muslim organisations drew a positive response to the tabligh activities he articulated. Second, his interfaith initiative found a receptive audience in the higher echelons of the church.

We now focus on the Islamic Cultural Centre in London.

Islamic Cultural Centre: London

As early as 1900 several efforts were made to build a mosque in Central London including the one initiated by Lord Headley (d. 1935), an English convert to Islam whose project was funded by the Nizam of Hyderabad (India). It was during his time in India that he first came into contact with Islam, and as a result, it had a lasting impact on him. His conversion to Islam took place after several years of intensive studying and reflection. As an active member of the Muslim community, he was largely instrumental in the establishment of the British Muslim Society in 1914, enlisting the services of prominent Muslim figures who became actively involved in *da'wah* activities.[29]

Abdullah Philby (d. 1960) was an activist Englishman, whose sojourn in the Middle East reflected the political turmoil in this region and the British expansionist designs. His writings included

---

[28] An excellent study on the Muslim communities in Britain is found in Humayun Ansari's *The Infidel Within: Muslims in Britain since 1800* (London, 2006), 24-51.

[29] Muhammad Mojlum Khan, *Great Muslims of the West: Makers of Western Islam* (Leicester, 2017), 419-20.

travelogues as well as his exploration of Arabia.[30] He was involved in running the Islamic Cultural Centre. In 1939 a mosque committee comprising various prominent Muslims and diplomats persuaded the British Government to allocate a site for Muslims in London as a tribute to the thousands of Muslim soldiers who had died defending the then British Empire. In 1944 King George VI visited the Regals Lodge and officially opened the Islamic centre. Construction work for the mosque complex was completed in 1977.[31] According to Ansari, the Islamic Cultural Centre was recognised as the central religious institution representing multiple Muslim communities in Britain.[32]

The speech delivered by Mawlānā Siddiqui at the Islamic Cultural Centre in 1950 covered important issues which were relevant to the Muslim community in Great Britain. Muslims were expected to realign their lives to the personality of the Holy Prophet (pbuh) who had brought "the most wonderful revolution of human history."[33] The Muslim encounter with the Western civilisation and culture required a proper dissemination of Islamic teachings against the anti-Islamic ideas and values rampant in these cities. The Islamic moral code as opposed to a 'social ideology' was in conformity with the "divine law in all aspect of life, individual as well as social."[34] Thus the totality of human experience must lead to Divine pleasure. If the Islamic ideal is followed then success is guaranteed. This was evident in the lives of the early Muslims who conquered the world. They were prepared to sacrifice their lives. The crowns of kings were placed at their feet. Allah opened the door of success for them and gave them eternal happiness in the Hereafter.

According to Mawlānā Siddiqui, the task of the Islamic Cultural Centre was to project an intellectual identity which was free from the superficialities of an Islam laden with rituals. Therefore, Muslims were urged to use the Centre as a 'rallying point'[35] for promoting Islam as the perfect code of life. He conceived the harmonious

---

[30] Ibid., 284-5.

[31] See. M.A. Sherif, *Brave Hearts* (Kuala Lumpur, 2011), 42.

[32] Ansari, *The Infidel Within*, 134.

[33] Siddiqui, "The Islamic Ideal" in *The Minaret*: June 2004, 15.

[34] Ibid., 16.

[35] Ibid., 15.

blending of all facets of human activity as the 'code' which was inseparable from *'ibādah* (worship). The road to saintliness was enshrined in this Islamic ideal. The following extracts capture the essence of the code as elucidated by Mawlānā Siddiqui:

Every code of life has a reference to a certain ideal. without fixing up an ideal we cannot have a code of life. The cause of the confusion which is prevailing in the world today is really that either the ideal is not well-defined, or it has been defined in a limited perspective, or it is not defined at all. For this reason, the first thing that Islam does is that it presents a rational ideal for man. The Holy Qur'ān says:

> *And I have not created the Jinn and mankind except that they shall worship Me.*[36]

The purpose of our creation is our attainment of the knowledge of Allah and His attributes. Furthermore, every particle of this universe is a manifestation of Allah's attributes. Hence, when a Muslim engages himself in scientific pursuit as a true Muslim, whether in the field of geology, or astronomy or chemistry, his goal is the knowledge of Allah. The Holy Qur'ān says:

> *Verily, in the creation of the heavens and the earth and in the alternation of the night and day, there are signs for men of understanding, who remember Allah, standing, sitting and reclining, and ponder over the creation of the heavens and the earth, and say: "Our Lord! You have not created all this in vain. Glory be to You! Preserve us from the doom of Fire."*[37]

Thus, even the purely scientific pursuit has a deeper significance in Islam. The true Muslim scientist does not stop at the discovery of physical causes, but proceeds further to realise the working of the "Great Beyond." Such an attitude can be possible only when the ideal of Allah-realisation (*taqwā*) remains constantly in the forefront. Hence, the Holy Quran says:

---

[36] Qur'an: 51: 56.
[37] Qur'an: 3: 190-1.

> *Say: Verily, my prayer and my sacrifice, my life and my death are all for Allah, the Lord of the Worlds.*[38]

Thus, when the ideal is Allah alone, it is natural that a Muslim should conform to the divine law in all aspects of life, individual as well as social.[39]

Mawlānā Siddiqui was well acquainted with the intellectual trends of the Islamic organisations representing these Muslim communities. Therefore, he selected a topic bearing the theme of an ideal. In other words, the power of positivity had strengthened the cause of Islam and brought about a revolution that remains unrivalled to this day. Muslims were not averse to facing the challenges of the day because they were inspired by the Islamic ideal as described in the Qur'ān.

Moreover, they shunned superficialities and strove to be the true representatives of the Prophetic conduct.

The Islamic Cultural Centre was patronised by dignitaries from the Arab world who were much impressed by its successful strides under the directorship of Dr Ali Hasan Abdel Kader. A graduate of Al-Azhar and London universities, Dr Abdul Kader's scholarly profile enhanced the prestige of the Centre. His studies on sufism have been critically acclaimed in the literary circles. To his credit is a definitive study on the famous sufi, Junayd al-Baghdadi,[40] a seminal figure in the early development of *tasawwuf*. Among Dr Abdel Kader's circle of friends was Abdullah Yusuf Ali, the famous translator and commentator of the Qur'ān in English. The turbulent period in Yusuf Ali's life, especially during his later years has been described in M.A. Sherif's *Searching for Solace*. He says:

> It is not known what befell his (Yusuf Ali) vast collection of books or the black steel box containing the diaries. The possession he did hold on to was a scrapbook containing newspaper cuttings about himself and some other personal

---

[38] Qur'an: 6: 162.

[39] Siddiqui, *The Islamic Ideal*, 16-7.

[40] Ali Hasan Abdel Kader, *The Life, Personality and Writings of Al-Junayd* (London, 1976.)

papers. He prepared a meticulous index for this collection, probably whiling away many a solitary hour in remembrance of past distinctions. In his diminishing circle of acquaintances was Dr Ali Hasan Abdel Kader, director of the London Islamic Cultural Centre, to whom he must have presented even this last possession. The scrapbook was uncovered many years later in the library of the Centre.[41]

Mawlānā Siddiqui's admiration of Dr Abdul Kader is expressed in these words:

> I do not find words to express my gratitude to my brother Dr Ali Hasan Abdul Kader, whom I had the honour to know for the first time in London. He is an embodiment of Islamic brotherhood. May Allah bless him for the valauable cooperation I received from him.

Another organisation which rendered sterling services to the Muslim cause in London was the Jami`at al-Muslimin (Muslim Association). As an active society it represented the various Muslim population in the city. The noted Islamic scholar, I.I. Kazi[42] (d. 1968) played a major role in expanding its network together with other Muslim institutions across Britain. Mawlānā Siddiqui was impressed by his commitment to translate the Islamic ideal into 'constructive applications.'

I.I. Kazi believed in the genuine transformation of Muslims living in Britain as practical models of Islam rather bringing about superficial conversions.[43] It is interesting to note that the practical models of Islam were a resonance of the tabligh efforts initiated by Mawlānā Siddiqui to his Islamic reawakening project.

An important point to consider was the robust scholarly exchange of

---

[41] M.A. Sherif, *Searching for Solace: A Biography of Abdullah Yusuf Ali, Interpreter of the Qur'ān* (Kuala Lumpur, 1994), 138.

[42] 'Allamah Imdad Ali Kazi was a distinguished scholar, jurist and educationist. He was a prolific writer on literature, education and tasawwuf. See *Allamah Kazi: Life and Thought* (Karachi, 1994).

[43] *The Ambassador of Peace,* 11.

ideas and *da'wah* efforts in Britain. This nexus was embedded in Mawlānā Siddiqui's vision of reaching out to the nascent Muslim communities who hailing from different countries rallied around the common cause of Islamic unity. Interestingly, several prominent Muslim converts who had direct links with Mawlānā Siddiqui were actively engaged in promoting Islam through lectures, writings and establishing Islamic organisations. His influence, therefore, had a direct influence on the collective identity of the diaspora Muslim communities. In more ways than one, he infused the dynamic spirit of Islam into these organisations, which may be regarded as his singular contribution to the cause of *da'wah*.

Abdullah Quilliam

William Henry Quilliam (d. 1932), better known as Abdullah Quilliam, was born into a middle-class English family. His parents were devout Methodists. Quilliam rose in prominence as a successful lawyer. Apart from his legal practice, Quilliam was widely read and well versed in philosophy, theology, history and science. During this period, he developed a spiritual crisis that led him to the path of agnosticism. The loss of faith in Christianity prompted him to travel to North Africa where he was exposed to the teachings of Islam. After his return to Liverpool in 1887 (during which time he presumably had accepted Islam) his scholarly articles focused on the Islamic culture and civilisation. His rational exposition of Islam is succinctly described in these words:

> Those who cannot understand how 'Islam can be accepted by a European' have no proper comprehension of Western peoples. In the British Isles we are taught to be logical, and to think and reason for ourselves. Islam as a reasonable and logical faith appeals to man's reason, and is therefore likely to be adopted by those who reflect and think and have the courage of their conscience.[44]

---

[44] Khan, *Great Muslims of the West*, 189.

In subsequent years, Quilliam's vision of Islam's presence in Liverpool bore tangible results. The establishment of the Liverpool Mosque and Institute (LMI) served as the hub of Muslim activities and within a period of twenty years Quilliam managed to establish the first indigenous community in Britain consisting of hundreds of British converts. As an editor, prolific writer and poet, he published widely and some of his notable publications include *The Faith of Islam* and *The Islamic World*. Through the pages of *The Crescent* Quilliam articulated the progressive trends of Islam which, however, did not compromise the teachings of mainstream Islam.[45]

Quilliam was not an `alim in the formal sense; however, his extensive reading of Islamic sources through English translations equipped him adequately to be a spokesman for Muslims in Liverpool. In recognition of his contributions and achievements, he was hailed as an 'alim by the prestigious University of Qarawiyyin in Fez, Morocco. In a similar vein, his pro-Ottoman caliphate support, which brought him in direct conflict with the British foreign policy, was recognised by Sultan Abdul Hamid who conferred on him the title 'Shaykh al-Islam'. Officially, Quilliam became a religious authority in his own right.[46] According to Ansari, "Shaykh al-Islam Quilliam made lecture tours in all parts of England and by his profound scholarship erased the rigid antagonism which prevailed in England of those days regarding Islam."[47]

Needless to add, Quilliam was a successful lawyer, charismatic *muballigh* and dedicated Islamic activist who worked tirelessly to raise an awareness and understanding of Islam in the backdrop of the deep misgivings by the majority Christians. Many individuals became prominent British or European Muslims who in many respects were influenced by the sterling efforts of Quilliam.

---

[45] Ron Geaves, *Islam in Victorian Britain: The Life and Times of Abdullah Quilliam* (Leicester, 2010), 127.

[46] Ibid., 205-8. Quilliam's pan-Islamic sentiments also was expressed in his unconditional loyalty to the Ottoman sultan.

[47] Ansari, *A New Muslim World*, 12.

Khalid Sheldrake

Like Quilliam, Lord Headley was instrumental in setting up the British Muslim Society in 1914. The key figure, Khalid Sheldrake brought new insights into the activities of the BMS. It attracted a considerable number of converts from the British aristocracy with the objective of providing a progressive understanding of Islam. The social norms of British society were maintained to allow the new Muslims to practise Islam in order to blur out the wide gaps between two different civilisations.

Unlike Quilliam's indigenous organisation, the BMS comprised a sizeable segment of South Asian immigrants. According to Sheldrake, there were prominent figures like Syed Ameer Ali, Muhammad Marmaduke Pickthall and Abdullah Yusuf Ali who delivered a series of lectures to both Muslims and non-Muslims. Sheldrake, too, was involved in "the Muslim societies and clubs that had emerged around the turn of the century. After the First World War, he played a significant role in the Islamic Society."[48] Through the publication of *Islamic Review*, there was a sustained attempt to present Islam to the new Muslim constituency whose intellectual and cultural temperament was rooted in the British soil. Therefore, Islam's appeal to the rising generation of British converts also opened up new vistas of understanding about its culture and civilisation. The rational and spiritual factor that drew them to Islam was, in indirect ways, a rejoinder to the Orientalist bias that had become pervasive in the academia. Overall, the steady growth of the inclusive Muslim communities spread across London and beyond was a reaffirmation of Islam's strong presence in the most powerful colonial country - Britain.

Lady Evelyn Cobbold

"Lady Evelyn Cobbold (d. 1963) embraced Islam at the hands of an Arab Imam in Egypt and performed *hajj* in 1933 at the age of 66. She had written her very valuable book, *My Pilgrimage to Mecca*.[49] The

---

[48] Humayun Ansari, *The Infidel Within*: 131.
[49] Ansari, *A New Muslim World*, 88-9 (Adapted).

first British woman to perform *hajj*, Evelyn Cobbold made her mark through her travelogue which detailed her spiritual journey to Islam. Her first exposure to Islamic culture took place in North Africa, after which her renewed interest spurred her to undertake an extensive study of essential teachings, guidance and wisdom. Her expressive description of Islam's positive impact and its remarkable contributions to human civilisation make interesting reading:

> Nearly 1300 years ago, when Christian Europe was in a state of semi-barbarism, its literature dispersed or lost, the finer arts extinct, Islam arose, binding the wild hordes of Arabia together in the brotherhood of a powerful faith; and in a short time, these Arabs built brilliant centres of advanced civilisation in the chief cities of Asia, Africa, and southern Europe. Baghdad became the home of philosophers, poets and men of letters, and in Cairo, Cordova, and many another city, libraries were collected, school of medicine, mathematics and natural history flourished, while Europe is indebted to Islam for the preservation of much of the classical literature of the ancient world. To the Arab his religion is a living thing, ever present in his daily life; a power to console in sorrow, a faith enabling him to face trouble with resignation, death without flinching. Truly is Islam a powerful and great force[50].

Muhammad Marmaduke Pickthall

Muhammad Marmaduke Pickthall (d. 1936) was a literary figure who embraced Islam in 1917. His travels to Egypt, Turkey, Lebanon and Syria brought him into contact with the Islamic culture and kindled his love for Islam and Muslims. In 1919 he served as the Imam of the Woking Mosque, Surrey, United Kingdom. The growing and subtle presence of Qadianism in a Sunni-controlled mosque was also reflected in the scholarly journal, *The Islamic Review*, edited by Pickthall. His exposure to Muhammad Ali's translation (1917), a

---

[50] Khan, *Great Muslims of the West*, 207. Cf. Ansari, *The Qur'ānic Foundations*, vol. 1, 219-39.

professed Ahmadi and other Orientalists' translations, dismayed him. Pickthall's brilliant contributions were visible during his stay in Hyderabad, a princely state ruled by Nizam Mir Osman Ali Khan. He edited the premier English language journal, *Islamic Culture* and also worked as an educationist and mentor. His series of lectures in Madras (Chennai) in 1926 were later published as *The Cultural Side of Islam.* The Nizam of Hyderabad sponsored his venture of the English translation of the Qur'ān which he completed in 1930. In consultation with the `ulama of Al-Azhar university, particularly Shaykh Mustafa Maraghi (d. 1945), Pickthall published his translation in 1930.[51]

Pickthall's personal reflections on the timeless message of the Qur'ān are lucidly conveyed in these words:

> No translation gives the least idea of the beauty and fire of inspiration of that book in Arabic, but no translation can conceal from you the fact that it contains a vision and a law for all humanity.[52]

Abdur Raheem Kidwai offers insightful comments on this translation. It is a faithful rendering of the original text. Unlike Yusuf Ali's loose paraphrasing, it avoids the pitfall of a literal translation. As an accomplished literary figure, Pickthalls's mastery of the language is imprinted in his elegance of style and diction. Unfortunately, the absence of adequate explanatory notes "fails to advance the understanding of uninitiated readers about the meaning and message of the Qur'ān."[53] At the same time, the notes, albeit brief, do not project dogmatic interpolations that characterise the translations of modernist scholars.

The Meaning of the Glorious Qur'ān was widely recognised after its publication. Mawlānā Siddiqui who was famed as the roving ambassador of Islam promoted the translation among the non-Muslim scholars. The following dialogue with the famous British playwright

---

[51] M.A. Sherif, *Brave Hearts, Pickthall and Philby: Two English Muslims in a Changing World* (Kuala Lumpur, 2011).

[52] Ibid, 40.

[53] Abdur Raheem Kidwai, *Translating the Untranslatable* (New Delhi, 2011), 12.

George Bernard Shaw about the Qur'ānic translation is illustrative:

As far as the translations of the Qur'ān are concerned, I would recommend you to read *The Meaning of the Glorious Koran* by Mr Marmaduke Pickthall, and I am sure that its perusal will enable you to appreciate considerably more the exquisite beauty, the sublime transcendence and the appealing and impressive style of the Qur'ān's perspective.[54]

However, I do not imply that it is a perfect version of the original, for you yourself can aptly judge, being an admittedly splendid writer, that, in spite of the translator being the ablest and the best, he can never transmit the force and brilliance of your original writings into his translations.

The translation was written during the tumultuous period of Muslim history when "military disarmament was followed by cultural disarmament - the door of *jihād* was obstructed, so too of *ijtihād*."[55] Like other emerging scholars, Pickthall resisted this trend and made every effort to steer away from the pernicious ideologies on the rise while focusing on the authentic interpretation of Islam.

The Qadiani distortion of the Qur'ān, which is discussed elsewhere in the chapter, also manipulated the supposed endorsement of its English translation by notable scholars like Pickthall. Ansari's rebuttal of these misrepresentation is emblematic of his scholarly acumen.[56] Essentially, *A New Muslim World* by Mawlānā Ansari is representative of the scholarly trends in Islamic studies in the early twentieth century. It covered a robust engagement with the Western scholarship and the sweeping tides of modernism and deviant movements like Qadianism.

---

[54] Cited in Abdul Kader Choughley, *Abdul Aleem Siddiqui and His Mission* (Springs, 2013), 141. Cf. Ibrahim Alladin, *Maulana Abdul Aleem Siddiqui: His Life, Thoughts and Message*, 122.

[55] Sherif, *Brave Hearts*, 56.

[56] Ansari, *A New Muslim World*, 90-1. Ansari's familiarity with Pickthall's literary contributions, and in particular *The Islamic Culture* is a conspectus of the former's scholarly erudition.

Islamic Activities in Cardiff

Besides London, Mawlānā Siddiqui selected Cardiff, the capital city of South Wales, for his tabligh visit. The Nur al-Islam mosque built largely through the tireless efforts of Shaykh Abdullah al-Hakimi[57] was the focus of Islamic activities. As early as the 1930s the Muslim community was disorganised; Islamic education was negligible and the missionary activities of the Christian evangelists among the Muslims reached a disturbing trend. In a specific sense, Muslims were vulnerable to the un-Islamic campaigns launched from all directions. For example, the Muslim students at Christian schools hardly possessed the rudimentary teachings of Islam. Furthermore, the community was not familiar with the Islamic rituals and practices.

The arrival of Shaykh al-Hakimi in 1931 was a turning point in terms of the corporate identity of the Muslim community in Cardiff. Islamic education was systematised; the *maktab* system was formalised for learning and teaching the Qur'ān, and most importantly, ties were strengthened with other Muslim organisations towards a more effective tabligh outreach network. According to Khan, "thanks to Abdullah's vision, leadership and dedication, the *zawiyas* (sufi lodges) he founded were open, inclusive, outward- looking and vibrant institutions that welcomed both men and women, young and old, rich and poor, and Muslims and non-Muslims alike. As a wise scholar and visionary leader, Abdullah was fully aware that he was operating in a non-Muslim country and, therefore, it was in the long- term interest of the Muslim community to establish contacts and strengthen relationships with the local authorities and institutions, as well as the wider society in general."[58]

A series of lectures was delivered by Mawlānā Siddiqui in the Nur al-Islam Mosque in Arabic, Urdu and English. The key theme of these lectures was based on *Islam: An Exposition.*[59] Mawlānā Siddiqui,

---

[57] Abdullah al-Hakimi of Yemeni descent was an influential figure in Cardiff. He is credited for initiating specific Islamic reform and widening his sphere of influence among the non-Muslims in the city. See Ansari, *The Infidel Within*, 100-101.

[58] Khan, *Great Muslims of the West*, 310-11.

[59] Mawlana Siddiqui's lectures were aimed at strengthening the Muslim `aqidah (belief), which was gradually eroded by Western values. Cf. *Ambassador of Peace*, 12-3.

keeping in mind the different backgrounds of the Muslim community and respective cultural temperaments, addressed important issues that were relevant to his unity (*ittihād*) vision. Two important points emerge from his visit to Britain. The evolution of the Muslim community was not an isolated phenomenon. Between integration and assimilation, Muslims had to consider a pragmatic option that would embrace change along realistic lines while allowing them to retain their distinctive Islamic identity. In other words, Muslims needed to be active participants in the British mainstream life without sacrificing their frame of reference - Islam. If Muslims were to succumb to the pervasive influence of Western civilisation[60] their roles as *du'āt* (missionaries) as described in the Qur'ān would be undermined. Mawlānā Siddiqui raised this concern during his lectures in America and Europe - a concern that formed the key theme of his tabligh activities in other countries like Japan and Kenya.[61]

Having mastered several languages, Mawlānā Siddiqui could address his audience in their 'mother tongue' with confidence. His study of Arabic, for example, went beyond the traditional course offered in the *Dars i-Nizāmi* curriculum. Likewise, his mastery over English enabled him to communicate the Islamic message in contemporary idiom.

Iqra: The Qur'ānic Paradigm

Mawlānā Siddiqui derived his understanding of the *iqrā* paradigm from the Qur'ān to present Islam's civilisational role. He makes insightful comments on this aspect in these words:

> Islam makes ideal provision for the utmost development of both the material and the spiritual aspects of life. If it

---

[60] As a polyglot, Mawlana Siddiqui was able to communicate with relative ease to a wider audience in the countries he visited. His impact in Japan was significant as his lecture at the Summer College in Tokyo indicated. Siddiqui, *Cultivation of Science by Muslims*, i-iii.

[61] Ansari explores these issues against the background of government's policies towards immigrants, see Ansari, *The Infidel Within*, 145-65.

dispenses instructions in secular progress, it does not stop at the elementary stage, but exhorts Muslims to aspire to its pinnacle by directing them to attain proficiency in all its branches of activity. In short, the Holy Qur'ān repeatedly refers us to the wonders of the creation and sets before our intelligent observation various phenomena of nature, thus encouraging the study of diverse sciences. In fact, the Book teems with logic and reason in this respect, and hundreds of verses (*āyāt*) and traditions (*ahādith*) can be quoted to demonstrate that a perfect knowledge of arts and sciences, including mathematics, geometry, trigonometry, astronomy, optics, etc. forms, as it were, the first chapter of the teachings of Islam. A Muslim's material progress is also accomplished to please Allah, so that he may enjoy the blessings of the world which are bestowed by Him.[62]

The message offered by Mawlānā Siddiqui may be framed from two angles. First, material progress is not frowned upon by the Qur'ān as is mistakenly assumed. Second, earning Allah's pleasure should be the ideal for every Muslim. As a *muballigh* and Islamic scholar, his persuasive approach to 'worldly matters' was marked by a sense of pragmatism. There was no semblance of the gloom and doom syndrome as was the case with many 'ulama who were his contemporaries. They could not appreciate the pace of modernity that affected the *ummah* as well. Their rigid interpretation of the Qur'ānic message to mankind did not suit the temperament of the rising generation of Muslims who were exposed to the new challenges in their daily lives. For this very reason, a scholar of Mawlānā Siddiqui's calibre was the ideal choice to address these issues.

Qadianism in Britain

Another centre which claimed to have Islamic legitimacy was the Ahmadiyyah group in London. An offshoot of Qadianism, the

---

Ahmadis have presented bizarre interpretations about the finality of Prophethood. Mawlānā Siddiqui paid a personal visit to the Centre to assess its activities. The Woking Mission, as he observed, did not have a functional mosque with a core Muslim community to express an 'Islam-in-action'. In fact, there were no markers of Islamic authenticity except the semblance of a professed *da'wah* among the Muslim converts who formed a threadbare minority in comparison to the established Muslim communities spread across London and other major cities.

The Mission had an 'elitist bias' and made efforts to serve only the interests of this particular 'Muslim' segment, thus deliberately ignoring the challenges posed by the imperialist status quo (British colonialism). Intellectuals like the Ahmadi lawyer, Khwaja Kamaluddin contributed to this distinct Islamic presence in London by engaging, in a seemingly academic level, on contemporary Islamic issues which were compatible with modernism. In its initial years, the Mission strengthened the Qadiani cause in a devious manner. According to Basheer Ahmad Masri, a former Imam of the Mosque, the Qadiani bureaucracy pre-empted the appointment of Sunni Imams in order to promote a heterodox version of Islam. Furthermore, they collaborated with the anti-Islam powers of the day by offering their clandestine services. Their missionary posts in foreign countries had served as a veneer to conceal their collusion with the anti- Islamic agencies.[63]

Through its official journal, *The Islamic Review*, the Ahmadis published the literary contributions of widely- acclaimed Islamic scholars in order to vindicate their 'Muslim' identity. Illustrative of their false claims were their propaganda techniques to present a garbled version of the Islamic beliefs under the guise of rigorous Islamic scholarship. Their publishing output euphemistically termed 'Free Islamic literature' had the sinister designs of luring the unwary public to the fold of Ahmadism. According to Mawlānā Siddiqui, the publications were mostly books written by Khwaja Kamaluddin, who was a staunch Ahmadi, while the literature of the Ahmadiyyah Anjuman of Lahore formed its guiding light.[64] The Mission officially promoted Maulvi Muhammad Ali's translation of the Qur'ān, which

---

[63] B.A. Masri, *The Bane of Mirzaiyat* (Benoni, 1988).
[64] *The Ambassador of Peace*, 15.

contains a full dose of Ahmadism in a subtle way, and which openly advocates Mirza Ghulam Ahmad as the 'special kind of Prophet', the Promised Messiah and the Mahdi.[65]

A common characteristic of these movements was their avowed aim to dismantle the *Finality of Prophethood* creed (*'aqidah*) and impose the so-called divine status (*kufr*-based) of their founder on the masses. Therefore, it was hardly surprising when they developed a parallel system of beliefs and practices to Islam. The element of charisma was employed to bolster their religious profile; new fangled interpretations were given on the established *'aqa'id* (beliefs) to vindicate their dubious presentation of prophethood. A cursory survey of articles in the journal during its formative period (1913-26) reveals the tempo of their missionary activities at the Woking Mission.[66]

In their sinister attempts to give credibility to their Qur'ānic contributions as the authentic expressions of Islamic beliefs, the Qadianis have the propensity to distort textual evidence in devious ways. For example, the renowned exegete (*mufassir*), Abdul Majid Daryabadi whose *Sidq* magazine was widely read among the literary circles was misquoted for his perceived endorsement of Muhammad Ali's commentary of the Qur'ān.[67] Worse still, they have created buffer zones to protect themselves against the critical writings of the ʿulama and Islamic scholars.

The mass distribution of the Ahmadi translation of the Qur'ān was also used by Elijah Muhammad, founder of *Nation of Islam*. He explicitly cited Muhammad Ali's commentary in his own work to defend his religious legitimacy and to interpret the significance of his mission by adapting terms from various Islamic textual sources. Hence, his reference to Ahmadi literature to strengthen his divine status claims.[68]

Ahmadism loomed large over the horizon and it was due to the relentless efforts of ʿulama and scholars like Mawlānā Siddiqui who exposed the hollow claims of this deviant sect.

---

[65] Ibid.

[66] *The Islamic Review* (Woking), 1913-26.

[67] See Gowhar Quadir Wani and Abdul Kader Choughley (editors), *Abdul Majid Daryabadi's Tafsir-ul-Qur'ān: A Critical Study* (Aligarh, 2021), 67-9.

[68] Curtis, *Black Muslim Religion in the Nation of Islam*, 46.

Interfaith Movement Initiatives

In the preceding years (1936-1949) Mawlānā Siddiqui had promoted his interfaith initiatives in Singapore for the purpose of "forging a united front on behalf of the world's great religions in order to combat the organised movements of irreligion and immorality."[69] His meetings with the high-ranking officials of the World Congress of Faiths and World Convention of Religions were aimed at the moral regeneration of society. Likewise, he contacted the Archbishop of Canterbury who through his chaplaincy extended his unconditional support to Mawlānā Siddiqui's interfaith initiative. To the end, Mawlānā Siddiqui delivered two important lectures, *The Universalism of Islam* and *Islam and Human Friendship* to reaffirm Islam's contributions on these issues.[70]

As stated elsewhere in the chapter, Mawlānā Siddiqui presented a well-knit analysis of Islam as a universal religion. The following extract reinforce this theme:

> [Islam] bases all its teachings on moral foundation and lays full emphasis on the moral reform of the individuals. Absolute moral values like truthfulness, justice, charity, etc. are its very life blood. The interests of the individuals and the society exist as co-centred realities. Equality of all human beings is one of the basic principles of Islam. Islam wiped off all distinctions of race and colour and taught in the most unambiguous terms the most practical and the truest form of human brotherhood. It is made up of individuals who are to be respected without attaching importance to any physical distinctions. In fact, Islam regards the individual as a world by himself, as representing the whole of humanity in his person.[71]

In a similar vein, Mawlānā Siddiqui presented the ideal relationship between morality and religion:

---

[69] *The Ambassador of Peace*, 16-7.
[70] Ibid.
[71] Siddiqui, *The Principles of Islam*, 18.

The concept of moral law and religion teaches one how best to live life in this world so that one may have peace always and that one's fellow-beings also may enjoy peace. Man must know his position as compared with his surroundings and should learn how to act in the different phases of life he is thrown into in the world. If a person fears the Almighty Creator and is afraid of breaking the religious law, he will be miles away from sin and would not commit crimes even secretly. He does not refrain from sin because a law officer may happen to note his actions, but because he knows that the Almighty Creator sees him no matter where he may hide himself.[72]

Taqwā and accountability are themes that are woven into his lectures for those audience seeking a rational explanation of the Qur'ānic message of salvation. According to Mawlānā Siddiqui, the transformation of the human spirit is only possible if spirituality permeates the lives of people. Again, the term spirituality as explained elsewhere in the volume has a distinct Islamic connotation. It has reference in the Qur'ān, the sunnah and the lives of the *salaf.* Therefore, it would be a misnomer to suggest that Mawlānā Siddiqui's lectures are limited to the rational explanation of the Islamic teachings. On the contrary, his elaboration of the Islamic moral code, for example, is clear: *wahy* redefines the concept of morality as opposed to man's liberal interpretations that offer no guarantee of peace and stability for society in general.

Islam in France: A Brief Survey

The history of Muslim settlement from North Africa in France dates back to the French imperialism in the Maghreb region. Like the British rule, the French colonial order attempted to perpetuate its hegemony and its culture on the North African Muslims. Opposition to French rule was consistent as is evident from the *jihād* movement of Shaykh Muhammad al-Khattabi (d.1963) of Morocco.[73] Like other

---

[72] Siddiqui, "Choice of One's Religion" in *The Muslim Digest:* November 1968: 3.

[73] Shaykh Khattabi was a *mujāhid* who represented a major political and strategic challenge to colonial rule. See "Muhammad ibn al-Karim al-Khattabi" in Alam, *100*

illustrious scholars, his experience in forming para-military organisations and his exceptional fighting qualities made him a worthy opponent to the otherwise well-trained European army.

The Muslim diaspora in France increased rapidly in the early twentieth century. Despite restrictions and discrimination by the French government, the Muslim communities in several cities organised themselves in order to retain their corporate Islamic identity. Paris in particular saw the emergence of Muslim organisations promoting Islamic education and *da'wah*. The number of *zawiyas* or sufi lodges increased substantially, thus retaining their sufi links with the existing orders in North Africa. In the 1950s the contributions of Sidi Cadour bin Ghabrit[74], a leading scholar consolidated the presence of Islam in Paris. His meeting with Mawlānā Siddiqui was a positive step in expanding the scope of *da'wah*. Mawlānā Siddiqui also met the veteran Moroccan leader, Shaykh Hadi al-Diouri who symbolised in his person the piety as well as the aspirations of the North African intelligentsia.[75]

During his brief stay in Paris, Mawlānā Siddiqui made extensive contacts with the Muslim activists and leading societies. His contribution is illustrative of his *ummatic* vision.

Mawlānā Siddiqui gave a comprehensive talk in polished Arabic and surveyed the missionary needs of Islam in general and the religious problems of the French-speaking Muslims in particular. He crystallised his argument by proposing the establishment of an Islamic Cultural Society which should undertake to launch a powerful Islamic literary movement in the French language. There was a discussion on the proposal, and all those present appointed a committee for the execution of the scheme. Mawlānā Siddiqui gave his own French *Catechism on Islam* for commencing the work of publications and donated 1000 francs to the society as a token of his love for the work.[76]

The *Catechism*[77]*on Islam* is a French translation of his popular *The*

Great Muslim Leaders of the Twentieth Century (New Delhi, 2005), 161-4.

[74] *The Ambassador of Peace*, 22.

[75] Ibid., 23.

[76] Ibid, 24.

[77] *Catechism* is a book giving a brief summary of the basic principles of Christianity in

Elementary Teachings of Islam which was originally written in English.

Islam to the West was Mawlānā Siddiqui's formulation of tabligh as a Qur'ānic paradigm. His methodology varied from country to country keeping in mind the multilayered cultural and religious traits of the respective Muslim communities. West Indies, for example, was a different landscape from the Western countries due to its strong link with the Indian subcontinent. In sum, his tabligh was in marked contrast to the approaches he adopted for Muslims living in East Asia.

---

a question-and-answer form.

Chapter 6

Moral and Spiritual Pursuits

The chapter examines the growth and development of two Muslim communities whose Islamic identity was in significant ways shaped by Mawlānā Siddiqui's tabligh. The period under review, 1930-50, illustrates the multiple strands of Islamic activism following the political developments in these regions. More importantly, the linkages through which the Islamic identity were forged are examined in the chapter.

Muslims in the Caribbean

The Muslim community in the post-indentured Caribbean witnessed several changes that influenced the character of their Islamic practices. As a way of institutionalising the faith, the community had established *masājid* (mosques), schools and several other organisations. Over the decades, foreign missionaries, particularly from the Indian subcontinent arrived in the Caribbean and imposed their interpretation of Islamic practices. The tension which arose resulted in the splintering of the community. As these streams of Islam evolved, key Islamic organisations were established at local and national levels.

These preliminary comments point out to the challenges Mawlānā Siddiqui and Mawlānā Ansari faced in their untiring efforts to reestablish unity among the disparate institutions across the Caribbean. Trinidad served as the focal point for the expansion of Islamic activities through the formation of the Anjuman Sunnat al-Jamaat[1] (AJSA) under the guidance of Mawlānā Siddiqui in 1937. Previously, the ʿulama from India imparted Islamic education in Urdu through which the linguistic and cultural links were maintained with

---

[1] The growth and development of the ASJA as a supreme body of Muslim affairs is discussed in the following articles: Omar Kasule, "Muslims in Trinidad and Tobago" in *Institute of Muslim Minority Affairs Journal*: 1986, 2-8; Aziza Javed, "A History of Islamic Groups in Trinidad" in *The E-Revolutionary*: September/October 2012.

their ancestral homeland. Parallel to these activities in the late 1920s, the Qadiani missionaries were making inroads in Trinidad, which posed a serious threat to Sunni Islam. A number of `ulama from India were employed in subsequent years to consolidate the Sunni cause.

The arrival of Mawlānā Siddiqui had a two-fold mission:

- To unite the various Muslim organisations under a central body.
- To forge links with South American Muslim bodies, principally those of British Guyana and Suriname.

These initiatives were aimed at fostering Islamic relations beyond the national boundaries.[2] The turning point of Islam and the transformation of Muslim life in Trinidad came with the visit of Mawlānā Siddiqui and Mawlānā Ansari who "gave new dimension to the Islamic image and gave new meaning to religious obligation, values and cultural practices."[3] The performance of *salāh*, shari`ah-compliant dress code for women and Islamic education fell under the purview of Mawlānā Siddiqui's *islāhi* (reformative) priorities. At the same time, he promoted *dhikr* as an exercise in spirituality. One of his major successes was his address to a crown of 7000 people at a rally organised by ASJA in the Queens Park Savanah, Port of Spain[4]. His impact on the crowd of different religious affiliations epitomised his pre-eminence as an orator. Like in several other countries, his public lectures inspired many non-Muslims to accept Islam. A case in point are the 'hundreds of conversions' at an address in Philippines.

According to Ahmad Alonto, Muslims in the Philippines in the middle of the twentieth century were on the brink of annihilation. The political upheaval in the country eroded the vestiges of Islamic consciousness and Muslims were placed in a precarious situation. The

---

[2] Kamal Hosein, *A Historical Review of the Anjuman Sunnat ul Jamaat Association*-ASJA.
[3] Pamphlet: AJSA Spiritual Development (n.d.)
http://www. caribbeanmuslims.com/articles/1131/3/A
[4] Kamal Hosein, *A Historical Review...* 1-2.

visit by Mawlānā Siddiqui and Mawlānā Ansari was an awakening call for the Philippino Muslims. His incisive analysis brings into sharper light about these *muballighs'* distinguished services to the cause of Islam:

Unexpectedly, a seemingly unimportant visit to the Philippine was made in 1949 by Mawlānā Abdul Aleem Siddiqui of Pakistan, accompanied by his assistant, Dr Fazlur Rahman Ansari. It is still sort of mystery as to why of all nations of the world, they chose to come to the Philippines, which was still bearing the ravages of war. As to why the trip had been made at that very opportune time when the Philippino Muslims, silent in their isolation and perhaps totally unaware, needed vitally an awakening call, which likewise could not be ascertained at this writing (of the article).

The visit produced a chain reaction among the Muslims of the country as it started movements for reorientation among the enlightened section. The Muslim Association of the Philippines - long dormant - was revitalised and became the first national socioreligious organ of these Muslims. It made contacts and re-established intercommunication with the Arab world and other Muslim states after the centuries-long disruption and isolation.[5]

Establishment of Islamic Organisations

Mawlānā Siddiqui mooted the idea of the Intercolonial Muslim organisations after his visit to British Guyana, Suriname, Barbados, etc. in 1950. His appeal for their establishment was based on the belief that a united front could perpetuate Islamic beliefs and practices in their pristine forms. Moreover, Mawlānā Siddiqui maintained that a progressive *ummah* could work successfully within these institutional frameworks to advance the cause of tabligh. The ASJA was representative of this trend that he suggested for the Muslim communities. During his six-month stay in Trinidad, Mawlānā Siddiqui made important contributions in the following areas:

- Hundreds of non-Muslims accepted Islam, some of

---

[5] Mohammad Manzoor Alam, *100 Great Muslim Leaders of the 20th Century*, 359-63. Cf. Alonto, "The Muslim Struggle in South Philippine" in *Muslim World League Journal*: July/Aug. 1996, 30-31.

whom rose to prominence in governmental ministries.

- His lectures captivated Muslims, Christian and Hindus who paid glowing tributes to him as *The Roving Ambassador of Peace.*
- He conducted regular Islamic classes (*dars*) at the Jami' Masjid Hall in Port of Spain. Among his students, the following individuals played a leading role in the Muslim affairs of Trinidad: Haji Mohammed Ibrahim (President of ASJA), Mohammed Yusuf Mitchell (Government architect and prominent Islamic worker) and Kamaluddin Mohammed (Government minister and acting Prime Minister).[6]

---

[6] Wahid Ali, *His Eminence Mawlana Shah Abdul Aleem Siddiqui* (Trinidad, n.d.).

Lecture Series

Mawlānā Siddiqui delivered a series of impactful lectures in Trinidad. Under the auspices of the AJSA he was able to reach out to a broader constituency comprising the `ulama, professionals and social activists. In this perspective, his reception at the Intercolonial Muslim Conference in the Jami Masjid Hall, Port of Spain inspired the establishment of the World Islamic Mission (WIM). In a similar vein, the welcome function was a landmark event that saw the beginning of the Muslim community in Trinidad taking the lead in unifying the disparate organisations under a central body. In this respect, the visionary leadership and guiding spirit of Mawlānā Siddiqui are impressed in these words:

> The welcome function for His Eminence was held at Queen's Park Savannah on 12 March 1950. Many thousands attended – Muslims and non-Muslims. In the audience there were government representatives and members of the diplomatic corp. At this event a soul-stirring recitation of the Qur'ān was rendered by Qari Ali bin Khamis of Zanzibar. Throughout his stay in Trinidad, and through tireless effort and dedication, Islamic propagation was always at the foremost priority, and to the Muslim masses His Eminence expounded on the principles of the *Ahl al-Sunnah.*

Two lectures mark out his approach to the challenges and future prospects of the Muslim community. These insightful counsels were meant to reawaken the dormant spirits of the Muslims and to realign their lives according to the noble conduct of the Holy Prophet (pbuh). For Mawlānā Siddiqui, societal reform has its roots in eradicating excessive rituals and practices associated with the simple acts of worship. The celebration of Eid is a case in point. Mawlānā Siddiqui deplored the overindulgence displayed by Muslim families on this occasion:

> O you who live in palatial buildings and luxurious homes, who rest on soft beds and fashionable couches, who ride in

costly cars! Think for a while of those unfortunate brothers and sisters also, who are unable to get a square meal or a full coverage of their body.

O you who dress in fashionable clothes and who decorate the dead earth of your houses with all sorts of vanities! Remember, your dress and your luxuries will not bring you honour while the rising generations of your community are totally deprived of that education which alone can make them honourable in this world as well as in the Hereafter. You will be regarded as truly honourable only when your community as a whole will be honourable, and only when it possesses faith, knowledge and *deeni* education.

In the same light, Mawlānā Siddiqui critiques the dissident voices in the community who engage in 'petty practices' that pose a serious risk to the unity of the *ummah*. They do not regard the Flood of irreligion and apostasy (*irtidād*) 'advancing in the world with all its fury.' The consequences are disastrous: "Moral vices are increasing at a rapid pace. The very foundations of religious outlook are under fire over the world."

Another perceptive lecture titled *The Law of Mutual Cooperation* is a deep reflection on Mawlānā Siddiqui's presentation of unity. The learned scholar draws upon the Qur'ānic verses to demonstrate the unity of purpose in the universe. Likewise, the cosmic unity is a pointed reference to the law of mutual cooperation for mankind. Essentially, mankind has the moral freedom to lead a life of obedience according to the divine scheme of things. On a similar note, Mawlānā Siddiqui reminds the Muslim community that worship, particularly *salāh* and *dhikr* are not rituals performed in a spiritless manner. These acts of *'ibādah* are meant to develop a spiritual affinity for and consciousness about the presence of Allah. Thus, the levels of spiritual growth require a positive plan to earn Allah's pleasure. The core message is clear:

We must try our best to accomplish the great task of spiritual and moral reform. We must carry the message of Allah to every home. We must preach the right type of faith in Allah and the higher moral values at the home and the school, at the market place and other places. Sadly, centuries of growing neglect have already played havoc. We had not succeeded in removing the evil effects of World War One when the Second World War burst upon us with all its miseries. Humanity seems to have forgotten that it cannot be rescued unless the root cause is removed. The warmongers are busy in deceiving mankind that religion is the cause of strife and war.[7]

Literary Contributions

In the field of Islamic education, Mawlānā Siddiqui made appreciable contributions. He produced the following books for both laymen and intellectuals. The motivation for preparing *The Elementary Teachings of Islam* is self- explanatory:

Preface to the *Third Edition*

It is a living miracle of the truth of Islam that, though it has neither a backing of huge missionary corporations, nor does it have any authentic literature in foreign languages, yet people after people, attracted to it by its inherent magnetic force, keep on embracing this religion of love and universal brotherhood. For, whenever either by dint of personal research and study or by a chance contact with, and the consequent guidance of a real Muslim theologian, they learn the true facts about Islam, the invariable conclusion they arrive at is that Islam is a very simple religion and all its teachings are perfectly rational and in complete consonance with the laws of nature.

The necessity of the presentation of the elementary teachings of Islam, explaining its cardinal articles of faith and the fundamental principles in the simplest possible English language is therefore obvious. Such a publication would not only serve to acquaint the English–knowing new Muslims with the essentials of Faith. [It] would also supply the long felt need of a handy book for imparting the rudiments of Islam to the Muslim children of those countries where

---

[7] Cited in *ASJA Eid al-Fitr Brochure*, 1967.

the English language rules supreme. Children are sent away to these schools using English as a medium of instruction, without having any knowledge, whatsoever, of their religion.[8]

This edition based on the Hanafi *fiqh* (Islamic jurisprudence) drew a positive response. Mohammed Ibrahim of Trinidad undertook the cost of printing of the book which was then widely distributed to the Islamic institutions. Much earlier the draft of the manuscript was serialised and published by *The Real Islam.* In the subsequent editions there appeared several changes to the original text of the work. For example, in the Australian edition the title was changed to *Genuine Islam*, ostensibly to meet the needs of the growing Muslim community of different backgrounds. The popularity of this work can be gleaned from the multiple editions in Egypt. In many instances, a print run of 5000 copies was distributed in different parts of the world for *da'wah* purpose. Again, the changed format of the text without the author's permission was glaringly evident. The commercial factor for many publishers illustrates the high volume demand of *The Elementary Teachings* in many parts of the world. The French edition was brought out by the Halqa i-Qaderiyah in Mauritius and widely circulated among the French readers by Egyptian admirers. The wide network of Mawlānā Siddiqui's tabligh outreach activitities prompted him to prepare a Shafi' version for readers in Colombo, Singapore, Java, etc.

The tenor of Mawlānā Siddiqui's Islamic activities extended to Islamic literature as well. This period also saw a steady growth of Muslim professionals in various sectors. They, too, were influenced by the liberal trends of Islamic intellectual thought during their study abroad, particularly in the Arab world which provided alternative readings to the traditional understanding of Islam. In view of these developments, there was a pressing need for Islamic literature which could suit their intellectual temperament. Mawlānā Siddiqui wrote *The History of the Codification of Islamic Law*[9], a testament to his profound learning in Qur'ānic and hadith studies. This work developed out of the lectures and public speeches delivered by Mawlānā Siddiqui in Trinidad during his world tabligh

---

[8] This work had seen several reprints during its first publication in 1934. A French translation was also completed in the 1940s.

[9] Siddiqui, *The History of the Codification of Islamic Law* (Karachi, 1982).

tour (1949-50). Two important points emerge from this work:

- The systematic study of hadith developed as a scientific discipline and its legacy continues to shape the Islamic discourse in the twenty first century.
- *Ijtihād* (independent legal reasoning) is a scholarly output and a rigorous discipline which is derived from the vast corpus of Islamic sources.

Therefore, any attempt to arbitrarily exercise *ijtihād* without the mastery of these *'ulum* as outlined by the Islamic scholars (past and present) compromises the intellectual legacy of the Islamic civilisation. According to Mawlānā Siddiqui, these persons dabbling with *ijtihad* matters discredit *taqlid* (adherence to authoritative guidance by the Imams) in order to establish their 'own hegemony and leadership' and thus ascribe false motives to the Imams.[10] His conclusive argument is based on the following Qur'ānic verse (*āyah*):

> ... Say: "Are those equal, those who know and those who do not know?

A telling example of the liberal views presented by the anti-*taqlid* scholars is summed up in these words:

> In mentioning this classification of Islamic sciences, my purpose is to give just an idea to my simple-minded brothers and sisters who are being thrown into confusion concerning the Islamic legal schools by certain unconscientious people, who wish to establish their own hegemony and leadership, and hence they propagate all sorts of confusion. Some of them have ulterior sectarian ends to gain. Most of them are ignorant of Islamic sciences and the safest way they can adopt their leadership is that of denial of the validity or the necessity of these sciences.[11]

---

[10] Ibid., 32-40.
[11] Ibid., 54.

According to Mawlānā Siddiqui, critics of hadith literature make egocentric claims. For instance, the founder of Qadianism, Mirza Ghulam Ahmad distorted the *ahādith* to suit his nefarious designs. He makes the following assessment of the Mirza's divine calling:

> [When] Mirza Ghulam Ahmad of Qadian found that his claims could not be comfortably lodged in genuine traditions (*ahādith*), he fell back upon the arbitrary association that he was the divinely appointed judge and could, therefore, accept any tradition (hadith) he liked and reject any other he did not like, the principles of logical and historical criticism notwithstanding.

The impact of Mawlānā Siddiqui's tabligh tour in the Caribbean produced manifold results. He highlighted the challenges faced by the Muslim communities and the practical efforts they should undertake to restore confidence about the primacy of the Qur'ān and the sunnah in their lives. Likewise, the Muslim communities were urged to build mosques, *maktabs* and organise themselves under a central umbrella body in order to maintain the spirit of unity. According to Mawlānā Siddiqui, divisive elements hampered efforts to create a dynamic society. It was in response to this concern that his rallying call '*Back to the Qur'ān and Sunnah*' must be understood.

Islam in Singapore

Mawlānā Siddiqui undertook his first visit to Malaya in 1927 which formerly included Singapore and Malaysia. He began his journey for "unity among his fellow Muslims and global harmony among religions of the world."[12] Singapore, a cosmopolitan country teeming with many languages and diversity of cultures, was on the threshold of a new era in terms of its entrepreneurial progress and urban redevelopment. The establishment of the All-Malaya

---

[12] *Footprints on the Journey of Human Fellowship: The History of Jami'yah* (Singapore, n.d.), 55.

136

Missionary Society (which later was renamed Jami'yah in 1932)[13] articulated the visionary leadership and the collective will of the Muslim community with different racial and cultural backgrounds. When Mawlānā Siddiqui arrived there during this period, Muslim leaders across the spectrum were "attracted by a certain charisma that he had crowded around him and gave him assurance of their support for ideals."[14]

He also founded *Real Islam* magazine which contained articles that had relevance to the aspirations of the Muslim community.

Among the pioneers of the Society, Syed Ibrahim Alsagoff,[15] played a prominent role in its establishment. Owing to his untiring efforts, the Society maintained transnational links especially with Saudi Arabia. It was Syed Ibrahim who was instrumental in securing donations from King Faisal of Saudi Arabia towards the construction of the Jam'iyah building in 1955.[16]

Challenges in Singapore: Mawlānā Ansari's Contributions

It was during the latter part of 1937 when Mawlānā Ansari was deputed on his first tabligh mission by Mawlānā Siddiqui. The rise of evangelist activities in the Far East Asia especially in Malaya Peninsula necessitated the presence of an articulate scholar who could stem the tide of this growing problem among the Muslim masses in this region. In his *Welcome Address* in Singapore he categorically stated that he came as the ambassador of the intellectual empire of Islam to negotiate for reinvigorating and reconstructing the Muslim intellectual life.[17] In other words, Singapore and by extension the Malay Peninsula required the renaissance of faith in all aspects of their lives. His pertinent remark about Singapore's future Islamic role vis-à-vis the decline of Muslim countries in other parts of the world reflected his sense of optimism.

---

[13] Ibid., 57. Cf. *The Muslim Digest*: Jan/Feb 1996, 177.

[14] Ibid.

[15] Syed Ibrahim Alsagoff belonged to an aristocratic family (*sharif*) who hailed from Hadramaut (Yemen).

[16] *Footprints ...*, 63.

[17] Foreword by M.A. Alsagoff, in Ansari, *Islam and Christianity in the Modern World*, (Karachi, 1965).

Mawlānā Ansari was ready to assist in raising up a great new edifice of Islamic civilisation among people "who entered the flow of Islam at a time when the Islamic world had lost its initial vitality and was on the way to succumb to the cultural onslaught of the anti-Western civilisation and could not therefore, enjoy the opportunity of building up enduring and vigorous national Islamic traditions and culture."[18] Therefore, he focused on three areas which could consolidate the presence of the Muslim community in this region:

- Providing constructive forms in the activities of the All-Malaya Muslim Missionary Society.
- Serving as honorary editor of *Genuine Islam* magazine through which he contributed a number of articles on comparative religion and contemporary issues germane to Muslims in the Malaysian peninsula.
- Organising the Far East Asia missionary front with clearly-defined goals.

In Singapore, the Christian missionary activities gained momentum, resulting in the proliferation of polemical literature. The onslaught against Islam as a universal religion intensified, judging by the spate of literature devoted to its missionary cause. Mawlānā Siddiqui's choice of deputing Mawlānā Ansari was indicative of his confidence in the latter's academic expertise. His critical study of comparative religions at Aligarh Muslim University prepared him to respond to the vituperative literature of Christian missionaries.

According to Mawlānā Ansari, the logical arguments developed by him in the monograph *Trends in Christianity* perturbed his Christian friends. They could not possibly challenge his contentions "except that any interpretation on the conclusions of researchers was biased and defective." Likewise, his refutation of *Muhammedans and Christianity - Twentieth Century* by Archbishop Wand of Brisbane (Australia) was reproduced in *The Straits Times* of Singapore (1938). He argued that the Archbishop's misrepresentations of Islam under the

---

[18] Ibid.

guise of mutual understanding of faiths only polarised Muslim and Christian communities. It was in the spirit of objectivity that the book was written to "clear the position of Islam of the charges levelled against it by the Archbishop and others of his way of thinking."[19]

Likewise, the attempts by Muslims to be governed by Muslim Personal Law drew the ire of the media. In 1938 a Bill meant to establish the supremacy of Islamic law in Malaya was introduced in the Federal Status legislature council. The entire press dominated by non-Muslims launched a scathing attack on the Federated Muslim States (FMS) Mohammedan Offences Bill. Among the press the powerful *The Straits Times of Singapore* led an editorial campaign captioned "Go to Mosque or Go to Prison" provoking a series of correspondence and articles undermining the proposed Bill. Mawlānā Ansari wrote a forceful reply in *The Straits Times* to refute the arguments of all the opponents of the Bill. The editor who was instrumental in writing a scathing editorial was deeply impressed by his rational exposition that he wrote another editorial, seemingly an apology and indirectly a tacit acknowledgement of Mawlānā Ansari's academic stature.[20] Thus Mawlānā Ansari in collaboration with Mawlānā Siddiqui resisted these campaigns which sought to undermine the shari`ah provisions in Malaya.

Inter-Religious Organisation

Mawlānā Siddiqui's last visit to Singapore in 1949-50 was a productive phase to his tabligh initiatives. His global mission culminated in the establishment of the Inter-Religious Organisation (IRO) movement on 18 March 1949. He said that he would like to see mutual love and cooperation between religious leaders of different faiths:

> There are undoubtedly differences between the various religions but as a student of comparative religion I have come

---

[19] Ansari, *Trends in Christianity* (Singapore, 1938), 4-5.
[20] A detailed discussion on the debate appears in *The Minaret*: 1974, 19.

to the conclusion that the religions of the world are united as far as the fundamental principles are concerned. The differences that there are, are largely of different interpretations. The Holy Qur'ān says that all divine religions are one and have the same source.[21]

Moral regeneration, according to Mawlānā Siddiqui, should permeate the scope and function of the Inter-Religious Organisation (IRO). He observed:

> As far as the common evils and accepted moral principles are concerned, no religion could have any difference and in the spirit of tolerance and sympathy and the desire to establish peace, all of them are one. The task of the religious leaders was to let the followers of each and every religion know the teachings of other religions, so that a spirit of fellowship might be created among them and so that they could all work together to spread the accepted moral principles and fight the common evils.[22]

The outcome of this conference was the consensus reached by the leaders from other faiths.[23] If truth was viewed through a prism, the jewels of faith would reflect many shining facets. Therefore, peace and goodwill were organically linked to the spiritual rearmament that Mawlānā Siddiqui advocated to the delegates in the Conference.

A more telling example of the IRO's commitment to the vision set out by Mawlānā Siddiqui was echoed by the Commissioner-General of Singapore, Mr Malcolm Mac- Donald. He remarked:

> [The] solution to mankind's present troubles lies in making our interest in economics and politics subordinate to religion

---

[21] Ibid.

[22] *The Straits Times*. Saturday, March, 19, 1949.

[23] The views of leading figures from other faiths reinforced the need for moral and spiritual reawakening.

and the sublime things of the past. What is needed more than anything else is a spiritual revival in man, arousing of a conscience, and a submission not only to the rule of law but the rule of God."[24]

Correspondence with the Vatican

The twin concept of moral regeneration and spiritual rearmament was reiterated in a letter written by Mawlānā Siddiqui to Pope Pius XII of the Vatican in 1950. The essence of his correspondence is encapsulated in these words:

> As your Lordship must be well-aware, the avalanche of Marxist philosophy is descending upon the world with its full weight and with great speed. It has already crushed religious activity out of existence from nearly half   the earth and bids to swallow the rest in   due course. The reservoir of faith in higher spiritual values seems to be drying fast.
> On the other hand, the general wave of moral laxity which originated in the West after the Industrial Revolution and which followed Western influences across Asia and Africa, has affected nearly the whole of humanity. The intelligentsia as well as the masses in every country seems to be in revolt - active or passive - against the accepted moral values. Humanity is in the grips of a mighty crisis and religious leadership is on trial. The process of disintegration in the domains of spiritual faith and moral action is developing in a manner which no religious worker can afford to look upon with equanimity and watch as a passive spectator.[25]

An important point clearly sets out Mawlānā Siddiqui's presentation of inter-faith dialogue: unity of religion does not presuppose syncretism (*wahdat al-adyān*). There is no apologia in Mawlānā Siddiqui's claims that in terms of religious stability, "[the] world of Islam is still perhaps the strongest unit and Islam still

---

[24] Ibid.
[25] Mohamed, *The Roving Ambassador of Peace*, 104.

possesses the initiative and remedy."[26] Mawlānā Siddiqui formulated practical steps for leaders of world religions to achieve the objectives contained in the resolutions adopted at the IRO conference:

o   They should set up a model of high-mindedness and tolerance for bringing about harmony and good fellowship among the masses of the world.

o   They should work shoulder to shoulder for wiping out the evils of race and racial prejudices and of economic exploitation and for bringing about a healthy order of human society.

o   They should cooperatively work, with the assistance of the statesmen and politicians, for introducing the moral education in all the institutions of learning, for propagating the accepted moral virtues, and for removing the agreed moral vices.[27]

To this end, a spirit of mutual tolerance and respect was indispensable for a new world order as discussed by Mawlānā Siddiqui.

Mawlānā Siddiqui served as the guiding spirit to the establishment of IR. His frame of reference was the Qur'ān and the sunnah, which gave the unequivocal declaration about the message for humanity. His speech which is contained in *The Contribution of Religion to Peace* sets out his goal of tabligh in the changed sociopolitical settings.[28] In many ways, he strengthened the scope and function of Islam's universal role with the clarity of vision and purpose, a singular contribution that carved a niche for himself as one of leading voice of Islamic revival in the twentieth century.

Mawlānā M.H. Babu

Among the luminaries who carried out Mawlānā Siddiqui's

---

[26] Ibid.

[27] Siddiqui, *What is Communism* (Karachi, n.d.), 10.

[28] H.B. Amstutz and Ahmad Ibrahim (editors), *The Contribution of Religion to Peace* (Singapore, 1949).

pioneering efforts, Mawlānā M.H. Babu (d. 2002)[29] deserves special mention. His academic activities reflected his sterling services to the organisation (IRO). He was inspired to take an active role in Muslim affairs of Singapore after attending the lectures of Mawlānā Siddiqui in 1950. Furthermore, he was a veteran and an esteemed member of the IRO and was nominated to represent the organisation in the interfaith dialogues[30] which were held locally and abroad. He maintained a cordial relationship with Mawlānā Ansari during his tabligh tours to Singapore.[31]

The Jami'yah (Muslim Missionary Society) represented the aspirations of Mawlānā Siddiqui who during his regular visits to Singapore mooted out the unity blueprint for the multi- ethnic society based on the Qur'ān and the sunnah. By the same token, A.A. Siddiqui Mosque was built in recognition of his pioneering work of spreading the faith and the message of peace in Singapore and elsewhere around the world.

Islamic Missionary Literature: An Assessment

Mawlānā Siddiqui witnessed the rising tide of Western civilisation which threatened the religious fabric of the *ummah*. He expressed alarm at the "anti-religious thought of the West"[32] that was gradually making inroads into the Muslim countries. In its early years Western materialism challenged metaphysical thought and influenced a marginal segment of the Westernised Muslims. But its fully fledged materialistic form of life was spawned by 'Marxian Communism' which in turn laid the foundation of atheistic thought.[33] The consequences of these ideological systems on Muslim culture were alarming. Mawlānā Siddiqui reminded the Muslims that the heretical movements in Muslim history were refuted by eminent scholars like Imām Ahmad bin Hanbal and Imām Abu Muhammad Ghazali. Their

---

[29] *Singapore's Past 'ulama: M.H. Babu Sahib*
http://ibnyahya.com/2002/moulavi-mhbabu-sahib
[30] Ibid. 4.
[31] Ibid. 3.
[32] Siddiqui, "Need for High Class Islamic Missionary Literature" in *The Muslim Digest:* 1952, 49.
[33] Ibid., 50.

intellectual endeavours resulted in the "defeat of these heresies so thoroughly that not a trace of them was left."[34] Therefore, an intellectual movement had to be initiated "not only to meet the attacks of materialistic literature but to sweep them off."[35] The intellectual reconstruction of Islamic thought as developed by Mawlānā Siddiqui was visible on two levels: critique of Western thought and the production of literature in English with strong Islamic ethos.

The following books written during this period are illustrative of the Islamic renaissance movements with which Mawlānā Siddiqui was associated:

- Muhammad Asad, *Islam at the Crossroads.*[36] A cogent presentation of the sunnah in the context of Asad's critique of Western civilisation.

- Shakib Arsalan, *Our Decline: its Causes and Remedies.*[37] An incisive analysis of the factors contributing to the Muslim decline in comparison to European sovereignty. This book became a masterpiece in the 1930s amid the political upheavals in the Muslim world.

- Muhammad Iqbal: *Reconstruction of Religious Thought in Islam.*[38] A collection of lectures originally delivered in 1928, Iqbal attempts to contextualise modern thought in the light of Islamic philosophy This classic work contains certain modernist views[39] which have not met the approval of the leading scholars of Islam.

In his writings Mawlānā Siddiqui makes reference to the above scholars to present his rational exposition of the Islamic beliefs and

---

[34] Ibid., 51.

[35] Ibid.

[36] Muhammad Asad, *Islam at the Crossroads* (Lahore, 1934).

[37] Shakib Arsalan, *Our Decline: its Causes and Remedies* (Kuala Lumpur, 2004).

[38] Muhammad Iqbal, *Reconstruction of Religious Thought in Islam* (Lahore, 1962).

[39] Notwithstanding Sayyid Abul Hasan Ali Nadwi's profound admiration of Iqbal's thought, he disagreed with certain concepts elucidated by the latter in his book. See Nadwi, *Glory of Iqbal* (Lucknow, 1973), 18.

practices. He provides a clearly-defined explanation of his Islamic views which he considers to be authoritative and representative of the illustrious scholars of the past. His standpoint is in marked opposition to the modernists whose writings are influenced by Western intellectual thought.

Apart from his thorough acquaintance with Western sources on philosophy and science, Mawlānā Siddiqui had an excellent grasp of Qur'ānic studies. He was familiar with the translations of the Qur'ān by Orientalists. His comment on John Rodwell's translation *The Koran* based on his conversation with George Bernard Shaw is revealing:

His Eminence: There is no doubt that Mr. Rodwell has expanded a great deal of energy and industry in translating the chapters of the Qur'ān in their chronological order, but as his knowledge of the Arabic literature and Islamic history was not sufficiently wide and profound, a considerable number of translated passages are so misleading and contain such flagrant mistakes that they are likely to create wrong impressions about Islam.[40]

In his review of Rodwell's translation, the noted Qur'ānic scholar, Abdur Raheem Kidwai states that this work (Rodwell's) is aimed at creating doubts about the authenticity and veracity of the Qur'ānic text. Even his comments on several verses (*āyat*) are "reflective of his malicious intent."[41]

Two translations of the Qur'ān written by Mawlānā Siddiqui's contemporaries are strongly recommended. Marmaduke Pickthall's *The Meaning of the Glorious Qur'ān* and Abdullah Yusuf Ali's, *Translation and Commentary of the Qur'ān* are considered to be authentic translations by Muslim scholars.[42] Many of the scholarly works written during the period under discussion were marked by rational thinking. This was a 'gestation phase' during which responses to Western culture especially in the domain of intellectual thought were assuming coherent forms. Likewise, the periodicals devoted to the cause of

---

[40] Siddiqui, *A Shavian and a Theologian*, 12.

[41] Abdur Raheem Kidwai, *Translating the Untranslatable: A Critical Guide to 60 English Translations of the Qur'ān*, 247.

[42] The insightful reviews of both these translations appear in Kidwai, *Translating the Untranslatable*: Pickthall (1930), 11-5 and Yusuf Ali (1934- 7), 16-34. Cf. Siddiqui, *Quest for True Happiness*, 9-10.

Islamic renaissance also shared the common traits of exemplary scholarship.

Islamic Magazines

Genuine Islam and Voice of Islam magazines published under the patronage of Mawlānā Siddiqui illustrated the trends of superior scholarship. Alongside the production of forceful Islamic literature was the urgency of monthly magazines to promote Islamic issues in a contemporary setting. To this end, the publication of *Genuine Islam* in 1936 was of immense importance. Mawlānā Siddiqui's tabligh pursuits were visible in many facets of Muslim life in Singapore. The unfailing support he received from influential individuals reinforced his status as *The Roving Ambassador of Peace*. The interest evinced in *Genuine Islam* may be gleaned from the following information:

A new Muslim magazine, entitled *Genuine Islam* has been founded in Singapore and the first number came out this month (January 1936). The editor is Mr Khalil Anwari and the publisher Syed Ibrahim bin Omar Alsagoff. The first number which came out contains a most interesting interview with George Bernard Shaw written by that eminent scholar and divine, Mawlānā Muhammad Abdul Aleem Siddiqui.

Seldom has the present reviewer come upon a clearer and more informative discussion of the Islamic religion that is reported in this meeting between two of the finest brains between East and West. Our generous patron Syed Alsagoff, the high-minded, benevolent and scholarly scion of the well-known Arab aristocratic family of Alsagoff has definitely undertaken to defray the expenses of the publication sufficiently long to make any magazine self-supporting.[43]

The editorial of the first issue of *Genuine Islam* outlined its mission statement: to present Islam in its pristine form in a contemporary idiom so that humanity may benefit from the ideals the religion of Islam has to offer.[44] The magazine published a series of articles that

---

[43] *Genuine Islam*: vol. 1: 1, 3.

[44] Maryam Jameelah (d. 2012), the famous Islamic author of books defending Islamic orthodoxy says that the books written from the early 1930s have been characterised

could be considered as the authoritative voice of the 'constructive aspects of Islam'[45] and could highlight a positive insight into the Muslim culture.

The pool of articles highlighted the progressive approaches[46] adopted by *Genuine Islam*. Eminent intellectuals like Khalid Sheldrake wrote articles of merit about the universal message of Islam and the Holy Prophet (pbuh) and his teachings.[47] Other articles surveyed the Islamic civilisation in Europe[48] and the future of *da'wah* in the West. An interesting feature of the magazine was the personal accounts of conversion to Islam[49] by distinguished scholars like Muhammad Asad (formerly Leipold Weiss).[50] In sum, *Genuine Islam* attempted to maintain a noteworthy balance in its projection of the message of Islam. Traditional `ulama like Sayyid Sulayman Nadwi contributed articles on the teachings of the Holy Prophet (pbuh). His compilation of lectures entitled *Muhammad The Ideal Prophet*[51] received critical acclaim in the Muslim world. Likewise, Iqbal's monograph *Islam and Ahmadism*[52] was serialised and served as an intellectual refutation to the Ahmadi beliefs.

Mawlānā Siddiqui also contributed illuminating articles which were interwoven with his dimensions of tabligh. In *Islam - The Golden Mean* he addressed the predicament faced by Muslims to interpreting the Islamic message as a harbinger of hope for humanity. He observed:

> Islam depreciates the separation of material from spiritual progress for it adopts the medium course for a Muslim. Thus, increased economic and social prosperity side by side with

---

by excellent scholarly traditions. See Maryam Jameelah, *Islam and Modernism* (Lahore, 1975), 233-8.

[45] Pamphlet: *Genuine Islam* (Singapore, n.d.), 1-3.

[46] Khalil Anwari, 'Ourselves' in *Genuine Islam*: Singapore, January 1936, 2-4.

[47] On Khalid Sheldrake's contribution to Islamic activities in England, *he Infidel*, 114, 130-1. Cf. Khan, *Great Muslims of the West*, 433-4.

[48] *Genuine Islam*, vol. 1: 5.

[49] Ibid., vol. 1: 12.

[50] A two-volume assessment of Asad's intellectual contributions is a useful study on this versatile scholar. See Ikram Chaghatai, *Europe's Gift to Islam*, 2 vols. (Lahore, 2006).

[51] Sayyid Sulayman Nadwi, *Muhammad, The Ideal Prophet* (Lucknow, 1976).

[52] *Genuine Islam:* vol. 5-7.

increased progress in the study of arts and sciences signifies an advancement which is more vital. These sciences should help him to penetrate the true essence of [life] and appreciate the intrinsic value of Allah Almighty's blessings and lead him to bow down his head before Him.[53]

Again, the relationship between science and religion is emphasised:

Scientific progress clearly indicates that a human being can differentiate between good and evil, thus imparting a lesson on human responsibilities. (It is) religion that provides guidance in this matter. Hence the progress of science and religion are complementary to each other.[54]

Mawlānā Siddiqui further states that as science and technology progresses, the revealed truth mentioned in the Qur'ān will unfold with the passage of time.[55]

In line with the intellectual movement initiated by Mawlānā Siddiqui were the thought-provoking articles written by Mawlānā Ansari for *Genuine Islam*. In a three-part series *Muhammad: The Ideal Reformer* he makes a comparative study of the Holy Prophet's (pbuh) contributions in the background of Orientalism. The following extracts summarise the theme of the articles:

The Holy Prophet (pbuh) came and reformed one by one all the evils which had crept into the various religions of the world. He proclaimed that the Message given to him by Allah superseded all the previous messages as they had lost their original purity and that his Message contained all the good points of the various creeds of the world, and the study of comparative religion in modern times has perfectly confirmed

---

[53] Siddiqui, "Al-Islam: The Via Media. The Golden Mean" in *Genuine Islam*: vol. 1:1, 1.
[54] Ibid., vol 1: 6-7.
[55] "Religion and Scientific Progress of the World" in *Genuine Islam*: February 1936, 8.

this claim. Some Christian authors opine that he claimed to be a teacher only to the Arabs and not to all mankind but let them revise their opinion in the face of the explicit enunciation in the Qur'ān in these words:

Proclaim! (or read!) In the name of Your Lord and Cherisher, who created-Created man, out of a (mere) clot of congealed blood: Proclaim! And Your Lord is Most Bountiful,-He who taught (the use of) the pen-Taught man that which he knew not.

The Message is a true Gospel for the uplift of humanity. It speaks of the bounty of Allah which He was going to confer on all His creatures by ushering in a new era of human progress. It predicts the dawn of a new age in which humanity will come to know of certain great implements of human progress - the Age of Modern Science.[56]

In Chapter 4, reference was made to Mawlānā Siddiqui's popularity in the Arab world, especially in Egypt. He was instrumental in giving shape to the unity of the *madhāhib* (taqrib) initiatives which served as a matrix for the interfaith movement based in Singapore. The address by the Rector of Al-Azhar University, Shaykh Muhammad Mustafa Al-Maraghi (d. 1945)[57] to the World Congress of Faith reinforced Mawlānā Siddiqui's consistent efforts in this regard. Entitled *Universal Fellowship*, Shaykh Al-Maraghi traces the factors that have led to moral degeneration and religious anarchy in the world. He deplores the 'religious tyranny' that has now exhumed the shameful past with all its horrors and defilements.[58] Against these bleak conditions, there is renewed hope that the religious figures from all faiths can play an important role in removing the past injustices inflicted against humanity. There is no doubt, Shaykh Al-Maraghi asserts, that the principles of Islam embrace the

---

[56] Ansari, "Muhammad The Ideal Reformer " in *Genuine Islam*: March- May, 1936.

[57] Shaykh Maraghi was active in encouraging substantive reform to the curriculum of Al-Azhar. For his contributions to the various facets of Islamic reform, see Zebiri, *Mahmud Shaltut and Islamic Modernism*, 18-20, 24.

[58] Muhammad Mustafa Al-Maraghi, "Universal Fellowship" in *Genuine Islam*: October 1936, 4.

universal fellowship which advocates peace and order.[59] It is in the "perfect noble conduct of the Holy Prophet (pbuh) (*uswah al-hasanah*)" that the vision of the World Congress of Faith can be exemplified." Another influential scholar, Amir Shakib Arsalan of Lebanon also contributed articles on the social aspects of Islam[60] which he maintained created a relatively unified society marked by a high level of morality and social justice. Needless to say, *Genuine Islam* represented a non-sectarian and cosmopolitan outlook articulating the vision of Mawlānā Siddiqui's tabligh.

It would be worthwhile to make a comment on two leading figures connected to Mawlānā Siddiqui's publications. His private secretary Khalil Anwari is credited with the publication of the bi-monthly[61] magazine *Voice of Islam*[62] in Singapore. Under the guidance of Mawlānā Siddiqui he served as its editor. He accompanied Mawlānā Siddiqui in his first visit to South Africa in 1934. The highly popular *A Shavian and a Theologian*[63] was edited by him. It contains the interview between Mawlānā Siddiqui and George Bernard Shaw, the renowned Irish playwright on a visit to Mombasa, (Kenya) in 1935.

Justice M.T. Akbar belonged to the eminent Akbar family of Colombo, Sri Lanka, who were responsible for the erection of important Islamic institutions in the country.

He was a senior disciple (*murid*) of Mawlānā Siddiqui and made substantial contributions to promoting the teachings of Mawlānā Siddiqui. His articles which appeared in important Islamic journals reflected his training in *tasawwuf* and Qur'ānic studies.

It can be safely said that the seeds of intellectual activity planted by Afghani and other Islamic reformers gradually began to blossom during this crucial phase of Muslim history. Mawlānā Siddiqui's contribution in this field thus cannot be ignored.

---

[59] Ibid. 7. Al-Maraghi maintains that it is in the principles of Islam that the strongest pillars of universal fellowship rest.

[60] Ibid., vol 1:7.

[61] The first issue of *Voice of Islam* was published in 1937.

[62] The monograph was reproduced from the *Tanganyika Herald* of Mombasa by Makki Publications in 1935.

[63] Refer to various issues of *Genuine Islam and Ramadan Annual.*

Chapter 7

Lecture Tours in South Africa

The historic lecture tours by Mawlānā Siddiqui in South Africa in 1934 and 1952 respectively were landmark events for South African Muslims. He was described as a great servant of Islam and ambassador of peace.[1] His lecture tours in the country were linked to several leading Islam figures notable among whom was Mohammed Makki (d. 2003), founder of Makki Publications.

Makki Publications

Mohammed Makki studied in Meerut city under the tutelage of Mawlānā Siddiqui and his brother, Mawlānā Ahmad Mukhtar Siddiqui. He came to South Africa in the mid-1920s with his father Essop Suleman Vadachia. His association with Mawlānā Siddiqui was further strengthened when he brought the latter for a lecture visit to South Africa in 1934. In that year Makki Publications was founded and Mawlānā Siddiqui served as its first patron. The title of 'Makki' was conferred upon him by his revered mentor.[2]

Makki was responsible for printing publications such as *Five Pillars, Paknews, The Muslim Digest,* an organ of the International Union of Islamic service, founded in Durban in 1950, and published by Makki Publications. He served as its first editor.[3] The *Muslim Digest's* primary aim was to "extend the Digest into all parts of the Muslim world for the purpose of inspiring and enriching the lives of those who read it, and to bring the Muslims in all parts into close communion and cooperation."[4]

According to Shamil Jeppie, these publications, showed a remarkable consistency and Makki produced them since the beginning on a

---

[1] *The Muslim Digest*: February/March 1995, 161.

[2] Goolam Vahed, *Ahmed Deedat: The Man and his Mission* (Durban, 2013), 93.

[3] "Editorial" in *Ramadan Annual:* December 1998/January 1999.

[4] Ebrahim Mahida, *History of Muslims in South Africa: A Chronology* (Durban, 1993).

151

shoestring budget and without administrative infrastructure.[5]

First Lecture Tour: 1934

Mawlānā Siddiqui's lectures in many parts of the country in 1934 galvanised the Muslims to take an active role in the community affairs. The establishment of the Muslim Youth League and Muslim Youth Brigade under his guidance stimulated interest among the youth to give concrete expression to the concepts of commitment and devotion as elaborated in the Islamic value system.

"It embodied the ideals of physical fitness and militancy and had done very useful service in making the Muslim youth conscious of his physical imperfectness, his lack of a militant spirit and communal pride. From the very inception, the movement stirred the imagination of the Muslim youth of Durban, and in a very short space of time its membership increased considerably. It formed its own band, and its red and white uniforms created a stir wherever it went. Durban, the home of its birth, saw many fine spectacles of the march of the Muslim Youth's Brigade. On many occasions, when well known personalities paid visits to the City, the members of the Brigade formed impressive guards of honour. In 1938 it travelled to Cape Town, and there, too, it created a very fine impression."[6]

Mawlānā Siddiqui enjoyed an iconic status due to his mastery over English and his profound grasp of contemporary issues. His constituency included the youth, intellectuals as well as many members of the `ulama fraternity. He had the gift of explaining abstract concepts "in a simple manner according to the intellectual capacity of his audience."[7] Likewise, his lectures and writings appealed to the intellectuals and laymen alike. Thus, he stood out head and shoulder above his peers in the presentation of Islamic faith and practice. *The Elementary Teachings of Islam*, also translated into Afrikaans, was an important contribution to Islamic studies.

---

[5] Shamiel Jeppie, *Language, Identity, Muslims: The Arabic Study Circle of Durban* (Cape Town, 2007).

[6] Ibrahim Haffejee, "Muslim Youth Brigade" in Ramadan Annual: 1941, 32.

[7] Mohamed, *The Roving Ambassador of Peace*, xix.

Islam and Science Lectures

Two lectures defined Mawlānā Siddiqui's intellectual calibre: his presentation of philosophy and modern science from the Islamic perspective. *Spiritual Culture in Islam* was delivered at the Theosophical Society of South Africa (Durban) in 1934. The focus of the lecture was on the Islamic view of the soul. The knowledge of the soul, according to Mawlānā Siddiqui "does not pertain to the material world and has a special correlation with the immaterial Being Allah."[8] Therefore, the Qur'ānic explanation of the soul in the following verse *(āyah)* is based on *wahy* which was revealed to the Holy Prophet (pbuh):

> *They ask you concerning the Spirit (of inspiration). Say: "The Spirit (comes) by the command of my Lord: Of knowledge it is only a little that is communicated to you"*[9]

In the final analysis, spiritual training, derived from the unimpeachable understanding of the Qur'ānic explanation, is only possible through the Prophetic model.[10] Citing the poet of the East, Iqbal and the lucid statements of Rumi, Mawlānā Siddiqui reinforces the need to cultivate 'angelic traits' to allow man to rise above 'earth-rootedness'. Simply put, man requires to develop the spiritual culture as the only way to achieve "spiritual illumination and union with Allah."

In a similar vein, the lecture entitled *Religious and Scientific Progress of the World*[11] provides an objective account of the Muslim contribution to science and technology. Mawlānā Siddiqui explored the relationship between Islam and the scientific tradition which was grounded on the *iqrā* (read) paradigm. Unlike several of his contemporaries who presented the Islam and science relationship in

---

[8] Ibid., 79.

[9] Qur'ān, 17:85.

[10] Mohamed, *The Roving Ambassador of Peace*, xix.

[11] The lecture was delivered at the M.K. Gandhi Library, Durban in 1935 and later published as *Cultivation of Science by the Muslims.*

apologetic terms,[12] Mawlānā Siddiqui based his understanding of scientific progress made by Muslims with reference to copious Qur'ānic verses (*āyāt*). This thought-provoking lecture had a major impact on many scholars of the day. In fact, Ahmad Deedat (d. 2005), founder member of the Islamic Propagation Centre International (IPCI) drew his early inspiration from the lecture which was delivered in Durban. He states:

The seeds of this booklet *Al-Qur'ān - The Miracle of Miracles*[13] was probably sown by the Roving Ambassador of Islam, the silver-tongued orator-Mawlānā Abdul Aleem Siddiqui. I was only a schoolboy when he visited South Africa on a lecture tour in 1934. Among his many erudite speeches, I heard him talk on *Cultivation of Science by the Muslims.* Subsequently, a booklet under the same title was published by the World Federation of Islamic Missions, Karachi, Pakistan, which brings back the earlier joy and thrill of the discourse I heard in my teens. In memory of that great servant of Islam, I reproduce here for posterity, a few words of what the Mawlānā had to say on the relationship between the Holy Qur'ān and the branches of scientific knowledge:

> "The intellectual upheaval created by Islam was a gigantic one. There is not a single department of learning which the Muslim scholars have left untouched and which they have not carved out a high position for themselves.
>
> "In truth, Islam intends the Muslim community to be a community of intellectuals, and the cultivation of science and all other forms of learning is one of the primary aims of Islam. Had it not been for the Muslims, Europe would never have seen its way to the Renaissance and the modern scientific era would never have dawned. Those nations who have received their knowledge of science from Europe are in fact indirectly the

---

[12] The Muslim modernists of the early twentieth century may be singled out regarding their penchant for scientific theories contained in the Qur'ān. For an incisive analysis on this aspect, see Muzaffar Iqbal, *The Making of Islamic Science*, 153-88.

[13] Ahmed Deedat, *The Choice,* vol. 1 (Verulam, 1993), 184-6.

disciples of the Islamic community of the past. Humanity owes to Islam a debt which it can never repay and gratitude which it can never forget."[14]

The silver-tongued orator (Mawlānā Siddiqui) ended his masterful exposition of the topic *Cultivation of Science by the Muslims* with the following words:

"Before I conclude, let me affirm once more that the Muslim community is out and out a creation of Islam which in its turn is rooted in Divine revelation. Nothing but belief in and the practice of Islam can make an individual a Muslim. Islam has laid it down as a religious duty that a Muslim should enquire into the reality of objects around him, so that his scientific enquiry may lead him to the knowledge of his Creator. Scientific enquiry in Islam is not an end but a means to the attainment of a higher end. And this is really the true end of humanity. *To Allah we belong and to Allah is our return.*"[15]

All Natal Muslim Conference

Efforts to unite the Muslim organisations under a central body in Natal for the purpose of articulating the Muslim interest particularly in the field of Islamic education culminated in the formation of the All Natal Muslim Conference in 1935. According to *The Indian Opinion,* the Conference "was the first of its kind in Natal."[16] There were delegates representing the various Muslim bodies from all parts of Natal." Mawlānā Siddiqui was invited to address this conference. The key issues discussed in the address were relevant to the Muslim community who were exposed to the blight of apartheid, and an uncertain future as a disadvantaged minority. Under these adverse circumstances, Muslim unity underpinned practical initiatives to build a well-knit Muslim society. More importantly, it

---

[14] Siddiqui, *Cultivation of Science by the Muslims,* 40.
[15] Ibid., 44.
[16] *The Indian Opinion:* 11 January 1935.

was the unity of purpose that chalked out guidelines for the unity of institutions.

Mawlānā Siddiqui highlighted the predicament and challenges faced by the Muslims in their interaction with both the white minority and the dispossessed black majority. They were reminded that they could remove the "shackles of slavery which are stigmas of humiliation"[17] by means of *da'wah*. He reiterated the belief that Islam's universal message of brotherhood offered the only solution to a racially polarised society in South Africa.

Da'wah and exemplary conduct in Mawlānā Siddiqui's view were ideals Muslims in the country should strive towards in their quest for justice and peace. Mawlānā Siddiqui noted:

I have made it a principle to invite people to Islam merely by portraying its beauties to them, and throughout my missionary career there seldom has been an occasion even to ask anyone directly to accept Islam. [No] sooner do the seekers after Truth realise it for themselves than they come forward of their own accord to proclaim their allegiance to it.[18]

Mawlānā Siddiqui urged Muslims to reassess the prevailing system of Islamic education against the background of socioeconomic changes. He outlined a blueprint for the preservation and propagation of Islamic teachings through a central body. It was an ambitious scheme that charted new pathways to the reconstruction of Islamic education in the country.

A sensitive soul, Mawlānā Siddiqui deplored the treatment of the 'ulama whose potentials were not fully utilised. Rather, pseudo-scholars were given prominence at the altar of the authentic teachings of Islam. In view of this precarious situation, he stated that a well-structured programme of action should take into account the needs of the youth. He urged the Muslim communities to set aside their petty differences in the form of sectarian bickering and focus on galvanising their energies by strengthening their collective identity.

---

[17] Siddiqui, *The Clarion Call* (Aligarh, 1935), 3.
[18] Ibid., 7-8.

Second Lecture Tour: 1952

After a lapse of eighteen years Mawlānā Siddiqui returned to South Africa in 1952. This lecture tour was memorable for the following reasons:

- Establishment of institutions to promote the collective Muslim identity.
- Coordination of Islamic activities in the principal cities of the country.
- Outreach programmes for the moral upliftment of the Muslim community.

The historic visit by Mawlānā Siddiqui was preceded by the publication of *Special Issues* and articles in several magazine, highlighting his missionary activities. *The Muslim Digest* eulogised his arrival in the following words: *Our Patron Arrives in South Africa*

When the S.S. *Kampala* docked in Durban on its arrival from Lourenco Marques (Mozambique), it brought to South Africa's shores our friend and patron, His Eminence Mawlānā Aleem Siddiqui Al-Qaderi. His Eminence was interviewed by news reporters and gave a happy message of goodwill through the columns of the *Natal Daily News*. He said:

> "I have preached in Protestant churches, Hindu temples, mosques and synagogues. Wherever I have been in the democratic countries I have found close cooperation. Tolerance towards others is one of the greatest virtues. We should invite people to love Allah. This is what I am trying to do; to bring a message of peace and love."[19]

The message of peace formed his keynote address at the reception given to him in the City Hall, Durban, to an estimated 8000 audience. Of particular significance was the presence of Jewish

---

[19] "Our Patron Arrives in South Africa" in *The Muslim Digest:* August 1952, 5.

rabbis and Christian priests in the *Welcome* proceedings. The report noted:

> ...[the] three constituents – religions of East and West - stood together represented by one or other of their ministers. These three religions are Christianity, Judaism and Islam. However, they may differ in practice and principle, the common ground between them is that they stem from the same inspiration, from the same Divinity.[20]

Mawlānā Siddiqui reinforced this theme by sharing his own experiences during his tabligh travels.

> His Eminence (Mawlānā Siddiqui) emphasised more than once, that his experience and his study of other contemporary religions convinced him more and more that all of them were basically the same: the search of man for Allah. That being so, he felt that on such common ground the various races of men, and especially the men of three great religions, should be able to find a foundation for peace and concern.[21]

Public Lectures in Durban

A similar protocol was followed in his public address at the City Hall in Pietermaritzburg.[22] He brought the message of peace and fellowship, a reminder that we are all equal before Allah though different in our individual characteristics.

Mawlānā Siddiqui stated categorically that he came to preach Islam. Peace was synonymous with Islam and, therefore, people could internalise the fellowship of peace by becoming followers in that sense. The role of the Holy Prophet (pbuh) was explained in these words:

> The Holy Prophet (pbuh) did not initiate a new religion or a new idea of Allah. He came to reaffirm and reestablish the

---

[20] "Durban's Great Welcome to His Eminence" in *The Muslim Digest*: August 1952, 8-9.

[21] Ibid., 9.

[22] For a detailed report, see *The Muslim Digest*: September 1952, 3-4.

old faith and the old religion which Allah had handed down to the Prophets from the time of Adam (pbuh). Islam was then not new but a reaffirmation of something old, something which all men could believe in, and in fact which all believers in Allah did believe in.[23]

Mawlānā Siddiqui was guided by the Qur'ānic view of Islam as the universal religion to which man must submit.[24]

In his message of Eid al-Adha[25] delivered at the Jumma Mosque (Grey Street, Durban), Mawlānā Siddiqui expressed his candour at the lack-lustre performance of Islamic practices among Muslims that was devoid of the spirit of sacrifice. He identified three areas of weaknesses that needed corrective measures:

- Poor standard of Islamic education that diminished the prospects of *da'wah* among non-Muslims.
- Absence of a strong publishing house that could effectively contribute towards the Islamic intellectual renaissance.
- Sectarian conflict that exacerbated the dynamism of the Islamic teachings.

Mawlānā Siddiqui deplored the malaise of sectarianism afflicting the Muslim society. He was unsparing in his condemnation of the divisive elements thriving on peripheral Islamic issues. The evocative image of imminent doom is succinctly described by Mawlānā Siddiqui:

They [mischief mongers] never considered that the flood of irreligion and atheism is advancing in the world today with its full fury. The scourge of immorality is blowing with its full force and burning the moral life of humanity. The weary foundations of religious outlook are under fire here and there, everywhere.[26]

---

[23] Ibid., 4.

[24] "We Remember His Eminence" in *The Muslim Digest:* June 1984, 294.

[25] Siddiqui,"The Message of Eid al-Adha" in *The Muslim Digest:* September 1952.

[26] Ibid., 10.

Mawlānā Siddiqui cautioned Muslims to be mindful of their duties towards Allah and cultivate the spirit of *taqwā* (Allah-consciousness). At the same time, Muslims should shun materialism which had assumed alarming proportions in the Muslim world:

> Modern man with all his material progress and technological advancement, is now experiencing the symptoms of his progress, but he is not taking steps to correct himself. Allah allows him to persist in his destructive practices, till he suffers due to his own neglect. Allah grants respite to the unbelievers: *Therefore, grant a delay to the unbelievers: give respite to them gently (for a while).*[27]

Islamic Education: The Madrasah System

During his international tabligh tours, Mawlānā Siddiqui had witnessed the deteriorating standards in madrasahs combined with the lacuna of textbooks catering for the needs of the Muslim students. He consistently advocated a review of the existing syllabi[28] and also made useful proposals for their improvement. There were, however, efforts, albeit limited, to introduce the integrated system of education, secular and Islamic, in schools like Ahmedia, South Coast Madrasah and Government State-Aided Indian schools. With the proven success and popularity of these schools in their implementation of the integrated system, the Anjuman Islam State-Aided Indian School also opted for its introduction.[29]

About this time Mawlānā Siddiqui addressed the Islamic Education Conference hosted by the Natal Muslim Council and openly encouraged the integrated system of education.[30] Permission was granted by the Natal Director of Education for Muslims to pursue this option in which Islamic education could be imparted alongside

---

[27] Mohamed, *The Roving Ambassador of Peace*, 65.

[28] Siddiqui, *The Clarion Call*, 23-8.

[29] Mahida, *History of Muslims in South Africa*, 68.

[30] Ibid., 65-7. A brief account about the formation of the Natal Muslim Council is provided.

secular education.

The Natal Muslim Council[31] advocated positive features of modern education which could be integrated with the traditional madrasah system. Two conferences in 1944 and 1952 were convened for this purpose. Among the other issues discussed were education for girls and training of Imams and the ʿulama in order to raise the standards of Islamic education in madrasahs and state-aided schools which were granted permission to offer an integrated syllabus. Another proposal submitted by the Council was the establishment of an institute for higher Islamic studies - dar al-ʿulum. The proposal hoped that graduates of this institution would be able to lecture on Islamic subjects and would be "qualified in religion, modern technique and modern education."[32] Mawlānā Siddiqui also laid great stress on the need to impart the teaching of Arabic at schools and tertiary institutions.[33] The focus of Mawlānā Siddiqui's activities was multidimensional and incorporated various facets of the Muslim collective life.

In his opening address at the conference, Mawlānā Siddiqui outlined the strategies that needed to be adopted to effect meaningful changes to the existing educational system:

> Every man certainly has the right to seek enlightenment from those in charge of affairs, but it does not mean that you should question their individual loyalties or sincerity, or you should level baseless accusation against them. Your religion forbids you to accuse another. You must learn to work in a spirit of tolerance and harmony.
>
> The biggest problem is whether or not you should educate your children; whether your children should take their rightful places as educated and self-respecting individuals in the community or do you wish them to remain illiterate and be a burden to the community in general?
>
> If you say that your children should receive their rightful

---

[31] Abdulkader *Tayob, Islamic Resurgence in South Africa: The Muslim Youth Movement* (Cape Town, 1995), 94.

[32] Ibid.

[33] *The Muslim Digest:* November 1952, 3.

education, that you want them to have education, then you have to decide what standard of education they should receive. Your religion does not prohibit you from receiving secular education. I say with all the power at my command, that the study of science, philosophy and every other branch of education, is open to you and is fully allowed by your religion. You must not differentiate; you must not demarcate between secular and religious education. You must accept both as being equally necessary.

Just as you teach your children you should gradually introduce Arabic as the medium of education in your madrasahs and I am confident that children will be able to understand the Holy Qur'ān in its original language in the next 10 or 15 years. You must also provide for the education of your girls, and set up a training-centre from where you can produce in your own country qualified teachers and `ulama."[34]

In Mawlānā Siddiqui's estimation, the lack of organised tabligh work among the indigenous people had hindered a strong Islamic foothold in the country. This appeal was previously made at Education Conference held in Durban in 1934.[35] A *muballigh* imbued with noble ideals, Mawlānā Siddiqui offered the following motivational advice to the delegates at the Conference:

Of the many diseases rife in the community one is the disease of lack of self-strength. Another is that the community has not confidence either in each individual or in its leaders. You have divided yourselves into groups, which is the bane of any society. For its remedy I recommend to you, that you should have no fear; you have in you, inherent strength that can shake off any opposition that you may encounter. Develop your spiritual strength, rely on it, and it will enable you to tide over all your difficulties.[36]

These problems could be overcome if Muslims displayed "a spirit of reconciliation, tolerance and understanding, and, above all, faith and

---

[34] See Siddiqui, *The Clarion Call.*
[35] *The Muslim Digest:* November 1952, 2.
[36] Cited in Siddiqui, "Muslim Education" in *The Muslim Digest:* November 1952.

confidence between man and man, between class and class."[37]

A similar conference was convened in Mombasa, Kenya, in 1953 on two important issues: education and tabligh. Mawlānā Siddiqui highlighted the need for the Muslim community to carry out its obligation among the indigenous people to counteract the growing Christian missionary presence in the country.[38]

Impact of Mawlānā Siddiqui Lectures

The impact of Mawlānā Siddiqui's lectures in Natal was summed up by A.C. Meer in a series of articles on the Indian history in South Africa and published in the Durban tabloid "Leader". He observed:

In 1952, we welcomed Mawlānā Siddiqui brought to us by Makki Publications. This great exponent of Islam took us by storm, creating a new pride in our Faith.

Makki Publications was in the forefront of promoting Mawlānā Siddiqui's worldview of Islam. The following excerpts offer a glimpse of the missionary zeal undertaken by Makki to advance the cause of Islam as a religion par- excellence.[39]

Islam

The Natural Religion - The Rational Religion - The Universal
Religion
The Religion
Taught by all the Messengers of God from Adam to Muhammad
{Peace be with them all} The Religion
Followed by six hundred million human beings belonging to
almost all races and countries
The Term "Islam" means

---

[37] Cited in Goolam Vahed and Tehembisa Waetjan, *Schooling Muslims in Natal: Identity, State and the Orient Islamic Educational Institute* (Pietermaritzburg, 2015), 162. This learned work covers Mawlānā Siddiqui's important contributions to the integrated school system Durban. Ibid., 161-4.

[38] Saleh Yakub, "His Eminence in East Africa" in *The Muslim Digest:* September 1953, 11-2.

[39] *Ramadan Annual:* 1989, 307.

Submission to the Divine Will and Guidance - Conformity to the
Divine Laws

The Term "Muslim" means

One who submits to the Divine Laws Every Particle of the Universe
Submits to Divine Commands and conforms to Divine Laws:
the Laws of Nature, and IS, Therefore, A "Muslim"

AS A FREE MORAL PERSON, EVERY HUMAN BEING

Is also under natural obligation to submit to the Revealed Law of
God, namely TO BE A "MUSLIM".

1. To consider all humanity as One Family and to treat all
   human beings as brothers and sisters, without attaching
   importance to the distinctions of colour, nationality and
   wealth. Further, to perform faithfully the obligation towards
   parents and other relatives, as laid down in the said Code.
2. To mould one's life as a whole in accordance with the Divine
   Moral Laws, eg. Justice, Truth, Fraternity, etc. and to abstain
   from indulgence in the evils described in the said Code, eg.
   Falsehood, intoxication, gambling, etc.

Alongside Makki's publishing output was the pivotal role played by
Haji Tarmahomed (d.1997), a businessman and philanthropist from
Durban. Makki who hosted Mawlānā Siddiqui in 1952 during his six-
month lecture tour in South Africa, gave Haji Tarmahomed
permission to have the lectures recorded, in those days on wire,
which were subsequently re-recorded on tape. All in all, there were 21
tapes of Mawlānā Siddiqui's lectures delivered both in Urdu and
English. These audio tapes were distributed free of charge - a
testament to Haji Tarmahomed's profound love for the revered
muballigh. The lecture series in Urdu were translated into English and
edited by Yasien Mohamed.[40]

---

[40] Yasien Mohamed, *The Roving Ambassador of Peace. The Lectures of Moulana Abdul Aleem
Siddiqui in South Africa* (Cape Town, 2005).

Mawlānā Abubaker Khatib

Mawlānā Siddiqui had a wide circle of *murids* and admirers who advanced the cause of his tabligh efforts. Among the many prominent figures, mention may be made of the eminent scholar, Mawlānā Abubaker Khatib (d. 1979). A leading 'alim, his association with Mawlānā Ahmad Mukhtar Siddiqui and his brother, Mawlānā Siddiqui strengthened the *da'wah* cause in the country. A graduate of the prestigious Islamic institution in Farangi Mahal (Lucknow)[41] which was noted for its formulation of the *Dars i-Nizāmi*, Mawlānā Khatib acquired mastery in the Islamic disciplines (*'ulum*) as well as in Arabic, Persian and Urdu.[42] He was also guided by the Islamic luminary, Mawlānā Abdul Bari Ansari (d. 1926)[43] who counted among his disciples political activists like Mohamed Ali of the Khilafat movement. Mawlānā Khatib's arrival to South Africa in 1944 marked a turning point in the consolidation of Islamic education, particularly in Kwa-Zulu Natal. His participative role in the establishment of the Jamiat al-'Ulama (KZN)[44] and the publication of the *Al-Haadil Ameen* magazine in 1956 were among his noteworthy contributions. His devotion to the Qur'ān was exemplary as can be gleaned from his tafsir of several surahs.[45] His son, Hafidh Abul Hasan (d. 2011)[46] continued with his father's *da'wah* activities by promoting both the *Al-Haadil Ameen* magazine and calendar, which "served as a valuable source of information about Islam and provided a means of spiritual enlightenment."[47] According Hafidh Abul Hasan, his beacon of inspiration was Mawlānā Siddiqui who emphasised the importance

---

[41] For a detailed study on the `ulama of Farangi Mahal, See Francis Robinson, *The 'Ulama of Farangi Mahal and Islamic Culture in South Asia.*

[42] *Al-Haadil Ameen:* December 1995, 2.

[43] An influential 'alim of his time, Mawlānā Ansari's impact as a sufi and politician was considerable. He wrote over 100 books on both Islamic and secular subjects. See Robinson, *Separatism Among Indian Muslims* (New Delhi, 1993), 419-20.

[44] Mawlānā Abubaker Khatib was one of the founder member of the Jamiat al-`Ulama (KwaZulu Natal) which was established in 1950. See Mahida, *History of Muslims in South Africa: A Chronology*, 70-1.

[45] See the following *Al-Haadil Ameen* issues: 2010: 1, 2011: 3, 2011: 4.

[46] Hafidh Abul Hasan passed away in front of the Ka'bah on 1 April 2011. For an obituary, see *Al-Haadil Ameen:* 2011: 3, 2-3.

[47] Mahmood Khatib,' Editorial' *in Al-Haadil Ameen:* 2010:1, 1.

of *da'wah* in the country during his lecture tour in 1952. The re-launch of *Al-Haadil Ameen*,[48] was meant to maintain the continuity of the inspiring ideals as set out by his spiritual guide and his father, Mawlānā Khatib. The inclusion of articles in Afrikaans, Zulu, Xhosa and Sesotho were praiseworthy efforts to spread the message of Islam among the indigenous communities in the country.

Lectures in Gauteng

Two cities in Gauteng (Johannesburg and Pretoria) which were part of the former Transvaal formed the nucleus of Mawlānā Siddiqui's *da'wah* activities. His powerful lectures enthralled his audience, his rational exposition of Islam appealed to both intellectuals and youth. In a particular sense, he blended classical Islamic traditions with modern trends that held sway in Egypt and India and which formed the hub of the intellectual discourse in those countries. The Queen Street Mosque in Pretoria represented an enlightened approach to contemporary Islamic issues. Mawlānā Siddiqui's lectures mirrored the aspirations of the vibrant Muslim community in search of the authentic representation of Islamic thought. In this regard, he elaborated on the theme *Allah's Greatest Gift* in relation to the status of the Holy Prophet (pbuh).

If we have no chance of counting Allah's blessings or gifts, we have even less chance of describing them. No words can do justice to them. And even if we have the words, we would not have ink sufficient to inscribe these words. If the ocean were ink, it would be exhausted and we would require another ocean.

> *Say: "If the ocean were ink to write the words of My Lord, sooner would the ocean be exhausted than would the words of My Lord. Even if we added another ocean like it for its aid."*

This is a graphic metaphor of the infinite blessings of Allah. The ocean is so vast and deep that it cannot be measured. If the ocean represents ink, the ink cannot be measured and it would be seemingly

---

[48] Hafidh Abul Hasan, "Editor's Message" in *Al-Haadil Ameen:* 4; 17-54.

unlimited in its quality. This vast amount of ink is not enough to write the blessings of Allah. The ocean would be depleted before the divine blessings can be described. We will require another ocean as soon as the first one is exhausted. What a powerful metaphor! The imagery suggests the incapability of man to describe the blessings of Allah. No matter how much ink, how many resources at his command, nothing will be enough to enumerate and express the infinite blessings of Allah. The human language itself can only express some idea of the magnitude of the divine blessings, but cannot depict for us an exact picture of them. The blessing of Allah is thus personified in the noble conduct (*uswah al-hasanah*) of the Holy Prophet (pbuh):

"And You (stand) on an exalted standard of character."[49]

According to Mawlānā Siddiqui, "Prophet Muhammad's character is all encompassing. It includes the virtues of his inner soul, the outer aspects of his character, the humility in his eyes, and the light in his face."[50] He gave this message of hope and optimism during a crucial period in the history of Islam when the Orientalist writings launched scathing attacks on the personality of the Holy Prophet (pbuh).[51] According to Mawlānā Siddiqui, tabligh in the broader sense was a projection of the exemplary conduct of Holy Prophet (pbuh) and inseparably linked to Islam as a universal religion. Again, the recurrent theme of *Back to the Qur'ān, Back to Muhammad* was a terse reminder for Muslims entrusted with this divine responsibility.

In another lecture titled *Know Thyself* Mawlānā Siddiqui draws several analogies to press home a key point: the toxic element of pride. People are "intoxicated by the pride of their own abilities and accomplishments" which is steeped in their *nafs al-ammārah* (lower self).[52] As a result, bloated pride and conceit permeates people's outlook on life and they become impervious to the timeless message

---

[49] Mohamed, *The Roving Ambassador of Peace,* 53-4.

[50] Ibid., 68.

[51] The plethora of polemical works by Orientalists in the early twentieth century indicated the tempo of their campaigns to vilify the Holy Prophet (pbuh) and his message. See Jabal Buaben, *Image of the Prophet Muhammad in the West* (Leicester, 1996).

[52] Mohamed, *The Roving Ambassador of Peace*, 3.

of the Qur'ān and the sunnah. Moreover, Muslims are reminded about their responsibilities as the 'best of nations' for the whole of mankind.

Peace and Dialogue in Tabligh

Peace and dialogue were Mawlānā Siddiqui's overriding concerns in a world dominated by materialism, Communism and racism. His meeting with the Prime Minister Dr D. F. Malan in 1952 was based on counsel (*nasihah*) and wisdom (*hikmah*). The Prime Minister expressed his satisfaction about the laudable work of Mawlānā Siddiqui and the stress he laid on moral and religious education to combat the evil forces.[53]

In cities like Pretoria where the Muslim population was considerable, Mawlānā Siddiqui focused on the inner dimensions of Islam. Spiritual rearmament and moral responsibility were indispensable guides for obtaining Divine pleasure (*ridā ilāhi*). Likewise, Islam as a code of life (*din*)[54] has a well-defined ideal as elaborated in the Holy Qur'ān.

The Universal Truth Movement

Founded in 1958 and led by Mawlānā Ismail Abdur Razzaq and Mawlānā Qasim Sema, the *Universal Truth Movement* (UTM) had the primary purpose of translating the Qur'ān into African languages and printing pamphlets by introducing Islam to a wider non-Muslim audience. The potential of printing pamphlets and books in order to promote the message of Islam is explained in the following words:

> Though the voice of preachers may reach ears of many millions, the thoughts emanating from the pens of authors travel farther to reach the eyes of many more. On looking closely at the immense power wielded by the ordinary daily newspapers, one finds that newspapers Xash their messages across many oceans and deserts, countries and continents in a

---

[53] *Ramadan Annual*: 1994, 37.
[54] For a detailed discussion on the term *din*, see Siddiqui, *The Islamic Ideal*, 15-7.

relatively short time, for the benefit of readers scattered on the surface of the globe. A similar effect is obtained when booklets, pamphlets and handbills containing religious material are published and distributed widely amongst the people. Islam, being the Universal Truth, must be propagated by every Muslim for any non-Muslim to read, understand and ponder about.[55]

The rhetoric of Islam being the Universal Truth was echoed by Mawlānā Siddiqui during his lectures in South Africa. He also stressed the importance of tabligh among the indigenous people. In fact, his vision preceded many institutions in chalking out appropriate strategies to reach out to the non-Muslims in the country. Both Mawlānā Abdur Razzaq and Mawlānā Qasim Sema[56] were charismatic religious figures who advocated tabligh on a more sustained level. The latter's activities among the indigenous communities in the Msinga Reserve have been adequately documented. Equally challenging was the systemisation of Islamic education for children attending the madrasah system. The UTM made inroads through their printing output and included the publication of Mawlānā Siddiqui's *The Elementary Teachings of Islam* which had been widely used in distant countries like Trinidad.[57] It was also translated into the Arabic and French languages and thus its impact was substantial. In a much more broader sense, Mawlānā Siddiqui's contribution as a *muballigh* was acknowleged by institutions of diverse religious orientations.

Tasawwuf Traditions in the Cape

Cape Town conjured up images of the struggle for human dignity and the quest for spirituality. *Tasawwuf* traditions were as old as the Muslim presence in the Cape, and by the end of the nineteenth century "a large number of *tasawwuf* practices had become an integral

---

[55] Universal Truth Movement, *Universal Truth Movement General Report,* 1964.
[56] For a biographical account, see Ismail Akoo, *Biography of the Founder and Principal Darul Uloom, Newcastle* (Newcastle, n.d).
[57] Brannon Ingram, *Deobandis Abroad: Sufism, Ethics and Polemics in Global Islamic Movement* (unpublished PhD, 2011), 115.

part of the Islamic religious fabric."[58]

The proliferation of the sufi *tariqahs* could be attributed to the local shaykhs who studied abroad in several centres of Islamic learning and assimilated their respective teachings during their stay there. There was also a sizeable number of *mashā'ikh* from the Arab world and the Indo-subcontinent who either stayed in the Cape permanently or during their visits "strengthened the already very deep-rooted *tasawwuf* traditions of the Muslim community."[59]

An important dimension of Mawlānā Siddiqui's visit to Cape was his elucidation of the *tasawwuf* perspectives in his lectures at the mosques and private *majālis*.[60] The following assessment by Yusuf da Costa of the *tasawwuf* tradition in the Cape is illustrative:

> There can be very little doubt that the practice of Islam at the Cape, by virtue of its very particular historical circumstances, has been considerably coloured by the *tasawwuf* tradition; and in a sense, this tradition has added a warmth and fervour to the practice of Islam that is not necessarily found where such a tradition is not flourishing. This has resulted in certain unique community practices and structures being established that are generally associated, in one way or another, with this tradition.[61]

In fact, Mawlānā Siddiqui's second visit to the Cape must be seen from the 'alim-sufi perspective.[62] This term gained greater clarity during the *jihād* struggles against British colonialism and French imperialism in the Arab world. The 'alim-sufi combined knowledge with action. Another dimension was added to this term - *jihād* - which was emblematic of the Muslim liberation from foreign rule. Amir Abdul Qadir (d. 1873) of Algeria[63] represented this trend in the

---

[58] Yusuf da Costa and Achmat Davids (eds.), *Pages from Cape Muslim History* (Pietermaritzburg, 1994), 135.

[59] Ibid., 138.

[60] *The Muslim Digest*: November 1952.

[61] Da Costa: *Pages from Cape Muslim History*, 159.

[62] Habibul Haq Nadvi, *Islamic Resurgent Movements in The IndoPak Subcontinent* (Durban, 1987), 53.

[63] On his biographical account, see Ahmed Bouyerdene, *Emir Abd el-Kader, Hero Saint*

Maghreb. According to Abdulkader Tayob, Mawlānā Siddiqui stressed the rational and philosophical aspects of the Islamic tradition[64] which had a positive impact on the professionals who were largely disillusioned by the ritualistic presentation of Islam. Hence, his visit to the Cape illustrated his popularity as a scholar-sufi.

Reception at the Grand Parade

At the Grand Parade, Cape Town,[65] Mawlānā Siddiqui received a tumultuous welcome as reported in *The Cape Times*. Accompanied by his host Mohammed Makki and the leading ʽulama of the calibre of Imam Ismail Talib (d. 1962) and spiritual luminaries like Sayyid Abdul Kader of Syria, Mawlānā Siddiqui's inspiring address touched on Islam as the pioneer of peace and justice. He stated in unequivocal terms that he had come to the shores of South Africa to serve all mankind which was the true meaning of Islam. The following report is a synopsis of Mawlānā Siddiqui's address:

> "Islam," he said "had never waged an aggressive war to further this belief. The very word Islam means peace. Had they done so there would today not be a single person in India, China or Europe who would be a Muslim. Instead, the Muslims tried to bring to people the message of universal brotherhood. (*His words were punctuated by loud applause.*)
>
> "But," he continued, "I feel that the people of Cape Town did not welcome me as Abdul Aleem Siddiqui in my personal capacity, but as an ambassador of the Holy Prophet (pbuh). *(loud cheers)*. For the enthusiasm you have shown in welcoming me, the Almighty alone will recompense you because you are actually respecting the government of Almighty Allah, whose humble servant I am."

---

of Islam (Bloomington, 2011).

[64] Tayob, *Islamic Resurgence in South Africa*, 88.

[65] Mawlānā Siddiqui's lecture at the Grand Parade, Cape Town was reported in *The Muslim Digest*: 1952. This article was reproduced in *The Muslim Digest*: February/March 1993.

Mawlānā Siddiqui then continued to give illustrations regarding the Oneness and Unity of Almighty Allah:

"Firstly, belief in one Allah; secondly, belief in all the divine religions of the world and belief in all the divine messengers of Almighty Allah who brought messages to mankind in different times and in different ages; and thirdly, all members of the human race are members of one great family as they are the sons and daughters of Adam and Eve, and all the human beings are just like different parts of one body." He went on to say that "Islam was never spread at the point of the sword, and he illustrated this with facts from history, showing that "Muslims ruled India for well over 700 years and if they had used the sword there would not have been a single non-Muslim left in the subcontinent. On the contrary, one finds that Muslims are even today in the minority there." He also stressed the fact that the growth of the Muslim community of South Africa was the result of humanitarian work carried out by the Muslim savants and saints of the early days, and that it was a false charge that Islam was spread at the point of the sword, which he repudiated with all the emphasis at his command.[66]

The testimony of faith was best expressed in the Cape Muslim community's appreciative response to Mawlānā Siddiqui's presence. He was escorted by a cavalcade of cars through the streets of Cape Town which was etched in the memories of those present. Mawlānā Siddiqui made history and it was "like a page written of spiritual inspiration and leadership by a magnificent figure; whose life to the service of mankind... [was] a model on which we might all found our lives in the future, in the service of faith of Islam."[67]

---

[66] *The Muslim Digest:* 1952.
[67] Ibid.

Lecture at Green Point Track

Another historic public lecture was delivered at the Green Point Track to an audience of 60.000 people on the occasion of the Holy Prophet's (pbuh) birthday (*Mawlud al-Nabi*). Mahmood Khatib's perceptive article about the Mawlud (2013) recounted the 1952 memorable lecture by Mawlānā Siddiqui. His poignant description of the function is instructive:

Let us Emulate the Past.

How beautiful was October, 1952! Cape Town was beautified by the love its inhabitants expressed for the best of Allah's creation. It seems inconceivable today that 60.000 people would gather and, in a unified manner, "express delight at the birth of The Light." It took one great scholar and Islamic missionary to attract over 36.000 people to welcome him at the Grand Parade, and 60.000 people to the Green Point Track to attach themselves to and rekindle their love for Muhammad Mustapha (pbuh). *It was a love story of note!*

The great poet, Safee Siddiqui (d. 2013) who accompanied the great 'alim to Cape Town, recalls that as the plane was about to land at Wingfield Airport, the captain asked the passengers to look down at the massive red carpet below. He was advised that it was not a red carpet but the red fezzes of the people waiting to meet the VIP on board the plane! It was a historical event and the largest Mawlud gathering of the last century. The question now is: will you be part of the historical and largest gathering of this century expressing love for the same personality?

Will you be part of the gathering to honour the one on whom Allah SWT conferred the title of "Mercy unto all the Worlds and a mercy unto everything other than Allah", meaning that he is a mercy even to the environment?

Mawlānā Abdul Aleem Siddiqui was a man of love and peace and he ignited those characteristics to those around him. Today, he rests peacefully at the feet of his lineage, and our spiritual mother, Sayyidah Ayesha (RA), in Jannat-ul Baqee.[68]

The theme of Mawlānā Siddiqui's lecture was *Mercy unto Mankind*.[69] The impact of the Prophet Muhammad's (pbuh) teachings shaped world civilisation over the centuries. His personal conduct served as the perennial source of guidance for mankind. Mawlānā Siddiqui says:

> Nothing deterred him from his message, no bribery, no persecution and no accusations. He won the hearts of people by his pure character, and today millions of people follow his teachings. He won the hearts of people through faith, not arms. His revolution was spiritual. People came into Islam by choice not force[70].

At the conclusion of this great gathering an address of gratitude from the Cape Peninsula was read out by Haniff Allie, former principal of the Habibia School:

> We the Muslims of the Cape, have much pleasure in presenting to you, Sir, a token of the high esteem in which we hold the noble and humanitarian work you are doing in the service of humanity and in the glorious cause of Islam.
> In this materialistic age when practically every individual is engaged with the accumulation of material wealth, and mankind is engaged in the waging of wars and bitter strife, it is an encouraging realisation that there are men of your calibre in the world who are prepared to sacrifice their all, and out of sheer love for mankind and without any financial or material support from any government, organisation or agency, are prepared to serve humanity at large.
> You have come to our country, Sir, as an *Ambassador of Peace* to teach us the true meaning of Islam, the religion of peace.

---

[68] Mahmood Khatib, "Let us Emulate the Past" in *The Muslim Views:* January 2013. Cf. "Mass Mawlid 1434" in *Al-Haadil Ameen*, 2013.
[69] Mohamed, *The Roving Ambassador of Peace*, 4.
[70] Ibid.

You have taught us that for the achievement of real and lasting peace, we should live in accordance with the divine laws and that truth and tolerance are essential. These lessons have been taken to heart by us, one and all.[71]

The inspirational lecture revealed unique insights into the personality of Mawlānā Siddiqui. His inexhaustible wisdom, profound sincerity and versatile knowledge pointed out to his unflinching faith in Allah and outstanding love of the Holy Prophet (SA'). The fluency of his lecture combined with the rare charms of eloquence infused a new zeal among the crowd to be committed Muslims. Mawlānā Siddiqui reminded them that the Qur'ān was a revealed guidance which empowered a believer (*mu'min*) to adopt a code of *taqwā* (Allah-consciousness). He cautioned Muslims to avoid a superficial interpretation of the Islamic teachings and attachment to the Holy Prophet (SAW) as these smacked of hollow ritualism. The outstanding aspect of Islam is emulating 'the model of excellence' and spreading his sublime teachings to the world at large. Mawlānā Siddiqui personified this ideal in word and deed. There was no 'gloom and doom' syndrome which was generally associated with the Islamic scholars of that period. On the contrary, he reinforced the vision of tabligh as conveyed by the Holy Prophet (SAW), which was a "timeless message for mankind." As such, the *Mawlid* was a tribute to the 'portrait of perfection' and Muslims were urged to project the values of compassion, altruism and tolerance, ideals which earn Allah's Divine pleasure (*ridā ilahi*). Even after a lapse of seventy years the lecture continues to resonate with a distinct message: *Back to the Qur'ān, Back to Muhammad (pbuh).*

Another dimension of Mawlānā Siddiqui's impressive lecture was the reiteration of the core Islamic values that typified the Muslim identity. He referred to the traditional Muslim attire worn in the country during that period which personified their admirable traits of integrity, transparency and accountability. Their (Muslims) outer appearance reflected their inner personality. He strongly maintained that any deviation from these ingrained values would no

---

[71] *The Muslim Digest*: 1952, 14-15.

longer signify one's commitment to the message of the Holy Prophet (pbuh), and by extension, an unconditional love for him. Mawlānā Siddiqui expressed his candour at Muslim formalism which lacked the spark of the genuine interiorisation of the Prophetic message. Instead, Muslims were gradually imbibing cultural practices that were alien to the Islamic spirit. He cautioned Muslims not to wear the borrowed robes of Western civilisation but to be worthy exemplars of the best values that the Holy Prophet (pbuh) represented in his personal life. The life-enriching lesson gleaned from the *sirah* of the Holy Prophet (pbuh) is aptly described by Mawlānā Siddiqui:

> His moral example is the key to the knowledge of the self and the knowledge of God. Without this higher knowledge, we cannot attain true happiness in this world and the Hereafter.[72]

Mawlānā Siddiqui himself was the embodiment of the Islamic ideal and invariably his lectures were an apt reminder that Muslims could only soar above other nations if they tenaciously upheld the Islamic teachings in their daily lives.

Love for the Holy Prophet (pbuh)

Mawlānā Siddiqui also lamented at the Muslims lack of commitment to the personality of the Prophet (pbuh). A soulless, ritualistic attachment was devoid of a passionate and sincere love for the Holy Prophet (pbuh). Using the following analogy, Mawlānā Siddiqui pointed out to the importance of following the exemplary model.

> Allah gave us Muhammad (pbuh) as our model to follow. To build a house, we must have a model. To build our character, we must have a model. If we do not follow the prescribed model, Allah will not stay in our house. Hence as

---

[72] Mohamed, *The Roving Ambassador of Peace*, 10.

we have been taught by our Lord: "We do not occupy heaven and earth, but We occupy the heart of a believer." Build your heart according to that model, so that Allah can live in it. Otherwise, it would be unpleasant to stay in. If the ornament does not match the model, you return it to the goldsmith to melt it again according to the prescribed model. We should remodel it till it is in accordance to that pattern. This is how we attain proximity to Allah. As dear creatures of Allah, we should reflect Him more than we reflect material things. So we should express the highest values of Islam in our moral character.[73]

The Prophetic model was a common refrain in Mawlānā Siddiqui's writings and lectures and expressed an organic unity in his presentation of Islam as the universal religion.[74] It was the same message and the same comprehensive model of perfection that 'stands out as the Beacon of Light' for all time.'[75]

Islamic Activities

Mawlānā Siddiqui's *islāhi* activities extended beyond his lecture itinerary. His pre-eminence as a Qādiri shaykh strengthened his relationship with the *mashā'ikh* of the day. Special mention may be made of Shaykh Mahdi Hendricks who had completed his studies in Makkah in 1936. The Azzawiya Mosque founded in 1920 also served as a nexus of *tasawwuf* activities. The name Azzawiyah had a *tasawwuf* connotation[76] and the activities under Shaykh Muhammad Salih Hendricks (d. 1945) were manifold. The institution of pedigree - the Alawi Maliki scholarship – was embedded in the profundity of his

---

[73] Ibid., 73-4.
[74] Siddiqui, *English Lecture in Cape Town,* 1952.
[75] Siddiqui, The Principles of Islam (Karachi, 2002), 22.
[76] *Tasawwuf* perspectives linked to the community practices were unique among the Cape Muslims. Many *mashā'ikh* settled in the Cape and retained their distinctive forms of *tasawwuf.*

Islamic knowledge and teaching methodology. His contributions to the field of *ta'lim* (learning) and *tarbiyah* (spiritual training) were admirable and even after his demise his sons "continued to nurture the structures that he had created in order to keep the torch of Islam burning."[77] Mawlānā Siddiqui maintained a strong bond with Shaykh Mahdi and Shaykh Ebrahim Hendricks and also guided them together with the Moslem Teachers Association of South Africa to draft an Islamic syllabus[78] for the primary schools. According to Yusuf da Costa, Mawlānā Siddiqui had a number of institutions and organisations named after him such as the Habibiyah Siddiqui Brigade, The Siddiqui Primary School and the Siddiqui Mosque in Elsies River.[79]

Mention may be made of the Habibia Siddique Muslim Brigade which was established in 1954 and was "the brainchild of Mawlānā Siddiqui, an Islamic luminary who visited Cape Town in 1952."[80] From the very beginning, the objective of the Brigade was to provide a programme of training and discipline to nurture a sense of Islamic responsibility. The formation of the Brigade was not a novel idea as Mawlānā Siddiqui had mooted this idea during his first visit to South Africa in 1934.

Haji Zubair Sayed: An Islamic Activist

The association of Haji Zubair Sayed, founder of *Muslim News* which was the forerunner to the present *Muslim Views* and Islamic Publication Bureau, with Mawlānā Siddiqui deserves particular mention. Haji Zubair was responsible for the publication of *Muslim News* in the 1960 which grew to acquire an international reputation for its informative articles and coverage of community affairs. Because of its stand against the draconian policies of the apartheid government, the newspaper faced much harassment from the Security Branch and other state authorities. Haji Zubair took a

---

[77] Da Costa, *Pages from Cape Muslim History*, 113.

[78] This information appears as *Appendix 3* in *The Roving Ambassador of Peace,* 110.

[79] Da Costa, *Pages from Cape Muslim History,* 138.

[80] *Muslim Views:* January 2013, 18.

principled stand against all forms of discrimination, which he deemed as *zulm* (injustice). His political activism drew him closer to the Pan African Congress (PAC), which conscientised and sensitised individuals to challenge the apartheid policies.

A successful entrepreneur, Haji Zubair focused on his 'service to humanity' (*khidmat al-khalq*) ideal. This philanthropic spirit was inspired by his interactive meetings with Mawlana Siddiqui through whom he cultivated an abiding interest in *tasawwuf*. Under his patronage, Haji Zubair established the Islamic Publications Bureau and also published his (Mawlana Siddiqui's) and Mawlana Ansari's monographs. The groundswell of interest in the Bureau's publishing output can be gleaned from the plethora of letters received from as far as Nigeria requesting its publications. These were posted free of charge.[81]

Ahmadiyyah Movement: A Critique

During the 1950s the establishment of the Ahmadiyyah centres in Cape Town also saw the emergence of literature purporting to contain authentic Islamic teachings. Of particular concern was the promotion of Maulvi Muhammad Ali's commentary of the Qur'ān in English. The Bureau in conjunction with Makki published booklets in refutation of the absurd claims of the Qadiani movement. The Muslim Judicial Council (MJC) also contributed a series of articles[82] to enlighten the Muslim community about the growing menace of Qadianism in the Cape.

Reference to the Qadiani movement has been made elsewhere in the volume. Scholarly works which critiqued the deviant sect were few, and by and large, reproduced extracts from the writings of Mirza Ahmad in their refutation of his claims. Presumably in the 1930s Mawlānā Siddiqui wrote *Al-Mar'at al-Qādiniyah*[83] in Arabic to alert the Muslims in the Arab world about the "true face of Qadianism." He

---

[81] A brief history of the Muslim News appears in Mahida, *History of the Muslims in South Africa*, 93.

[82] The Bureau published *The Truth about the Ahmadiyyah and Qadiani Movement*, which was prepared by Shaykh Abubakr Najjar of The Muslim Judicial Council.

[83] Qadri, *Azim Muballigh*, 46.

analysed the movement from different angles and cogently revealed the Qadiani complicity with British colonialism. The missionary agenda of the movement was obvious: to undermine the *Seal of Prophethood* belief[84] in order to bolster its devious interpretation to the Muslim masses.

In South Africa, the anti-Qadiani campaign gained momentum. Under the patronage of Mawlānā Siddiqui, Makki published a number of articles and books which exposed the hollow claims of Qadianism. M.O. Abbas, a noted journalist of Dar-as-Salam (Tanzania) wrote *The Mirror*[85] showing "the living picture of the relation between Mirza Ghulam Ahmad and the British government." The book was edited by Mawlānā Siddiqui. Other articles contributed by 'Phoenix' (a pseudonym) also highlighted the inconsistencies of the founder's claim to prophethood. An important contribution to the critique of Qadianism was the work of the distinguished academic, Professor Mohammed Elias Burney. An admirer of Mawlānā Siddiqui, he was guided to write *Qadiani Movement*[86] as a rejoinder to the Qadiani propagandist in Nigeria, Naseem Saifi. The infiltration of Qadianism in that country was a disturbing development. According to Makki, "[Elias's] books on Qadianism are recognised as authentic on the subject, particular his vast critical analysis, named *Qadiani Madhab* (Urdu), a masterpiece of thorough research. It is an exhaustive compilation of numerous quotations and references systematised on psychological basis and a most interesting and instructive psycho-analysis of Mirza Qadiani and his adherents..."[87]

Mawlānā Siddiqui actively supported the publication of the book and promoted its distribution in the Far East during his tabligh tour in 1949-50.[88] On the question of prophethood, Mawlānā Siddiqui was vociferous in his condemnation of (Maulvi) Mohammad Ali who sought to dismantle the creed of prophethood in his commentary of the Qur'ān. The points enumerated by Mawlānā Siddiqui on prophethood express the unanimous view of the *ummah* on this

---

[84] Ibid.

[85] M.O. Abbasi, *The Mirror* (Durban, 1953).

[86] The serialised articles appeared in *The Muslim Digest*: 1952 issues.

[87] M.E. Burney, *Qadiani Movement* (Durban, 1955), viii.

[88] Ibid.

subject.[89]

Under the guidance of his spiritual mentor, Mawlānā Ansari wrote a critique on the Ahmadi movement. As a student of Aligarh Muslim University, the book which was written in 1934 was considered a masterpiece in Islamic missionary literature. Mawlānā Ansari exposed the hollow claims of the Ahmadis and their professed claims to be the true representatives of Islam. Their sinister workings in the United Kingdom and Germany are critically examined by the learned author.[90] The first edition (1934) was published by The All Malaya Muslim Missionary Society, Singapore.

Bahaism in the Cape

In South Africa, Qadianism was not the only deviant sect that challenged the belief concerning the finality of prophethood: Bahaism made similar claims. During the mid 1950s, Joseph Perdu (d. 1978) surreptitiously promoted Bahaism in the country. His intellectual sophistication was misread as an authoritative exposition of Islam. The Arabic Study Circle (Durban) played a leading role in the dissemination of Perdu's unorthodox presentation of the Islamic teachings. However, his claims that "Islam will be taken away by God because a second prophet would emerge after 1000 years,[91] did not go unchallenged. Makki together with Ismail Bawa and Adam Peerbhai formed a vanguard against 'Perduism'. They embarked on an exhaustive program of action to expose Perdu and The Arabic Study Circle. Perdu's hasty departure did not stop Makki from his unabated campaign against the Circle members whose motives he suspected. Shamil Jeppie observed:

He (Makki) believed it was his duty to promote the basic purified Islamic creed through his publications, and to criticise anyone who deviated from what he understood to be the religion of Islam.[92]

---

[89] For a further elaboration on this subject see Siddiqui, "True Prophethood" in *The Muslim Digest*: March 1968, 9-11.

[90] Fazlur Rahman Ansari, *A New Muslim World in the Making* (Karachi, 2018).

[91] Shamil Jeppie, "Identity Politics and Public disputation: A Baha'i missionary as a Muslim Modernist in South Africa" in *Journal for Islamic Studies*, vol. 27: 2007, 150-7.

[92] Ibid., 167.

Makki's close association with Mawlānā Siddiqui ensured that the channels of communication regarding the latter's extensive tabligh travels were covered through his publications. The array of articles in *Ramadan Annual* and *The Muslim Digest* illustrated Makki's prolific activities.

Stellenbosch University

Mawlānā Siddiqui had a busy schedule in the Cape. His meetings with the distinguished academics from Stellenbosch University included discussions on contemporary religious thought and moral rearmament against the backdrop of sociopolitical developments in the country. According to Mawlāna Siddiqui, the twin evils of materialism and Communism loomed large over the horizon and it was Islam 'as the most creative of an active faith' that could counteract these ideological systems. Twenty years later, his successor, Mawlānā Ansari, also attended a symposium at Cape Town. His topic was *Do the Different Religions of the World offer a Solution to the Problems of the Twentieth Century?* Speakers besides Mawlānā Ansari were Professor Cumpsty, Head of Department of Religious Studies and the Chief Rabbi of Cape Town. Mawlānā Ansari's vast learning and depth of study of comparative religion was truly recognised. His logical presentation and well-structured reasoning were his outstanding traits that brought out the tenor of his lecture on comparative religion. The absence of polemics which otherwise tends to mar an objective analysis of the dogmas and beliefs of the Abrahamic faiths, was a marked feature of his exposition of Islam as a world religion.[93]

There is no doubt that Mawlānā Siddiqui's lectures strengthened the Muslim resolve to establish a distinct Islamic presence in the country.

---

[93] Cited in Choughley, *Fazlur Rahman Ansari: Life and Thought*, 164-65.

Assessment

Among the historic tabligh tours of Mawlānā Siddiqui, his lecture tour, particularly of 1952 stands out for his singular contributions to the growth and development of the Muslim community in South Africa. From Durban to Cape Town, his message was clear: Muslim identity flowed from unity (*ittihād*). In the same strain, he urged the Muslim organisations to develop a well-structured Islamic educational system that was compatible to the needs and aspirations of the community. *The Elementary Teachings of Islam* had a global reach among the English speaking Muslims and was a template for developing textbooks along this line. Mawlānā Siddiqui believed that progressive ideals were consistent with the Islamic ethos within the framework of the *iqrā* vision. Overall, Islam promoted a scientific temper by realigning the Islam and science discourse. His lectures and writings reflected his overriding concern for the *ummah* to assume their role as the saviours of humanity.

Chapter 8

Islamic Identity in Mauritius

Early Visits to Mauritius

As mentioned elsewhere in the volume (Chapter 2), Abdool Razack Mohamed (d.1978) was instrumental in arranging Mawlānā Siddiqui's visit to Mauritius in 1928. Our focus is on the legacy of this remarkable figure who in many ways reconfigured the collective identity of the Muslim community on this island.[1]

A timeline approach reveals interesting facets into the tabligh activities of Mawlānā Siddiqui. The demographics – a sizeable Muslim population with deep roots in the Indian subcontinental culture - shaped his contributions in the various fields of Muslim life. Apart from the speeches delivered in several mosques, Mawlānā Siddiqui, in his unique way, introduced Islam to many aspirant seekers- after-truth. For him there had to be a tangible expression of the Islamic identity: the establishment of the Volunteer Corps of Worshippers was the first step in this direction.

In 1931, his second visit to the country established his fame as an influential 'alim-activist who worked tirelessly with the community leaders to build a strong Muslim society. Sheikh Yacoob Ramjan who founded the Quatre Bornes Sunnee Mosque in 1927 also collaborated with Mawlānā Siddiqui to establish the Mauritius Muslim Orphanage in 1932. Like his illustrious brother, Mawlānā Ahmad Mukhtar who was the leading spirit behind the Dar-al-Yatama in Durban, he, too, saw the pressing need of establishing similar institutions to cater for the social welfare of the disadvantaged children as well as widows in the community. In a similar vein, a medical facility, the Currimjee Jeewanjee Infirmary, expanded his vision of Islam-in-action.

---

[1] I acknowledge the principal source of this chapter to Ibrahim Alladin's *Maulana Abdul Aleem Siddiqui.*

According to Alladin, Mawlānā Siddiqui was the embodiment of the three pillars of sufism (*tasawwuf*): charity, humility and truth. His charitable disposition extended beyond the conventional understanding of this philanthropic term. Alladin makes a perceptive observation:

> As he travelled around the world to promote peace and goodwill, he (Mawlānā Siddiqui) also urged Muslims to be charitable and build orphanages for the helpless youths, infirmaries for the destitute, hospitals for the suffering, spiritual assemblies for spiritual discipline, libraries for the preservation of the Islamic traditions and intellectual heritage, masjids, Muslim youth brigade and Muslims scouts for the physical and moral discipline of the youth.[2]

Mawlānā Siddiqui believed that the Islamic organisations should also reflect the inner dimensions of Islam. To this end, the Halqah Qaderia[3] was formed to develop a spiritual affinity with the rich repository of the Islamic traditions. As the name suggested, Mawlānā Siddiqui was a distinguished figure who belonged to the Qadiri *silsilah* (order). His inspirational talk on Shaykh Abdul Qadir Jilani (d. 1116), eponymous founder of the Qadiriyyah, expressed his profound love for this pre-eminent *mujaddid* (revivalist) of Islam. His decades- long tabligh personified two distinguishing traits of Shaykh Abdul Qadir: sacrifice for knowledge and upright character.

The popularity of Mawlānā Siddiqui in Mauritius was evident: the MBS (Mauritius Broadcasting Service) broadcasted his speeches and lectures, which evinced much interest among the non-Muslims. In a similar vein, the conversion of renowned personalities also took place at the hands of Mawlānā Siddiqui, among whom was the French statesman, Governor Merwat of Reunion Island. Charisma and spiritual grace were embedded in his unassuming personality. This period (1932) saw a flurry of tabligh activities in the far-flung areas of the island. It was not un-often that Mawlānā Siddiqui was

---

[2] Ibid., 156.

[3] Halqah Qaderi as it was known in other countries.

preoccupied with instructing the villagers on the basic tenets of Islam. *Salāh* was prioritised and so were the practical teachings of Islam.

It is generally assumed that Mawlānā Siddiqui addressed largely professionals, Islamic organisations or Muslim elites. This misperception stems from the image built around his personality. One account refers directly to his spiritual aura, which was the success story of his tabligh endeavours. An English officer disembarked at the port in Port Louis and decided to visit the Jumma Mosque. At the time, Mawlānā was delivering a lecture. The Englishman was enthralled by his magical voice and magnetic appeal. He was overcome by an unexpressed restlessness and insisted that he meet Mawlānā Siddiqui. The conversation lasted for half an hour and, thereafter, conversion was a lifetime experience.[4]

The subsequent visits by Mawlānā Siddiqui to Mauritius focused on the corporate identity of the Muslim community. He instituted the creation of the Waqf Board, which inter alia, oversaw the efficient administration of the mosques and other Islamic institutions. Another noteworthy contribution by him was the national celebration of the *Yaum al-Nabi* (Prophet's Day) in the presence of the Governor of Mauritius. This Islamic event was later declared a public holiday on the island. Mawlānā Siddiqui promoted the concept of good governance and in this respect the Muslim Unity Board was established. Given the diverse composition of the Muslim population and their respective historical backgrounds, he ensured that they were well represented in the various organisations.

Two salient matters were addressed by Mawlānā Siddiqui in his 1949 visit to Mauritius. First, he mooted the idea of the Inter-Religious organisation, which was carried forward by the Halqah Qaderi together with other executive members of the various committees. This was in line with the unity vision which he propagated in countries that he visited during his forty years of extensive tabligh travels. Second, Mawlānā submitted a memorandum to J. D. Hartford, the Governor of Mauritius "for the introduction of the

---

[4] *Al- Faqih* (Amritsar). March 14, 1932.

Muslim Personal Law to enable the people of Islamic faith to live according to the prescription of their religion."

Historic Visit: 1953

If 1952 was the landmark visit of Mawlānā Siddiqui to South Africa, then 1953 was equally significant for the Muslims of Mauritius. First, he was the special guest to commemorate the centenary of the Jumma Mosque on 9 April 1953. Second, the foundation stone for the Aleemiah College was laid by him in June. Of particular importance was the proposed Dar al-'Ulum which was aimed at providing a comprehensive course in ' Islamic theology and learning.' As the name of the Halqah Qaderi suggested, it strove to disseminate (*ishā'at*) the pristine teachings of Islam framed from the perspective of tabligh. This approach was in line with Mawlānā Siddiqui's lifelong mission. His key message in his farewell address was the unity of the Mauritian community. They were urged to follow the Islamic teachings in their totality; any deviation from the Prophetic model would lead to misguidance. This was an implicit reference to the threadbare Muslim groups who were advocating a rigid interpretation of Islam that was shorn of the spiritual values. He advised these committees to strengthen the Muslim Unity Board, which was representative of the collective aspirations of the Muslims. Its constitution was based on the Qur'ān and the sunnah, the unerring guides for Muslim success.

For the Mauritian nation, Mawlānā Siddiqui struck a positive note. He was overwhelmed by the changed atmosphere on the island and the mutual love and harmony engendered by his lectures. It was a revolution that was discernible in the lives of those men and women who had attended his inspirational lectures and pledged to work tirelessly to promote the spiritual values that were the common heritage of mankind. In the same strain, Mawlānā Siddiqui renewed his appeal to the citizens of Mauritius to shed the complexes of race and colour and build a stable society in the spirit of true brotherhood.

Mawlānā Siddiqui's message had a magnetic appeal: politicians like Seewoosagur Ramgoolam who later became the first prime minister of the country after independence of the country from British colonial rule, were mesmerised by his thoughts and open-mindedness. Overall, his call echoed the moral regeneration theme that shaped his tabligh mission.

Mawlānā Siddiqui had singled out the rural villages as his base for tabligh. First, the people were poor and earned a meagre wage on the sugar plantations. They were victims of exploitation by the landowners. Second, they led simple and austere lives. Education was hardly accessible to them and the rudimentary Islamic knowledge was a rarity. This was the plight of the poor villagers that Mawlānā Siddiqui strove to assist by teaching them the Islamic beliefs and practices. His regular visits brought about a transformation in their lives. In the thinly populated and remote village of L' Assurance, he laid the foundation stone for the madrasah - a testament to his selfless dedication and unconditional love for the Muslim communities, regardless of their financial and social status.[5]

Promoter of World- Fellowship and International Harmony

A versatile scholar and *muballigh*, Mawlānā Siddiqui was inspired to open up new pathways for developing the Islamic consciousness among the Muslims of Mauritius. His singular achievement was creating forums to institutionalise Islam on the island. His tabligh acuity brought about a revolution that had not been witnessed over the last century. Keeping in mind that his activities were not limited to Muslim affairs, his iconic status was equally recognised by the higher echelons of politics and society. State dignitaries were enthralled by his perceptive lectures. Likewise, the faith-based communities drew their inspiration from his knowledge of comparative religions and his spirit of tolerance. For the Muslim organisations he had a clear message: bigotry stifles the creative spirit of Islam. Essentially, this was the 'sweet fragrance' of his towering personality. Muslims had to access the foundational sources of Islam to build an ideal Islamic society.[6]

---

[5] Alladin, *Maulana Abdul Aleem Siddiqui*, 161-4.
[6] Souvenir: *The Roving Ambassador of Peace.*

Chapter 9

Inner Aspects of Faith

Mawlānā Siddiqui typified the tabligh-*tasawwuf* amalgam[1] which assumed importance in the twentieth century. Elsewhere in the volume the challenges created by the colonial and post-colonial situations are discussed with reference to the `ulama's response in the subcontinent. The rise of Marxism and Communism meant an onslaught on the universal values of Islam. Parallel to these ideological developments was the entrenched presence of materialism sweeping across the Muslim world. Thus, the need of the hour was to expand the base of tabligh with a strong spiritual orientation.

Tasawwuf: Content and Context

The multiple *tasawwuf* orders in the subcontinent were in the forefront of consolidating the *tajdidi* (revivalist) trends through the untiring efforts of the illustrious spiritual guides in the early twentieth century. A distinctive feature of the *tasawwuf* hierarchy was the initiation of *murids* into these multiple orders.[2] Their spiritual affinity or overlapping characteristics demonstrated the integral role of *islāh* (reform) in specific historical contexts. As a Qadiri shaykh, Mawlānā Siddiqui also belonged to the Sabiriyya Chistiyyah sub-order[3] enjoying a transnational affiliation. The sufi orders

---

[1] The tabligh-*tasawwuf* concept is a variant term for the `ulama and *mashā'ikh* who combined multiple roles in the promotion of Islamic beliefs and practices. The term denotes the scholarly and spiritual traditions reflected in these Islamic luminaries' lives. See Syed Habibul Haq Nadvi, *Islamic Resurgent Movements in the IndoPak Subcontinent* , 53.

[2] See Metcalf, *Islamic Revival in British India,* 158. A plausible explanation for this practice was to emphasise the synthesis of *tasawwuf.*

[3] No detailed study has been undertaken on the Sabiriyyah-Chistiyyah order. A brief account is found in Carl Ernst and Bruce Lawrence (eds.), *Sui Martyrs of Love* (New York, 2002), 118-27.

sought to update their relevance and reconfigure the network of their activities in the changing religious settings. Thus, Mawlānā Siddiqui personified the –continuity and change vision' associated with *tasawwuf* in its crucial period during the twentieth century.

Mawlānā Siddiqui's presentation of *tasawwuf* is lucidly discussed in his *Kitāb al-Tasawwuf*.[4] His other writings contain brief comments about the inner dimensions of the spiritual culture within the *tasawwuf* tradition. The conflict that exists between the practitioners of *tasawwuf* and its vocal critics rests primarily on the technical definitions of this discipline. Two terms fall under the rubric of *tasawwuf*: *tazkiyah al-nafs* (purification of the soul) and *Fiqh al-bātin* (jurisprudence of the inner aspects).

The following comment sheds light on the nature and function of *tasawwuf*:

> There are two very difficult and unavoidable stages encountered in all doctrines, be they ethics, education and training, reformation or the values. In the one stage the means becomes the object and in the other, technical terms obscure the realities. Without them the propagation and teaching are impossible. [If there exists no balance] between the means and technical terms, they become detrimental instead of beneficial. The matter of *tasawwuf* is very similar. The aims and objectives are self-evident. However, when the means were exaggerated in importance and the technical terms were over-emphasised, *tasawwuf* was adversely affected. A poet has appropriately said:

> *Wise men do not get involved with words*
> *Are the divers' interests in shells or the pearls?*[5]

Historically, *tasawwuf* and its variations (*tazkiyah and Fiqh*) underwent considerable changes over the centuries. Beginning from sufis in the early period of its formation,[6] it met with resistance from

---

[4] Siddiqui, *Kitāb al-Tasawwuf* (Karachi, 1994).
[5] Muhammad Iqbal, *The Achievement of Love: The Spiritual Dimension of Islam* (Montreal, 1987), 5.
[6] Mawlānā Ansari has given an interesting overview of the evolution of *tasawwuf* in

certain sections of the `ulama fraternity who regarded its rituals and practices as *bid'ah* (blameworthy innovation).[7] In fact, one of the contributory factors for the ambivalent reception towards *tasawwuf* was its terminology[8] which tended to blur out its aims and ideals. There was no doubt that *tasawwuf* as a discipline did not always align itself to the shari`ah norms and standards through which the outward form of *Fiqh* could be entrenched. To this end, *tazkiyah* is a progression of *mujāhadāt* (spiritual endeavours)[9] that ultimately leads to *ihsān* (spiritual perfection). All the spiritual struggle and exercise are undertaken to achieve this condition of perfection. Regarding *ihsān*, the hadith says that the Messenger of Allah was asked "What is perfection (*ihsān*)? The Messenger of Allah replied, "That you worship Allah as if you see Him, for though you do not see Him [know] that He does see you."[10]

Purifiying the Heart

The cleansing of the *nafs* (self) is elaborated by Mawlānā Siddiqui in his *Kitāb al-Tasawwuf*. The source of the transformative energy is the heart (*qalb*) which in sufi parlance is a "receptable of Allah's grace and is spiritual in substance."[11] The following hadith emphasises the pivotal role of the heart in relation to the human personality:

> *Indeed, there is a body in the flesh which if it is sound then the whole body is sound, and if it is corrupt then the whole body is corrupt. Indeed, it is the heart.*[12]

Mustafa Alvi, *Al-Haqā'iq* (Karachi, 1963).

[7] The term *bid'ah* has become a contentious issue between the reformists and *tasawwuf*-aligned `ulama. Shaykh Muhammad al-Ghazali (d. 1996), the eminent Egyptian scholar has made a critical study about *bid'ah* from the legal and *tasawwuf* perspectives. Ghazali, *Within the Boundaries of Islam: A Study of Bid'ah.* Translated by Aslam Farouk-Alli (Kuala Lumpur, 2010).

[8] Ibid, 85-95.

[9] Siddiqui, *Kitāb al-Tasawwuf*, 36-7.

[10] Muslim: *Kitāb al-Iman.*

[11] Mir Valiuddin, *Contemplative Disciplines in Sufism* (London, 1980), 11.

[12] Bukhari and Muslim, Cf. Siddiqui, *Kitāb al-Tasawwuf*, 36.

The classical writings of the early sufis reinforce the role of the heart in the human body. Imam Ghazali in his intellectual masterpiece, *Ihyā 'Ulum al-Din* (Revival of the Islamic Sciences) wrote in detail about the human heart:

> Although the spiritual heart (*qalb*), which is the controlling centre of the soul, is different from the physical human heart, its functioning is related and directed by it ... Every quality that appears in the heart will have its influence flowing to the organs so that they act only in accordance with that quality. In the same manner, the effect of every action that is committed from the organs may reach the heart. And this keeps on occurring in a circular fashion.

Abdur Rahman Ibn al-Jawzee, in his book *Minhāj al- Qāsidin* expressed the following views about the human heart:

> We should understand that the heart holds the supreme position in the human body. It is this organ that recognises Allah and works to get close to Allah. Other organs are its subordinates. The heart by its nature quests for the path of righteousness. It is true that whoever has recognised his heart has recognised Allah.[13]

The human heart is the place of constant change and fluctuation. It is the isthmus (*al-barzakh*) between this world and the Hereafter. The battlefield of the greater *jihād* is the heart where the lower self is confronted by the yearning spirit (*ruh*). The high and low tendencies in the heart are inseparable from the status of the self (*nafs*) which is associated with the ego.

According to Mawlānā Siddiqui, if the ego submits to the dictates of the compulsive obsessive self (*nafs al-ammārah*) it is the blaming self (*nafs al-lawwāmah*) that acts as a monitor and warns of the evil consequences that follow.[14] The blaming self is a counter force that can

---

[13] Cited in Gohar Mushtaq, *The Intelligent Heart, The Pure Heart* (London, 2008), 5-6.
[14] Siddiqui, *Spiritual Culture in Islam,* 101.

maintain checks and balances against our inclination to commit evil.[15]

It is the shari`ah that has prescriptive methods for controlling the *nafs al-ammārah*. The institution of fasting (*sawm*) brings the animal appetite under control and to a large extent suppresses the evil tendencies. Likewise, the institution of *zakāh* reduces the obsession to amass wealth at the expense of neglecting one's duties towards society. Thus, the shari`ah has built-in safeguards against the inclinations of the ego. A regimen of spiritual training is required for the soul to progress during its onward journey to the pursuit of spiritual perfection: 'the tranquil self' (*nafs al-mutma'innah*).[16]   A reference is found in the *āyah*:

> *O you peaceful soul! Return unto your Lord, well-pleased and well-pleasing. Enter among My righteous servants. And enter My Garden.*[17]

According to Iqbal, the heart is a kind of inner intention or insight which brings us into contact with Reality (*ma'rifah*). It reflects the spiritual reality in the heart and is beautifully captured in the following verse of Rumi:

> *Purify your heart from the rust (of sins)*
> *Then you shall perceive that light of Reality (ma'rifah).*[18]

Tasawwuf and Prophetic Culture

Mawlānā Siddiqui's *tasawwuf* is grounded in the Qur'ān and the sunnah. According to him, spiritual culture emanates from imbuing divine attributes personified by the Holy Prophet's (SAW) personal conduct. The Divine attributes which are the core values advocated by the *mashā'ikh* can be manifested in the following ways:

The Holy Prophet (pbuh) said: "Imbue yourselves with

---

[15] Siddiqui, *Kitāb al-Tasawwuf*, 110-111.
[16] Siddiqui, *Spiritual Culture in Islam*, 102-3.
[17] 89 : 27-30. Cf. Mahbub Ahmad, *Shifā i-Dil* (Allahabad, 2005), 118-40.
[18] Siddiqui, *Spiritual Culture in Islam*, 105.

divine morals," which means: Allah is Pure; hence, you also should strive after purity. Allah is Perfect; hence, you also should work for the elimination of your defects and shortcomings and strive after perfection. Allah is the embodiment of truth; hence, you also should imbue yourselves with truthfulness. Allah is Just; hence, you also should practice justice and eliminate the desire of oppressing anyone. When the vision of the soul is focused on its Origin (Allah), the human personality which is a lamp for the spiritual light begins to reflect the divine morals. Or, you might say, that, as the soul has special affinity with Allah, it realises at this stage that it is itself a mirror in which the Divine attributes reflect themselves and that it is the repository of the divine morals.[19]

The exemplary conduct of the Holy Prophet (pbuh) is borne out in the following *āyah*:

And you (stand) on an exalted standard of character.[20]

All facets of the Holy Prophet's (pbuh) life were fused with spirituality; therefore, it was the inner dimensions that drew man spontaneously and unconditionally to Allah. All actions were directed to earn Allah's pleasure. In this regard, Mawlānā Siddiqui makes an insightful comment:

It is the unique and distinguishing feature of the Holy Prophet's (pbuh) character that he was a "man of the world" and a "man of Allah" at one and the same time. His devotion to and communion with Allah and the performance of his multifarious duties as the leader of the faithful, went side by side. He was the human personification of Islam, which combines in its harmonious system the "religious" as well as the "secular" aspects of human activity. [It] destroys the very foundations of the popular notion of "secular things" by

---

[19] Ibid., 103.
[20] Qur'ān, 68: 4.

supplying a spiritual basis for each and every conceivable aspect of our life.[21]

In a similar vein, shari`ah and *tariqah* (the spiritual path) are complementary ideals which make the spiritual journey possible. It is the *tariqah* that is rooted in the Qur'ān and the shari`ah and is "like a tree whose branches stretch outwards towards heaven."[22] The *silsilahs* (spiritual orders) as the name suggests have preserved the means of spiritual realisation that go back to the Holy Prophet (pbuh) and transmit his special *barakah* (grace) from generation to generation.[23]

Contemplative Disciplines in *Tasawwuf*

The contemplative disciplines of *tasawwuf* have raised important questions about their validity and efficacy. Mawlānā Siddiqui maintains that the methods of *dhikr* (remembrance) have life-enriching elements of focus and vision. They are effective techniques to the transformation of the human personality to reach the goal of *ma'rifah* (divine knowledge).[24] These contemplative disciplines may vary from one *silsilah* (spiritual order) to another but their goal leads to the unitary experience where the potential for spiritual perfection is limitless.[25] The primary spiritual technique of *tasawwuf* is *dhikr*, which ultimately becomes unified with the rhythm of life itself. In Arabic the word *dhikr* conveys the meaning of supplication and remembrance. They are forcefully captured in this *āyah*:

> *Those who believe, and whose hearts find satisfaction in the remembrance of Allah. For without doubt in the remembrance of Allah do hearts find satisfaction.*[26]

---

[21] Siddiqui, *The Universal Teachings*, 256.

[22] Seyyed Hossein Nasr, *Ideals and Realities of Islam*, (Lahore, 1993), 135. Cf. Qur'ān: 14: 24.

[23] Ibid., 144. Cf. Siddiqui, *Kitāb al-Tasawwuf*, 112-3.

[24] Ibid., 38-9.

[25] Ibid., 116-7.

[26] Qur'ān: 13:28

Likewise, there are many *ahādith* that extol the virtues of *dhikr*. These Qur'ānic and prophetic sources form the basis of the sufi methods of *dhikr*.[27]

According to Mawlānā Siddiqui, a believer's pursuit of true happiness "is born of the remembrance of Allah."[28] It has two vital functions: power and goodness proceed from Allah and, therefore, our actions should be guided by the revealed laws under every circumstances. Hence, *dhikr* has an all-pervading presence that governs a believer's *(mu'min)* life towards true happiness and abiding peace. This affinity between a believer and Allah develops into a *qurb* (nearness) which is established through *dhikr*. This is clearly shown in the following *āyah*:

We indeed created man and We know what his soul whispers to him, and We are nearer to him than his jugular vein.[29]

Elaborating on the above *āyah*, the eminent commentator of the Qur'ān, Abdul Majid Daryabadi makes a pertinent observation:

Allah is even more minutely conscious of his (man's) innermost feelings than is his own self. That is the exact relationship, in Islam, between Allah and man. Of course, there is no identity between the two; we remain ourselves, and He the great Other. Yet His communion with us is of an even more intimate nature than is that of ourselves with ourselves. The verse also does away entirely with the idea of Allah being remote and unapproachable, and stresses His all-pervading character and His intimacy with all His creatures.[30]

---

[27] The *Kashful Mahjub* by Syed Ali Hujweri is the earliest text on *tasawwuf*. It shows how the Sahabah embodied the true meaning of *dhikr* in their everyday lives. The method may have varied with the later generations but the essence permeated the lives of the sufi masters. Ali Hujweri, *The Kashful Mahjub*, Translation with Special Commentary by Wahid Baksh Rabbani (Kuala Lumpur, 1997).

[28] Siddiqui, *Quest for True Happiness*, 12.

[29] Qur'ān: 50: 16.

[30] Daryabadi, *The Glorious Qur'ān: Text, Translation and Commentary* (Leicester, 2008), 933.

True *dhikr* is a spiritual state (*hāl*) in which the devotee concentrates his physical and spiritual powers on Allah, so that his entire being is united with Him. This true remembrance is not merely an expression of the tongue, but of the heart. Constancy and focus lead to this ideal without which it becomes a soulless practice. By drawing the following analogy, Mawlānā Siddiqui illustrates the conflicting relationship between the inner forces. The lower self (*nafs*) stands between the disengaged spirit (*ruh*) which is light and the corporeal body (*jism*) which is darkness. A spiritual battle is waged against the downward pull of the *nafs* which tends to seduce the heart (*qalb*) away from the *dhikr* of Allah.[31] Thus, *dhikr* is a 'feeder for the soul'[32] which sustains the human personality; it derives inner strength and vision in order to create a harmonious pattern with the Divine Will. In this realm, the emotional and psychological obstacles are diminished; the lodestar of true happiness guides the devotee to the promised glad tidings in the Holy Qur'ān:

> *We are your protectors in this life and in the Hereafter: therein shall you have all that your souls shall desire; therein shall you have all that you ask for!*[33]

The Islamic spiritual discipline[34] as Mawlānā Ansari terms it, possesses the innate power to combat alien ideologies or systems that sway man from Allah's remembrance. A spiritual orientation is required to thwart evil deeds which act as a barrier to the divine realisation. Islam has defined the concept of worship (*'ibādah*) in the Holy Qur'ān:

> *I have only created Jinn and men that they shall worship Me.*[35]

The focusing of attention upon Allah, Mawlānā Siddiqui states, will

---

[31] Mohamed, *The Roving Ambassador of Peace,* 47-8.
[32] Siddiqui, *Quest for True Happiness,* 11.
[33] Qur'ān: 41: 31-2.
[34] Foreword to Siddiqui, *The Forgotten Path of Knowledge,* 16.
[35] Qur'ān: 51-56.

produce a two-fold result. On the one hand, we will have a realisation of ourselves, a clear grasp of the reality of the soul and on the other our belief in Allah (*imān*) will be transformed from mere words into a practical and living reality.[36] This is a form of *ihsān* that a believer strives for in his quest for true happiness. The various aspects of *dhikr* are contained in the techniques adopted by the sufis. Ghazali, for example, has elaborated on the names of Allah (*asmā al-husnā*) as the transformer to our human personality. Through the simple process of repetition, the *dhikr* (remembrance) is 'transferred' from the tongue to the mind, from the mind to the feelings and the deeper levels of the personality until its reality (*haqiqah*) is established in the core of the human being. Mawlānā Ansari's presentation of the Islamic spiritual discipline bears close resemblance to his mentor, Mawlānā Siddiqui. In his major work, *The Qur'ānic Foundations*, Mawlānā Ansari outlines the integral aspects of *dhikr* which are inextricably linked to *tazkiyah* (self-purification).

Remembrance of Allah (*dhikr*) as the fundamental exercise is directed to seeking the nearness of Allah, and cannot, therefore, be something formal. As such, firstly it should be undertaken in a state of 'withdrawal' - withdrawing attention from everything else and concentrating it solely on Allah. Secondly, it should be undertaken abundantly under all conditions and at all times. Thirdly, it should be joined to contemplation of the Signs of Allah, which pervade the entire universe. Fourthly, it should be combined with a study of divine guidance as contained in the Holy Qur'ān and with a serious exercise in moulding one's life in accordance with it to the fullest extent possible. Fifthly, this entire exercise should proceed more conscientiously as well as most intelligently in order that the practical results and the tangible fruits of all this labour of love may be grasped at every step for enabling the pilgrim of eternity to undertake his spiritual flights and moral development at higher and higher levels with the attainment of ever-increasing refinement of the soul, on the one hand and purity of will for moral action, on the other.[37]

---

[36] Siddiqui, *The Forgotten Path of Knowledge*, 17.

[37] Ansari, *The Qur'ānic Foundations and Structure of Muslim Society*, vol. I, 306-7.

Spiritual Rearmament

Like Mawlānā Siddiqui who had been advocating the spiritual rearmament as the alternative to materialism, Mawlānā Ansari envisioned *tazkiyah* as a guarantor of Islamic leadership. In the history of Islam, Mawlānā Ansari says, it was the spiritual luminaries (sufis) who fought with their spiritual armour[38] alone against the hostile forces to establish the supremacy of Islam. It was through their *tazkiyah* that they "acquired the glorious distinction of becoming the sole pioneers of converting vast and widespread communities to Islam."[39]

A critical analysis of the Muslim predicament in the world today reinforces the need for a surge of Islamic spiritual values. Mawlānā Ansari says:

> The world of Islam will have to revive the pursuit of comprehensive *tazkiyah* in accordance with the norms and principles laid down in the Qur'ān and Sunnah. [in order] that genuine Islamic leadership of the Muhammadan pattern (*uswah al-hasanah*) emerges on a high level and in a large measure, and acts fruitfully for the fulfilment of the mission of Islam.[40]

There is a general tendency among the misguided sufis[41] to marginalise the exalted status of the Holy Prophet (pbuh) in preference to the practices of their respective *silsilahs*. This attitude militates against the shari'ah-*tariqah* dimension. Likewise, these trends have a detrimental effect on the true nature of *tasawwuf* and

---

[38] Ibid., 313.

[39] Ibid., 314.

[40] Ibid.

[41] Mawlānā Ansari makes the of following assessment of this situation: "With the awful degeneration of society... the understanding and practice of *tasawwuf* also has degenerated in more dimensions than ever. Also, its name has been misused for certain wrong notions and ideas in certain quarters." *The Qur'ānic Foundations,* vol. I, 152.

have also given rise to scepticism among certain segments of the *ummah*. The practical approach adopted by Mawlānā Siddiqui is a summative assessment of *tasawwuf*:

> Shari`ah is the sacred law as enunciated by the Holy Prophet (pbuh). Prayer (*salāh*) is the obligation of the law, but *tariqah* is the inner attitude towards one's actions and *haqiqah* is the state manifested in the heart of a believer when praying. The sacred law provides the foundation for true knowledge and noble character traits. Those who "know" Allah and the beloved Holy Prophet (pbuh) will never leave shari`ah.
> Their love for Allah and the Holy Prophet (pbuh) preserves them from letting the scale of the law slip from their hands.[42]

Love for the Holy Prophet (pbuh)

In the *tasawwuf* realm, *fana i-Rasul*[43] is pervaded by the spontaneous and overwhelming love for the Holy Prophet (pbuh). This love which surpasses all forms of attachment has a direct bearing on the hadith literature. Mawlānā Siddiqui maintains that the journey to spiritual perfection is not possible without the unconditional attachment to the Holy Prophet (pbuh). His personal conduct is our model to follow. On a higher realm of love for the Holy Prophet (pbuh), he counsels the believers:

> Close your eyes and the inner eyes will open. This does not mean to blink the eyelids, but to annihilate one's eyes in the eyes of the Holy Prophet (pbuh). This is when the believer's eyes are overwhelmed and nothing seems dearer to him than the love for the Holy Prophet (pbuh).[44]

The importance of the sunnah is beautifully summed in these

---

[42] Mohamed, *The Roving Ambassador of Peace*, 35.

[43] The *fanā* (annihilation) theory may be gleaned from *Dhikr al-Habib*, a collection of articles written in praise of the Holy Prophet (pbuh). See Siddiqui, *Dhikr i-Habib* (Karachi, 2018).

[44] Mohamed, *The Roving Ambassador of Islam*, 37.

words:

> It is inconceivable that these virtues [of the sunnah] could
> have been practised through the centuries down to our time if
> the founder of Islam had not personified them in the highest
> degree; it is also inconceivable that they should have been
> borrowed from elsewhere - and one cannot imagine from
> where since their conditioning and their style are specifically
> Islamic. For Muslims the moral and spiritual worth of the Holy
> Prophet (pbuh) is not an abstraction or a supposition; it is a lived
> reality, and it is precisely this which proves its authenticity
> retrospectively.[45]

This 'lived reality' is an expression of Muslim devotion to the
beautiful conduct of the Holy Prophet (pbuh). The declaration of the
Holy Prophet's (pbuh) status is discussed in several Qur'ānic *āyāt*
(verses).[46]

Dhikr i-Habib encapsulates the cumulative veneration of the Holy
Prophet (pbuh) by Mawlānā Siddiqui. It is a treasure trove of poetic
elegance gracefully crafted in sublime prose. The readers navigate
the life and teachings of the Holy Prophet (pbuh) and immerse
themselves in the ocean of love. The soul-stirring descriptions evoke
a sense of deep reference, a spontaneous expression of tear-filled
supplications (*munājāt*) in the spiritual presence of the *Mercy to the
Worlds*.

Tasawwuf: The method of spiritual pursuits in Islam

This position is reflected in Mawlānā Siddiqui's presentation of
tasawwuf as the inner dimension of Islam. It is the 'soul of Islam' which
is sustained by *imān* (belief), Islam and *ihsān*.[47] These three levels form

---

[45] Schimmel, *And Muhamad is His Messenger*, 29.

[46] Qur'ān: 68:4.

[47] This hadith defines the framework of *tasawwuf* and reaffirms the primacy of the outer
(*zāhir*) and inner (*bātin*) aspects of Islam to the development of the human
personality. For a detailed discussion on this concept, see Ibn Hajar Askalani, *Fath
al-Bāri*, vol. 1 (Cairo, 1980), 144-8.

the basis of *tasawwuf* and are the markers of the Islamic authenticity. Mawlānā Siddiqui laments at attempts to misrepresent *tasawwuf* by groups giving embellished and perhaps incredulous accounts of the *mashā'ikh* who were the upholders of the sunnah. On the contrary, they epitomised Islam in their pure lives and guided others by their exemplary conduct. The spiritual ethos was a living tradition which removed the crust of superstition and syncretic practices accumulated over the centuries by Islam's encounter with the alien philosophies.[48] Mawlānā Siddiqui deplored the encroachment of the mystical systems that distorted the simple message contained in *tasawwuf* as these thoughts alienated Muslims from appreciating the essence of the spiritual pursuits propagated by the *mashā'ikh*.[49] Therefore, any attempt to assign blame to them is a travesty of justice. In a similar vein, Mawlānā Siddiqui urged Muslims to reassess their attitude towards *tasawwuf* as quite a number of people had come to believe in its so-called un-Islamic character. The Qur'ān provided the method as the following *āyah* shows:

Truly he succeeds that purifies it (soul)[50]

In this connection, he says:

It consists in the purpose of *tazkiyah*- cultivation of traits that lead to the development of the human personality in the spiritual dimension.[51]

According to Mawlānā Siddiqui, man's quest for spiritual

---

[48] Islam's encounter with the different cultures since the early Muslim conquest is critically examined in M.M. Sharif (ed), *A History of Muslim Philosophy*, 2 volumes. (Karachi, 1983).

[49] Mawlānā Siddiqui refers to the spiritual illumination which was evident in the lives of the eminent *mashā'ikh* over the centuries. See Siddiqui, *Spiritual Culture in Islam*, 109.

[50] Qur'ān: 95:9.

[51] In a similar strain, Mawlānā Ansari maintains that *dhikr* (remembrance of Allah) and *Fikr* (probe into the mysteries of Creation) lead to *falāh*, which has a wider connotation in the Qur'ān. Ansari, *The Qur'ānic Foundations and Structure of Muslim Society*, vol. 1, 153.

perfection (*ihsān*) is derived from the knowledge that our full focus of attention is on Allah. With spiritual exercise, *tazkiyah* will take place through which our spiritual faculty will develop. The infirmities and diseases associated with negative traits (*akhlāq al-razilah*) will give way to the spiritual power which can realise its full potential through acts prescribed in the Qur'ān and the sunnah. He observes:

> This increase in spiritual power will lead us towards spiritual perfection which will manifest itself in high and sublime morals and will enable us to fight those diseases which arise in the moral sphere. And the more we advance on that path, the nearer we will be to the concept of the Perfect Man (*insān al- kāmil*).[52]

The methodology that Mawlānā Siddiqui proposes is consistent with the teachings of the *mashā'ikh* of the past. Its essence remains unchanged as it is grounded in the perennial sources of Islam. A distinctive feature of Mawlānā Siddiqui's presentation of *tasawwuf* is the absence of cluttered terms that tends to obscure its true purpose and function. Instead, he employs his mastery of modern science and philosophy to present the 'Qur'ānic sufism' which is compatible with the temperament of modern man. This approach had endeared him to the hearts of thousands of Muslims across the world. His charismatic presence exuded the inner energy that transformed many lives to be aligned to *taqwā*. His message was far-reaching and served as a model for the spiritual quest in a world mired in materialism and other deviant ideologies. In the final analysis, the essence of *tasawwuf* is clearly explained:

> The message is: Remember Allah and regard Him as Omnipresent and All-Knowing in every moment of your life. Search for His Message in its authentic form, and when you have found it, practise it. Mould morals and your habits in conformity with the Divine laws. Remain conscious that Allah

---

[52] Siddiqui, *The Forgotten Path of Knowledge,* 16.

alone is your real Master and King. Bow down to His commands, and take as your model His Messengers, the last of whom was the Holy Prophet (pbuh). Follow this course and preach the same to others. Walk on this path and attain real success, abiding peace and true happiness.[53]

Embodiment of *Tasawwuf*

Two incidents related by Mawlānā Ansari regarding Mawlānā Siddiqui's trust and reliance in Allah (*tawakkul*) are a testament to the status of the *mashā'ikh*. In sufi language they are endowed with *karāmat* and *kashf* by the will of Allah. These states are not acquired (*kasb*) nor do the *mashā'ikh* strive towards perfecting them. Within the sufi hierarchy, *karāmat* refers to the charismatic gift or supernatural action or miracle which Allah the Generous (*al-karim*) bestows upon His friends (*awliyā*). Moreover, the power of *karāmat* manifests itself in different ways by the Divine Command.[54]

Mawlānā Siddiqui's trust in Allah was unwavering that he was able to remain calm and focused under adverse circumstances. The following account narrated by Mawlānā Ansari points out to the course of events as the manifestation of *karāmat*:

Let me tell you about Mawlānā Abdul Aleem Siddiqui. I was with him on a world tour during 1950 and we visited the capital of the Philippines, Qutabatu. A function was to be held on an open square scheduled to begin after Maghrib. After Dhuhr (*salāh*), dark clouds appeared and by Asr, conditions worsened with signs of a big storm. After Asr, I mentioned to my teacher about the dark clouds and the rolling thunder and the impending storm, and he replied: "My dear son, why are you worried? We have come here to deliver the message of Allah – the rain is sent by Allah, the earth belongs to Allah and the human beings are

---

[53] The term 'Qur'ānic Sufism' is employed to prove the interrelationship between the Qur'ān and *tasawwuf*. See Mir Valiuddin, *Qur'ānic Sufism* (Lahore, 1991).

[54] Amatullah Armstrong, *Sufi Terminology, The Mystical Language of Islam*, 108.

creatures of Allah, and if He wants me to deliver the message it will be done."

After Maghrib we went to the open plain, where a huge crowd was waiting. The governor was the chairman and the Chief Justice who was a Roman Catholic was also there. His Eminence, Mawlānā Siddiqui just began to deliver this talk when huge drops of rain started to fall. The huge crowd started to get up in order to flee to their homes when Mawlānā Siddiqui said: "My dear friends, don't be worried, the rain is going to stop right now." And the rain stopped. Mawlānā Siddiqui assured them that "[it] will not rain for as long as this function is on. However, after the function is over you will have ten minutes to get to your homes, and then a very big storm will come."

Not one drop of rain fell after the announcement and Mawlānā Siddiqui delivered one of his finest lectures in an utmost carefree manner and spoke for about one and half hours. The rumbling and thunder was there all the time. Then the chairman gave the vote of thanks. When the function was over, the people rushed to the platform in order to shake hands with Mawlānā Siddiqui who again said: "My dear friends, you were running away from here earlier and don't you see what is happening in the sky? Please, for Allah's sake, you have ten minutes to get to your homes and I am going to my hotel." Exactly ten minutes later the storm came and the following morning, the water in the roads was about two metres high. Thousands of those who were Catholics, became Muslims. This happened in 1950! This is *khalifat-Allah and this is Islam.*[55]

Likewise, Allah blessed Mawlānā Siddiqui with *kashf* through which the Divine mysteries and knowledge of reality were unveiled to His servant *('abd).* In essence, the divine self-disclosure not only increases his knowledge of Allah but love of Allah.[56] The following incident shows the power of *kashf* which in many instances was characteristic of the *mashā'ikh's*

---

[55] Mohamed, *The Roving Ambassador of Peace,* xvi -vii.
[56] Armstrong, *Sufi Terminology,* 109.

extraordinary lives.

Mawlānā Siddiqui's itinerary to Canada during his 1949-50 tabligh tour included a public lecture at the Edmonton Mosque. His scheduled flight from New York to Edmonton was, therefore, confirmed. According to Mawlānā Ansari, that evening after Maghrib *salāh*, Mawlānā Siddiqui called him aside and informed him to cancel the booking to Edmonton. He was perplexed at Mawlānā Siddiqui's change of plan and even attempted to dissuade him as the arrangements for his public lecture were finalised. Mawlānā Siddiqui was adamant and instructed Mawlānā Ansari to inform the travel agency accordingly. When asked about a rescheduled date for his visit to the Edmonton Mosque, Mawlānā Siddiqui was non-commital. The following morning, the 'breaking news' on several radio stations covered the aircraft disaster. Mawlānā Ansari narrated the tragic turn of events:

The aircraft carrying hundreds of passengers (exact number not specified) left from New York. Not long it exploded in mid-air killing all passengers aboard. It was one of the worst aviation disasters in recent times.[57]

The concept of *khilafāh* has important implications. First, there are concrete proofs that the elements of nature are subservient to a *mu'min* (believer) by Divine permission. Second, the notion of `*abdiyat* - total surrender to the will of Allah - raises a believer's rank in which he is blessed with 'divine gifts'. Last, contemplation (*dhikr*) opens up the pathways of spiritual harmony. In this way the heart, the fulcrum of moral and spiritual equilibrium, becomes the repository of true happiness and abiding peace.[58]

Assessment

Tabligh embedded in the *tasawwuf* framework chalked out new opportunities for Mawlānā Siddiqui in his international travels. The establishment of *halqahs* became centres of Islamic learning where

---

[57] Lecture: *Sufism, The Method of Spiritual Pursuit in Islam* (Durban, 1970).
[58] Siddiqui, *Quest for True Happiness*, 13.

the shari`ah merged seamlessly with *tariqah*. Mawlānā Siddiqui's multifaceted personality endeared him to thousands of people from different religious backgrounds. His sincerity of purpose and intense love for the Holy Prophet (pbuh) spurred him to present the comprehensive message of Islam to Muslims and non-Muslims alike. His personal life embodied the Prophetic model, and his mission was aimed at promoting unity, peace and harmony to mankind.

Chapter 10

Reflections

The message of humanity was the overriding concern of Mawlānā Siddiqui's tabligh mission. His forty years of extensive travels of tabligh, *tarbiyah* (spiritual training) and interfaith dialogue transcended the sectarian and ideological boundaries. Several key concepts were developed on his interpretive understanding of Islam as a universal religion. Unity (*ittihād*) among the Muslim communities irrespective of their sectarian backgrounds was based on mutual respect and the decorum of disagreement (*ikhtilāf*).[1] Mawlānā Siddiqui deplored the sectarian divide particularly in the subcontinent which inevitably created a fissure in the *ummah* with no collective voice to articulate the corporate Islamic identity (*tashakkhus*). Sadly, the theological debates dominated the Islamic discourse and the result was obvious- a divided *ummah*. To redress this imbalance, Mawlānā Siddiqui undertook rigorous tabligh tours to bring Muslim organisations and communities closer together in their pursuit of a common ideal: to be an exemplary model for humanity. This indeed was an extraordinary accomplishment in view of the enormous hurdles he had to face to restore the primacy of Islamic textual sources as the guidance the mankind.

It was no fortuitous circumstances that his meetings with influential non-Muslim organisations and eminent personalities paved the way for the interfaith forum that advocated the unity (*wahdat*) of humanity. Mawlānā Siddiqui envisioned the organisation to promote universal values of morality and spirituality as precursors to the new world order. The formation of the IRO was meant to stem the tide of materialism, Marxism and Communism sweeping across the world. Muslim countries were no exception to their pervasive influences. According to Mawlānā Siddiqui, Islam as

---

[1] The polemical literature on *ikhtilāf* has been a major cause for sectarian bickering. The refinement of disagreement (*adab*) has been displaced by extremism (*tashaddud*), which does not augur well for any prospect of reconciliation for the *ummah*. See Taha Jabir Al-Alwani, *The Ethics of Disagreement in Islam* (Herndon, 1993).

a universal religion remained uncorrupted in its divinely- revealed mission to establish unity among humanity. This did not in any way imply that a syncretic religion had to evolve to achieve this goals. Rather Mawlānā Siddiqui emphasised the intrinsic values like justice, truth and morality in his presentation of global unity as opposed to unity of religions (*wahdat al-adyān*).[2] This clear distinction must be made to appreciate Islam's role as the *ummatan wasatan* - a religion maintaining harmonious balance to the development of the human personality. It is through Islam that man may find meaning and fulfilment in life.

Mawlānā Siddiqui's missionary fervour bore distinct imprints of his unwavering commitment to establish unconditional devotion to the Holy Prophet's (pbuh) personality and love for humanity. His personal life mirrored the Prophetic conduct in its practical form; his vision embraced Islam as a *din* - a comprehensive way of life. There were no political overtones to his tabligh nor were there vested sectarian interests to advance a particular version of Islam. He eschewed both rigidity and extremism–two reactionary impulses that have impacted negatively Islam's legacy as a civilisational force. In fact, these two traits have raised the spectre of the clash of civilisations that the world of Islam is witnessing. On the contrary, Mawlānā Siddiqui's profile as a scholar and sufi had opened up the pathway for mutual understanding and tolerance. Obviously, geopolitical developments have changed the religious landscape; globalisation has invoked new interpretive readings of the Islamic discourse.

There is no doubt that Mawlānā Siddiqui's multidimensional personality foregrounded the progressive orthodoxy paradigm developed by Mawlānā Ansari as an alternative to the modernist interpretation of Islam. Like the sufi scholars of the past, he maintained that transparency and *taqwā* (Allah consciousness) were the beacon lights which illumined the Muslim understanding of being

---

[2] The Sufi International Order, founded by Inayat Khan (d. 1927) employed the Chishti tradition to develop his theory of the fundamental oneness of all religions. As a result, Islam was marginalised as other faiths were given equal status through Inayat Khan's Universal Worship service.

Allah's *khalifah* (custodian).[3] Thus, the message for humanity assumed greater clarity to his definition of tabligh.

The following article is a conspectus of Mawlānā Siddiqui's visionary spirit and commitment to tabligh.

In my old age, I have undertaken the present world- tour, with all its attendant hardships, only with the mission of delivering the message of peace and goodwill to my fellow-beings so that they might be able to avoid conflicts and quarrels and to live in harmony. After years of serious thinking, I have come to the conclusion that the real cause of human strife and wars consists in selfishness, on the one hand, and the forgetfulness of Allah on the other. When people begin to act in utter self-interest, when the social obligations are forgotten, when one can stoop down so low as to pursue one's interest at the cost of the rights of others, harmony and concord recede into the background. Similarly, when men become so engrossed in earth-rootedness that they do not find the occasion to remember their Creator even formally, when the relations with that Supreme Source of Power are cut off, when we cease to feel that by breaking the divinely-appointed laws of nature, we are only destroying the harmony of human existence, peace must become a thing unattainable.

We all experience it in our daily lives that whenever we break the laws of nature, we fall ill and have to endure bodily pain. Similar is the case of the divinely-ordained moral laws. By breaking them, we invite nothing else than misery. If one breaks the heart of someone today, one must be ready to suffer a similar pain tomorrow.

Beautiful faces and beautiful things come before you day and night and enchant your hearts. You say that you consider the face of so and so as beautiful, and you declare your love for that beauty. At this occasion I would not drag you into a discussion on the nature of love. I might tell you later on that what people call love today is not love in the real sense of the term, but only a name for vulgar appetites, rooted in the lower forms of human desire. Actually, love denotes

---

[3] For a comprehensive discussion on man's role as *khalifah* see Ansari, *The Qur'ānic Foundations and Structure of Muslim Society.* Cf. Yasien Mohamed, *Islam to the Modern Mind*, 128.

that holy state of mind which has no reference to self-interest and baser passions.

However, even if you think that love is nothing but an inclination which is sensuous in nature, I would like you to consider the problem: from where came those superior distinctions which make you to bow down? Could these material bodies become so beautiful and seemingly so perfect by themselves, or, is there some Supreme Power who creates this beauty and imparts distinctions? If you doubt the existence of that Supreme Being, we might discuss it at some other occasion. But if your nature itself and your inner voice tells you that there is someone who is the Maker of this universe, then rest assured that all this beauty and perfection which you see in this world is only a manifestation of that really Beautiful and Perfect Being whom all sensible people and the followers of religions call Allah. One step further and you shall be able to feel that, if the beauty and perfection of created things is so attractive, how beautiful and perfect should He be who is the Creator.

You allow yourselves to be absorbed by the beauty of created things. But I would like you to focus your attention on Him, the really Beautiful and the really Perfect Being, in whom is the origin of all life. Think of Him and love Him. Your attitude of love will help in increasing your consciousness of Allah's omnipresence, until you will find impossible to act against His law. Then you will hurt none. You will break the heart of none. You will cheat none. You will speak lie to none. You will insult none. On the other hand, you will feel that the Blacks and the Whites, the poor and the rich, the lowly and the high-placed are all Allah's family and consequently your own brothers and sisters. Your love for Allah will compel you inwardly to love your fellow beings. When this attitude of mind has been attained, the world will have peace in the true sense of the word.

You are accustomed to hear the melodies of human song from the radio. Today you have heard about the melody of Divine Harmony. Let us henceforth think of Allah and love Him with ever-increasing devotion. Let us adopt the higher forms of human morals. Let us endeavour to build up a true humanity.[4]

---

[4] Siddiqui, "Divine Harmony" in *The Muslim Digest*: January 1951, 18-20 (Adapted).

My Beloved Murshid[5]
His Eminence Mawlānā Abdul Aleem Siddiqui

By: Abdullah Hoosen Deedat

(On the First Death Anniversary (1955)[6] of His Eminence by a
Durban youth now studying in Cairo)

His voice in my humble ears still rings to my heart a great
pleasure it brings as a true slave of the King of kings
He cared nought for all worldly things.

He loved the Prophet with fullest heart He loved his Master with
God-loved art to praise his love when he used to start He was with
his Love from us apart.

When serving he cared not for his health nor worked to
accumulate wealth
He showed all the world his lack of stealth As Islam was his
manifest wealth.

He distributed to everyone
His spiritual wealth many hearts won
He showed them the path showed by the one Allah Himself
deemed Second to none.

---

[5] Spiritual guide.
[6] The dedication was written by Abdullah Deedat after the passing away of
Mawlānā Siddiqui in 1954.

The most beautiful Madinah where He used to satisfy his heart
His Master no doubt is resting there He desired rest there in his
care.

Allah granted this great desire He rests today we all admire
In Yathrib[7] by Ahmad and Sire[8] Abubakr.
Weep not, oh crier!

---

[7] Madinah.
[8] An honorific title employed for the second khalifah of Islam.

Short Reviews

Abdul Aleem Siddiqui and His Mission. By Abdul Kader Choughley. Durban, South Africa, Ahsan Publications. 2013, ISBN: 978-0-920-58293-3, Pp. 229.

Fazlur Rahman Ansari: Life and Thought. By Abdul Kader Choughley. Durban, South Africa, Ahsan Publications. 2012, ISBN: 97806254784, Pp. 285.

In recent years Abdul Kader Choughley, a South African scholar, has made a mark as the chronicler and analyst of the Islamic intellectual tradition, particularly of the Indo-Pak subcontinent. His area of expertise is Islamic resurgence in 20th century in South Asia. Since Sayyid Abul Hasan Ali Nadwi (1913-1999) prominently figures among the Islamic revivalists in the region, it is not unsurprising that Choughley's earlier works were *Islamic Resurgence: Sayyid Abul Hasan Ali Nadwi and his Contemporaries* (2011) and *Sayyid Abul Hasan Ali Nadwi: Life and Works* (2012). Ahsan Academy, headed by Choughley, has published also the intellectual biography of another leading Islamic scholar, *From Darkness Into Light: Life and Works of Mawlānā Abdul Majid Daryabadi (1892-1977)*.

Abdul Aleem Siddiqui (1892-1954) was both an Islamic scholar and *muballigh* (*da'wah* activist) par excellence and a Sufi master in his own right, with a non-sectarian approach. Born in Meerut, India, he turned his attention to *tabligh* (preaching of Islam) before Mawlānā Ilyās's trend-setting, global Tablighi Jama`at movement. Siddiqui was thoroughly grounded in Islamic scholarship and adept at English, Arabic, Persian and Urdu. As part of his mission he toured extensively the Arab world, Europe, the Caribbean islands, Singapore and South Africa. Apart from delivering lectures on Islam, he bought out two Islamic magazines, *Genuine Islam* and *Voice of Islam.* As an activist he championed also the cause of the Pakistan movement in 1940s in the Arab world and secured Hasan Al-Banna's help and support for this cause. As early as in 1949 he set up in Singapore the Society for the Promotion of Inter-Religious Cooperation, which engaged major faith leaders Amid his several works, the following deserve special mention: i) *Dimensions of Islam* ii) *The Principles of Islam,* iii) *The Forgotten Path of Knowledge* iv) *A Shavian* and a *Theologian* and v) *Cultivation of Science by Muslims.* His writings in Urdu deal with *sirah,* Sufism and repudiation of Qadianism. Choughley's work succeeds remarkably in unravelling various aspects of Siddiqui's multidimensional personality, especially his religious fervor for promoting Islam and his inspiring works. Another laudable feature of Choughley's work is his cross-referencing, which enables readers to gain fruitful acquaintance with most of the publications on the intellectual history of Islam in the Indo- Pak subcontinent. Choughley is to be complimented for both his lucid presentation and his insightful scholarship.

In his *Fazlur Rahman Ansari: Life and Thought,* Choughley vividly brings into relief the accomplishments of Siddiqui's illustrious disciple, Fazlur Rahman Ansari (1914-1974) who carried further his mentor's mission. Born in 1914 in Muzaffar Nagar, India, Ansari first pursued Dars-i Nizami at Madrasah Islamiyah, and then pursued his, BA, MA. B.Th and Ph.D. in philosophy at the Aligarh Muslim University. It was in 1932 that he first came into contact with Abdul Aleem Siddiqui who initiated him in both Sufism and *Tabligh.* Ansari served as a member of the Education Planning Committee set up by M. A. Jinnah for the new state of Pakistan. While following in Siddiqui's footsteps, Ansari delivered lectures on Islam in various countries and contributed to inter-faith deliberations.

The Aleemiyah Institute established by him in Karachi went a long way in honing some bright Muslim scholars. Amid Ansari's several books, the following won a wide acclaim: i) *Foundations of Faith,* ii) *Islam and the Western Civilisation,* iii) *Islam versus Marxism,* iv) *The Qur'ānic Foundations and Structure of Muslim Society* and v) *Through Science and Philosophy to Religion.* Throughout his life long *da'wah* Ansari placed premium on *tawhid* (the concept of the One True God), Sufism anchored deep into the Qur'ān and Sunnah, and Islam as the natural way ensuring the success of man in both the worlds. He exhorted fellow Muslims to internalize the Islamic concept and practice of *islāh* (individual and social reform) and *tazkiyah* (self-development and self-purgation). He devoted his considerable time and energy to preaching and consolidating Islam in its pristine purity in South Africa and Seychelles and hence Choughley's glowing tribute to him. For Ansari's invaluable mission led to the Islamic resurgence across the world.

Choughley has done well to document the biography, methodology and achievements of these two laudable Islamic revivalists. It is hoped he will continue this invaluable series both for inspiration and posterity. We look forward to many more such tracts.

Abdur Raheem Kidwai
Aligarh Muslim University, Aligarh India

BIBLIOGRAPHY

Abbasi, M.O. *The Mirror*. Durban, 1953.

Alam, Manzoor. *100 Great Muslim Leaders of the 20th Century*. New Delhi, 2005.

Alladin, Ibrahim, *Maulana Abdul Aleem Siddiqui: His Life, Thoughts and Message*. Curepipe, 2019.

Ansari, Fazlur Rahman. *Islam and Christianity in the Modern World*. Karachi, 1965.

Anwari, Khalil. *A Shavian and Theologian*. Durban, 1953.

—. *Islam and Western Civilisation*. Karachi, 1983.

—. *The Qur'ānic Foundations and Structure of Muslim Society*.

Karachi, 1994.

Ansari, Humayun. *The Infidel Within: Muslims in Britain since 1800*. London, 2006.

Armstrong, Amatullah. *Sufi Terminology: The Mystical Language of Islam*. Kuala Lumpur, 1995.

Arnold, T.W. *The Preaching of Islam*. Lahore, 1979.

Banna, Hasan. *Memoirs of Hasan al-Banna Shaheed*. Karachi, 1981.

Burney, Elias. *Qadiani Movement*. Durban, 1955.

Choughley, Abdul Kader. *Fazlur Rahman Ansari: Life and Thought*. Springs, 2012.

--. *Fazlur Rahman Ansari: Aligarh Years (1933-1947)*. Aligarh, 2021.

Da Costa, Yusuf, and Davids, Achmat (eds.) *Pages from Cape Muslim History*. Pietermaritzburg, 1994.

Deedat, Ahmad. *The Choice,* Verulam, 1993.

Faridi, Shahidullah. *Inner Aspects of Faith*. Kuala Lumpur, 1979.

Ghazi, Mahmood: *Islamic Renaissance in South Asia 1707-1867*. Islamabad, 2002.

Haq, M. Anwarul. *The Faith Movement of Mawlana Muhammad Ilyas*.

London, 1972.

Hourani, Albert. *Arabic Thought in the Liberal Age 1798-1939*. London, 1962.

Iqbal, Afzal. *Life and Times of Mohamed Ali*. Lahore, 1979.

Iqbal, Muhammad. *Islam and Ahmadism*. Lucknow, 1982.

Iqbal, Muhammad Sufi. *The Achievement of Love: The Spiritual Dimension of Islam*. Montreal, 1987.

Jeppie, Shamil. *Language Identity Modernity: The Arab Study Circle of Durban*. Durban, 2007.

Kidwai, Abdur Raheem. *Translating the Untranslatable: A Critical Guide To 60 English translations of the Quran*. New Delhi, 2011.

Kriel, Mahdie. *Islamic Intellectual Revival of the Modern Mind*. Cape Town, 2011.

Levinskaya, Maria. *Scientific Religion or Reverent Science*. Karachi, 1983.

Mahida, Ebrahim. *History of Muslims in South Africa: A Chronology*. Durban, 1993.

Masri, B.A. *The Bane of Mirzaiyat*. Benoni, 1988.

Masud, Muhammad Khalid. *Travelers in Faith*. Leiden, 2000

Mohamed, Yasien. *Islam to the Modern Mind*. Cape Town, 2006.

—. *The Roving Ambassador of Peace*. Cape Town, 2006.

Nadvi, Syed Habibul Haq. *Islamic Resurgent Movements in the Indo-Pak Subcontinent*. Durban, 1987.

Nadwi, Abul Hasan Ali. *Qadianism: A Critical Study*. Lucknow, 1976.

—. *Western Civilisation, Islam and Muslims*. Lucknow, 1974

Qadri, Muhammad Younus. *The Greatest Propagator in Islam*. Karachi, 2003.

Faridi, Shahidullah. *Inner Aspects of Faith*. Kuala Lumpur, 1979.

Ghazi, Mahmood: *Islamic Renaissance in South Asia 1707-1867*. Islamabad, 2002.

Haq, M. Anwarul. *The Faith Movement of Mawlana Muhammad Ilyas.* London, 1972.

Hourani, Albert. *Arabic Thought in the Liberal Age 1798-1939.* London, 1962.

Iqbal, Afzal. *Life and Times of Mohamed Ali.* Lahore, 1979.

Iqbal, Muhammad. *Islam and Ahmadism.* Lucknow, 1982.

Iqbal, Muhammad Sufi. *The Achievement of Love: The Spiritual Dimension of Islam.* Montreal, 1987.

Jeppie, Shamil. *Language Identity Modernity: The Arab Study Circle of Durban.* Durban, 2007.

Kidwai, Abdur Raheem. *Translating the Untranslatable: A Critical Guide To 60 English translations of the Quran.* New Delhi, 2011.

Kriel, Mahdie. *Islamic Intellectual Revival of the Modern Mind.* Cape Town, 2011.

Levinskaya, Maria. *Scientific Religion or Reverent Science.* Karachi, 1983.

Mahida, Ebrahim. *History of Muslims in South Africa: A Chronology.* Durban, 1993.

Masri, B.A. *The Bane of Mirzaiyat.* Benoni, 1988.

Masud, Muhammad Khalid. *Travelers in Faith.* Leiden, 2000

Mohamed, Yasien. *Islam to the Modern Mind.* Cape Town, 2006.

—. *The Roving Ambassador of Peace.* Cape Town, 2006.

Nadvi, Syed Habibul Haq. *Islamic Resurgent Movements in the Indo-Pak Subcontinent.* Durban, 1987.

Nadwi, Abul Hasan Ali. *Qadianism: A Critical Study.* Lucknow, 1976.

—. *Western Civilisation, Islam and Muslims.* Lucknow, 1974

Qadri, Muhammad Younus. *The Greatest Propagator in Islam.* Karachi, 2003.

Photo Essay

The opening issue of the Star of Islam. Photo: Sri Lanka Malay Association and South Asia Open Archive

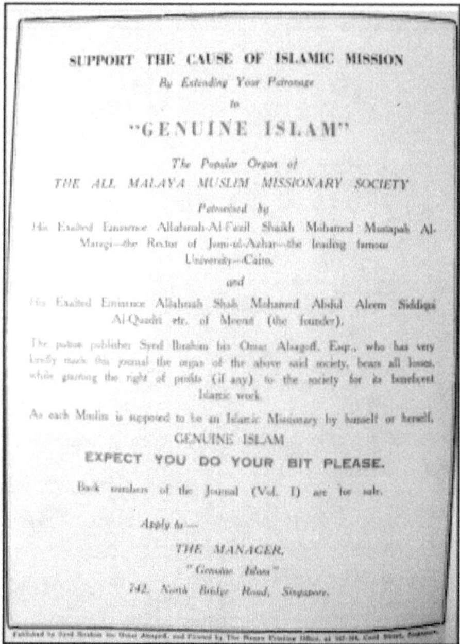

PRICE 25 Cents.
India, Burma & Ceylon—8 As.
Foreign 1s.
CONSTANTINOPLE IN 1913
By Dr. Mohd. A. R. Khan.
Voice of Islam
Under
the Royal Patronage of
H. H. Tunku
Temenggong Ahmad of
Johore.
AN ILLUSTRATED MONTHLY DEVOTED TO GENUINE TEACHINGS OF ISLAM.
(Dedicated to H. E. E. Maulana M. A. A. Siddiqui and Richard Taylour, Esq.)
Vol. I.
SINGAPORE,
Z-HADJ. '56, MOHARRAM. 1357.
FEBRUARY/MARCH, 1938.
No. 4.

The Muslim Digest
INTERNATIONAL MONTHLY OF MUSLIM AFFAIRS
Vol. 16   Nos. 5 & 6   Ramadan 1385   Dec. '65/Jan. '66
Founded by
His Eminence Mohammed Abdul Aleem Siddiqui, Al-Qaderi
Organ of
THE WORLD FEDERATION OF ISLAMIC MISSIONS
31st YEAR OF PUBLICATION
Published under the Distinguished Patronage of
His Eminence Muhammad Fazlur Rahman Ansari Al-Qaderi

Built in 1954, it is named after the renowned Islamic scholar, spiritual master, and author – Maulana Shah Muhammad Abdul Aleem Siddique, who dedicated his entire life preaching and propagating Islam in Singapore and around the world.

Masjid Abdul Aleem Siddique.

Foundation stone laying of Nygoya Mosque (Japan) in 1936.

The Hindustan Times (Delhi) August 08, 1933

M. ABDUL ALEEM

Returns Home From Pilgrimage

MEERUT, Aug. 6.

Maulana Mohamed Abdul Aleem Siddiqui, a famous Muslim traveller and missionary, arrived here after performing the pilgrimage. He was received at the station by a large gathering of Muslims amidst shouts of "Alla-Ho-Akbar". A huge procession then started from the station and passing through the Clock Tower, Khairnagar and Sipat Bazaar reached his residence.

Detailing his experiences of the tour at a largely attended meeting in the Juma Masjid, he said that travelling in the Hedjaz was quite safe, but he deplored that condition of the roads to the improvement of which, he said, no attention was being paid by the Government. Trade suffered greatly owing to abnormally high customs duties.—A. P. I.

البيـــــان

لما جرى بين

جلالة الملك عبد العزيز بن عبد الرحمن الفيصل آل سعود ملك المملكة العربية السعودية

وبين

كبار العلماء الأعلام وزعماء الاسلام من حجاج بيت الله الحرام

في سنة ١٣٦٤ هـ

ثم ما جرى

بين جلالته وأعيان دولته

وبين

الداعي إلى الله صاحب الفضيلة والارشاد الأستاذ الشيخ

محمد عبد العليم الصديقي القادري

رئيس وفد الرابطة الاسلامية المتحدة ومندوب مسلمي الملايو والجزائر الشرقية وبلاد الشرق وجنوب افريقية إلى المملكة السعودية

في سنة ١٣٦٥ هـ

وذلك

[illegible]

Historic document on the *Hajj Tax*.

Reception at the Edmonton airport (Canada).

Jumu'ah khutbah at Al-Rashid Mosque (Edmonton).

Distinguished visitors: Mawlana Siddiqui and Mawlana Fazlur Rahman Ansari at Al-Rashid Mosque.

Arrival at Port of Spain (Trinidad).

Islamic Mission of America, Brooklyn, New York.
Shaykh Daoud Ahmad Faisal: Spiritual Head.

San Francisco
A memento presented to Mawlana Siddiqui in recognition
of his pioneering *contribution to da'wah.*

A dinner reception hosted by Muslim dignitaries from
various embassies in New York.

Dinner reception. *Poster* in Urdu.

Our History

Jamiyah Singapore, also known as Muslim Missionary Society Singapore, was founded in 1932 by the Roving Ambassador of Peace from Meerut (India), Moulana Abdul Aleem Siddique. Continuing Moulana's legacy, our mission is to serve and provide welfare services to the less privileged and disadvantaged, regardless of their race or faith.

Over the decades, Jamiyah has expanded with several enhanced programmes and services to address the ever-changing needs of the community.

> "If it was ever necessary to create harmony among leaders and followers of different religions, it is more necessary and more urgent today when the world is living in fear of Third World War. With this very idea the Inter-Religious Organisation was founded"
>
> **His Eminence Maulana Abdul Aleem Siddiqui, Founder of IRO, 1949**

The Contribution
of
Religion
to
PEACE

Edited by the Rev Dr. H. B. Amstutz
and Ahmad Bin Mohamed Ibrahim

————◆————

MALAYA PUBLISHING HOUSE, LIMITED
STAMFORD ROAD, SINGAPORE
1949

Malay Congregational Committee.

WELCOME RECEPTION.

IN HONOUR OF

Moulana Mohammed Abdul Aleem Siddiqui, B. A.

THE EMINENT MUSLIM LECTURER AND THEOLOGIAN

AT THE

NASERIA SCHOOL,

23rd STREET, VREDEDORP, JOHANNESBURG.

On Sunday, 18th November 1934,

AT 2-30 P. M.

THE MAULANA'S MASTERY OF THE ENGLISH, FRENCH, ARABIC, URDU, AND PERSIAN LANGUAGES ENABLES HIM TO ADDRESS ALL GATHERINGS IN ANY OF THE ABOVE LANGUAGES.

The Transvaal Muslim Lads Brigade will form a Guard of Honour.

All are cordially invited to Attend.

આવકારનો જલસો.

મૌલાના મોહંમદ અબ્દુલ અલીમ સાહેબના માનમાં

તા. ૧૮ નવેંબર ૧૯૩૪ને રવિવારે બપોર બાદ ૨-૩૦ વાને "નસહીઆ સ્કૂલ" ૨૩ મી સ્ટ્રીટ ફ્રિડીઓર્પમાં અખબ પ્રોફીશ્યન કમીટી તરફથી આવકારનો જલસો કરવામાં આવશે, સર્વ ભાઈઓને પધારવા વિનંતી કરવામાં આવે છે.

GARLANDED and smiling, His Eminence is seen on the docks with his brother, Moulana Bashyr Siddiqui. On his left is Mr. E.I. Haffejee and on his extreme right, Mr. Mohammad Makki.

Welcome on Durban docks: Mawlana Siddiqui (garlanded).
Picture shows Mawlana Abubakr Khatib (white turban) and
next to him his son Hafidh Abulhasan Khatib

The late Hajee Ebrahim Tarmahomed (seated with grandson)
seen with his sons (left to right) Hashim, Allymahomed,
Omar and Yunus, a year before he passed away in May 1997.
His younger brother, Moosa Tarmahomed is seated next to
him, while at inset is the distinguished *Shaykh al-Hadith* from
Makkah, Shaykh Muhammad al-Alawi al-Maliki.

Seated from left: Mawlana Bashir Siddiqui, Essop Paruk, Mawlana Aleem Siddiqui, Mawlana Abdul Kader.

Natal Muslim Educational Conference: 1952

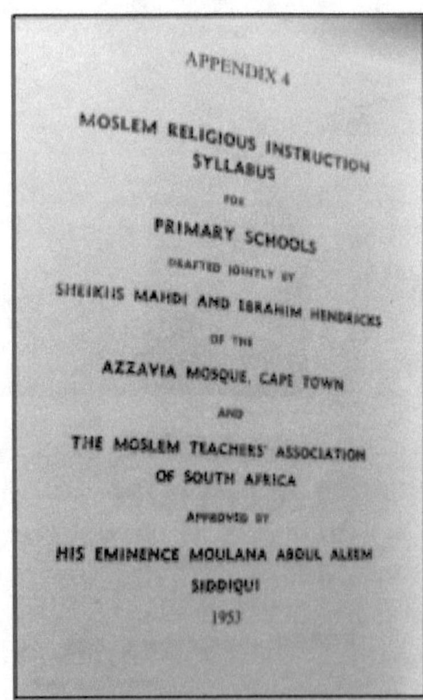

APPENDIX 4

MOSLEM RELIGIOUS INSTRUCTION
SYLLABUS

FOR

PRIMARY SCHOOLS

DRAFTED JOINTLY BY

SHEIKHS MAHDI AND IBRAHIM HENDRICKS

OF THE

AZZAVIA MOSQUE, CAPE TOWN

AND

THE MOSLEM TEACHERS' ASSOCIATION
OF SOUTH AFRICA

APPROVED BY

HIS EMINENCE MOULANA ABDUL ALEEM
SIDDIQUI

1953

Moulana Siddiqui (centre), Shaykh Mahdi Hendricks (left) and Shaykh Ebrahim Hendricks (right) in the library of the Azzawiya mosque.

A memorable lecture was delivered at the Grand Parade, Cape Town by Mawlana Siddiqui in 1952. A crowd of 36 000 Muslims had gathered to await his arrival in the Cape on his second visit.

Mauritius: 1953

(Photo: Courtesy: Yacoob Ebrahim Dawood)

In 1949, H. E. Maulana Abdul Aleem Siddiqui (R.A.) visited Mauritius for the third time as the guest of the **Jummah Mosque** and posed for a souvenir photo with some of the dignitaries of the Muslim community who accompanied him to the Town Hall during a courtesy call on the Mayor of Port Louis, His Worship Abdul Razack Mohamed.

Seated (left to right): Dawood (Seth) Abdool Raman; His Worship Mayor Abdul Razack Mohamed; H. E. Maulana Abdul Aleem Siddiqui (R.A.); Goolam Mahomed Dawoojee Atchia; and Ahmad Hassam Batchoo.

Standing (left to right): Jackaria Abdul Raman; Eshack Abdulatiff; and Aziz Peeroo

Tabligh mission in Mauritius

The Abdul Alim Building, named in honour of Maulana Abdul Aleem, at Aleemiah College, Phoenix, Mauritius and Mohseen Owasil, staff at the College, 2018. Aleemiah College was founded by Maulana Abdul Aleem in 1953.

Source: Mohseen Owasil

The Jummah Masjid in Port-Louis, lit for the centenary celebration in the presence of Maulana Abdul Aleem in 1953.

Source: Vintage Mauritius, vintagemauritius.org